A Portfolio Primer

Other Books by Geof Hewitt

Just Worlds (poetry)
Living in Whales: Vermont Public School Stories & Poems (ed.)
A Preservation Primer (with Bethany Kaiman)
Quickly Aging Here: Some Poets of the 1970's (ed.)
Selected Poems of Alfred Starr Hamilton (ed.)
Stone Soup (poetry)
Working for Yourself (nonfiction)
Writing Without Walls: Boise Writing in the Schools (ed. with James Hepworth)

A Portfolio Primer

Teaching, Collecting, and Assessing Student Writing

Geof Hewitt

HEINEMANN
Portsmouth, NH

Heinemann
A division of Reed Elsevier Inc.
361 Hanover Street
Portsmouth, NH 03801-3912
Offices and agents throughout the world

We would like to thank those who have given their permission to include material in this book. Every effort has been made to contact the copyright holders for permission to reprint borrowed material where necessary. We regret any oversights that may have occurred and would be happy to rectify them in future printings of this work.

Reprint from "Nontechnical Assessment," by Peter Johnston, *The Reading Teacher,* September 1992. Permission granted by International Reading Association.

Reprint from Vermont's portfolio-based writing assessment program; Vermont Writing Assessment: the Portfolio, "This Is My Best," Analytic Scoring Guide. Permission granted by the Vermont Department of Education.

Reprint from *The Art of Change,* as printed in *Our Own Horns,* the student magazine of the Governor's Institute on the Arts, 1990. Permission granted by Danny Osman, Governor's Institute on the Arts.

Reprint from *A Language For Life.* Permission granted by Pam Beckley, Copyright Assistant, and reproduced by permission of the Controller of Her Majesty's Stationery Office.

Reprint from pages 38, 48, and 70 of *Fourth Generation Evaluation,* by Egan G. Guba, Yvonna S. Lincoln. © 1989. Reprinted with permission of Sage Publications.

Poems and stories from *Living in Whales,* ed. Geof Hewitt © 1972 by Vermont Council on the Arts, pages 36–42.

Reprint from "Glossary of Writing Techniques," from *Writing as a Road to Self-Discovery,* 1993 by Barry Lane, pp. 184–189. Used with permission of Writer's Digest Books.

Reprint "Improvised Drama," by Geof Hewitt, from IDEAS *Plus Book Eight,* published by the National Council of Teachers of English, 1111 W. Kenyon Road, Urbana, IL 61801.

Reprint "Vermont's Portfolio-Based Writing Assessment Program: A Brief History," by Geof Hewitt, from the May-June, 1993 (Vol. 24. No.5) *Teachers & Writers Magazine,* published by Teachers & Writers Collaborative.

Library of Congress Cataloging-in-Publication Data
Hewitt, Geof.
    A portfolio primer: teaching, collecting, and assessing student writing / Geof Hewitt.
    Includes bibliographical references and index.
    ISBN 0-435-08834-3
    1. English language—Composition and exercises—United States–Ability testing.
2. Portfolios in education—United States.
I. Title.
LB1576.H344 1994
808'.042'071—dc20   94–24748
                                                                              CIP

Editor: Dawn Boyer
Production: J. B. Tranchemontagne
Cover design: Darci Mehall
Cover drawing by Amanda Taylor

Printed in the United States of America on acid-free paper
98 97 96 95 94 EB 1 2 3 4 5 6

Contents

Introduction

Most of the writing samples in these pages come from students in grades four through twelve, but the principles of writing, portfolios, and assessment apply to all grades and, I think, all subjects. A writing portfolio should by no means be limited to "language arts" or "English." Teachers who don't know a comma splice from a run-on sentence can concentrate, in their response to student work, on expression or content, rather than try to fill the shoes of the precise grammarians who may have discouraged them so many years ago. What's important is that the students are writing!

Equally important is that the teacher write too. Life is actually easier for the teacher who enters the community of writers by writing with the students. When students see that the teacher is busy scribbling away, they are much less likely to ask questions than if the teacher is merely sitting at the head of the class overseeing the work of others. When students see a teacher struggling to write a meaningful essay or a poem that cuts to the heart, they realize that writing can be hard work — even for adults.

Our concept of scholarly writing too often harbors stale models from a dark, academic past. Can't students demonstrate their understanding of a historic period more thoroughly by producing an original play or video than by each writing a five-paragraph essay in the third-person, past tense? This book focuses on ways to stimulate "creative writing" in all classes; writing which is, I claim, the keystone to any thoughtful curriculum.

As a writing zealot, someone whose life has focused since junior high school on the act of writing, I have two strong biases that may help the reader weigh the ideas in this book:

1. No one really knows how to "teach" writing. People learn to write by writing. As in sports, the more one practices, the greater the improvement in certain basic skills. The teacher's job is to guide this process.

2. Many teachers allow too much classroom time for writing! Given a forty-five-minute writing period, students often develop a writer's worst habit — chewing on the end of the writing implement. Instead of expecting students to write for one full class period a week, perhaps we should ask them to write daily in every classroom, for only five or ten minutes — just enough time to get a good start!

It's important for me to think back on my own formative years and to think about the teachers who helped me most. I do not recall ever being asked to keep a portfolio, or even a folder, of my work. But I had teachers who stand out in memory and somehow link to my development as a writer. Starting with Miss Clough (rhymes with *rough*), my fourth-grade teacher, I've worked with a wondrous variety of people whose special concerns — their quirks and biases — each had unique influence on my writing. As much as I complain about Miss Clough, who often used writing as a punishment and who doggedly sniffed out each error in every paper (ignoring content and with never a word of encouragement), I must admit I learned a lot from her, although, try as she might, she never succeeded in killing my respect for the power of a run-on sentence! Nor the allure of occasional fragments.

As a college undergraduate, tirelessly submitting my work for publication and papering my walls with rejection slips, I learned to set type and run a small press, self-publishing my poems on broadsides and in chapbooks. In graduate school, I discovered that persistence pays — two or three editors weakened, and a few of my poems and essays began to find little audiences, scattered and ill-defined, but *there*. Yet I realized that I'd probably never be able to support myself as a writer, and I began to teach in colleges and at any grade school where the adults in charge would let me through the door.

I understand the frustration people often express about "not having time to write," yet I believe not writing is a kind of starvation, a cultural vitamin deficiency.

Call it an obsession; I don't mind at all. My lifelong focus on writing actually shaped my career! So it was as a writer and sometime teacher that, in 1988, I responded to the Vermont Department of Education's classified advertisement for a writing consultant, someone who would work with teachers and (I later learned) coordinate the development of a statewide, portfolio-based writing assessment program. In this capacity, learning about a variety of writing assessment programs across the country, I have witnessed the use and abuse of "accountability" as justification for telling teachers what to do and how to do it. The automatic presumption is that mandated testing will drive the limousine of "classroom improvement."

Probably no human activity offers a fuller picture of a learner's growth than writing — thought and feeling made visible in a language the reader shares with the writer. The concept of a shared language should not be taken lightly. It presumes a contract between two individuals: they have both learned a language for the purpose of communication. One's interest in sharing that language with others depends on their level of sophistication with the shared language. I probably won't engage in a diatribe about writing and writing instruction with someone who only knows enough English to ask what I do for a living unless I happen to be fluent in that person's language.

Recognizing the significance of writing as a record of any student's development as a thinker, schools across the country are asking their students to keep folders — portfolios — of their writing. No longer limited to certain English classes, a "writing portfolio" may well be part of the curriculum in every subject. Some schools have had such portfolio programs for years. At least two Vermont high schools observe a long-standing tradition of presenting students with their completed high-school portfolios, in addition to the diploma, at graduation; I'm told the students value their portfolios more highly than the diploma.

Other schools design portfolio programs in response to mandates from above. Within these schools, some teachers see portfolios as a valuable tool for learning about their students, for student learning, and for teacher-parent conferences. Other teachers fear that the writing portfolio will be used to judge their teaching performance, that the judgment may be harsh, and that high stakes will be attached to the judgment. Such judgments are unfair; see Chapter 11, The Future of Portfolio-Based Writing Assessment, for a discussion of this misguided use of portfolios.

A school's reasons for requiring portfolios and a teacher's fears aside, what does the portfolio accomplish for the *student*? And who, ultimately, is supposed to benefit from the portfolio?

1. Asking students to keep portfolios of their work suggests that the work has value, importance.

2. Students who keep portfolios have tangible evidence of their progress.

3. Students who keep portfolios have tangible evidence of their effort. Many writers who keep carbon copies of their correspondence admit they are amazed to see how quickly the pages pile up. Students who do not keep folders of their work may not realize how much effort they have invested in their education. Portfolios may make it harder for some students to drop out!

4. Portfolios suggest that the important comparisons are not to be made with one's peers, but with one's own past accomplishments.

5. Portfolios may provide a means of formal assessment that is based on a system of shared values, such as "clarity of expression," "sentence variety," etc. When students understand these values, they may attempt to demonstrate them in their day-to-day work, a selection of which, after all, will eventually wind up in the portfolio.

In this portfolio primer, I shall attempt to describe ways to design student writing portfolios, and ways to respond to the work therein, with ideas and anecdotes about creating a system for formal assessment.

But no matter how well designed and thoughtfully assessed our students' portfolios are, our efforts are wasted if we fail to provide challenging opportunities for writing, including a variety of topics and topic treatments, a varied sense of audience, and frequent opportunities to write for "real situations." Without the sense of excitement provided by such challenges and opportunities, students' portfolios reflect a depressing sameness. The challenge in designing portfolio assessment programs is making sure that individuality is valued and nurtured. That is why I cannot write only about "assessment." The portfolio and what goes into it are inextricably linked to the usefulness of any assessment, which should be designed to set a model for and to encourage the best possible writing.

So as much as I'll try to offer information and ideas on portfolios and assessment, I also intend to describe the best approaches I know to writing and teaching writing. For students to write well, they need to anticipate an atmosphere of acceptance and support, an atmosphere that develops almost automatically when the teacher writes with the students. Writing is nearly always enjoyable when the author anticipates an audience that is friendly, understanding, and (because all members of the audience have tackled the same challenge) empathic. Maybe the teacher doesn't write in response to every assignment, but on a regular basis accepts the same challenge the students receive, creating a portfolio and publishing or reading work to others as frequently as students are asked to publish or read their work.

To overtly state, "now we're going to write a piece for the portfolio . . ." makes the portfolio the writing prompt, creating an enormous misinterpretation of writing process and portfolio in one fell swoop. The portfolio should act as a ravenous clam, sneaking up on and then enveloping only those pieces that are suitable to its dietary interests. To suggest that a piece be composed for the portfolio is to impose notions of high quality on an act that should be exploratory ("risk taking," as often as not) in nature. Through the writer's concern for and engagement in the first draft should emerge revision and, possibly, sufficient regard for inclusion in a portfolio.

I bring these considerations to any group I can find that wants to discuss writing and how we teach it. A couple of years ago, Teachers & Writers Collaborative asked poet Gary Lenhart and me to chair a two-day miniconference for teachers on responding to student poetry. In my introductory comments, I found myself citing William Stafford's assertion, at a conference of the National Council of Teachers of English, that he offered no judgment on his college students' writing, essentially forcing evaluation back to the source: self-assessment, arguably the one practice we should expect of every high-school graduate. Extending Stafford's stance to the primary grades, I heard myself intoning, "Maybe we should leave our youngest writers alone, free of concerns for quality, focusing our efforts instead on inculcating a love for writing. Make it fun so that by seventh grade our students are writers. Let the seventh-grade teacher hit 'em with the rules!"

Behind this suggestion is the whispered belief that no teacher should have to spend more than half a period on any of the "domains" of writing, given a group of willing young writers. The persuasive essay should be a piece of cake for any student who is sufficiently comfortable as a writer to capture his or her own narrative voice. "If you can tell a story," you explain, "you can write a persuasive essay or anything else the teacher or life demands. Just listen to yourself the next time you negotiate a curfew or use of the car with your parents. You get the main reasons out as fast as you can, and you return to those themes often, adding little embellishments. You acknowledge and explore opposing points of view, and you summarize with the most important point last."

1. I want to borrow the car.
2. I'll drive carefully, and the car will be clean when I return it.
3. I will admit that I stripped the gears and dented the fender last week, but I've learned my lesson.
4. I'll take good care of the car, I'll drive carefully, and I won't ask for it again until next month.

Given assurance of the validity of their individual speaking voices and an awareness of the strategies of argument, students can almost teach themselves the persuasive essay. Ditto for any other domain because — no matter how arcane — they have already covered this material (and developed the skills) orally.

My argument at the miniconference presupposed that a child who has frequent and varied opportunities to write will become a writer with only a minimum of critical response from the teacher, and by the seventh grade will want to tackle the formal and genre-specific demands that, imposed earlier, would have killed the natural connection of mind/heart-tongue/hand. That presupposition seems a little extreme, but far better an absence of teacher judgment than a heavy concentration on teacher judgment! It's a matter of balance, and throughout the primary grades the balance should be heavily weighted toward experiment and pleasure. "When a baby starts to speak," one teacher told me, "we don't correct grammar or pronunciation; in fact we often reinforce the baby's use of language with our own baby talk. When children start to write, why is our attitude so different?" Does this difference in attitude explain why so many people, who have no difficulty expressing themselves in conversation, nonetheless suffer from "writer's block"?

Richard Scarry, the noted children's author-illustrator, died in the spring of 1994. His wife of forty years, Patricia Murphy Scarry, told the press: "Richard considered himself an educator more than anything. He thought any child could learn to read and absorb other things if they were having fun." If, especially during the elementary school years, we can make the act of writing *fun*, we'll find that students are eager, by the time they reach junior high school, to satisfy the standards of correctness we too often attempt to drill into them at too early an age.

In *A Language for Life* (1975), the Committee of Inquiry appointed by Great Britain's secretary of state for education and science under the chairmanship of Sir Alan Bullock, F.B.A., reports: "Curiosity about language is widespread among children and enables them to engage successfully in occasional studies or linguistic 'experiments' arising out of their reading, writing, listening, and talking. The teacher encourages this curiosity and seizes the opportunity of pursuing some general question about language as it arises from usage, collecting and organising further examples for the purpose of answering the question. Studies of this kind may develop an experimental attitude toward language and provide a method of enquiry which helps pupils solve their own problems of language usage as they meet them" (162). While *A Language for Life* does not advocate abandoning our concerns for mechanics and conventions, it claims that the "first task for the teacher is one of encouraging vitality and fluency in the expressive writing that is nearest to speech. Children will move out into other modes in their own various ways and at various times that no one can predict in any detail" (166). The report maintains that all but the simplest lessons on usage should wait until students are ready for a systematic study of language. Until that time, sixth or seventh grade in my opinion, minilessons should arise from the context of *the students'* writing, not from textbooks.

If too much emphasis on correctness may be damaging, it is equally true that praise can derail a child's natural interest in writing. I recently heard a psychologist define praise as a form of manipulation, a way of congratulating the subject for meeting the praise-giver's standards. Yet if those standards are honored by the receiver of the praise, and if the praise is deserved (and not overstated), I think the psychologist might relent.

The hope is to create a love of writing for its own sake, not the slavish mentality some students develop because writing is something they are forced to do.

For me, the miniconference came together in its final half hour, when an English teacher who'd been asking all weekend, "How do we make it possible for elementary students to value the act of writing?" said: "All these response-and-evaluation strategies we've been discussing are irrelevant if we're not providing good writing prompts and a valid sense of audience."

We don't need reliable assessment devices one-tenth as much as we need strategies for helping young people find themselves as communicators-in-writing. I say, "Give me good writing prompts and a valued sense of audience, and I can write very well, thank you. Assess *that*! Here, it worked for me, and it's not so personal that I wouldn't want a stranger reading it — I think I'll put it in my portfolio."

Teachers who write with their students are more likely to come up with engaging assignments than teachers who never participate in the exercise. If writing and the keeping of portfolios are seen only as a student's job, how will students come to recognize the significance of these activities? A teacher's writing or writing portfolio may or may not serve as a model of excellence, but the teacher's effort will, indeed, demonstrate the type of commitment students should make to their own work!

"But where will I find the time?" you may ask. Try it for the first six weeks of school. If it works, you'll find the time. Ask your students for help and advice during these critical six weeks: How do they feel, how do *you* feel, about this activity? Make your writing program a group effort, where the opinions of the intended beneficiaries are considered and discussed. Some teachers ask their students to write about every piece of writing in their portfolio. These responses, from students, to their own completed assignments, provide an excellent source of feedback.

---

1. (Choose one):

  ☐ I like this piece of writing because . . .

  ☐ I don't like this piece of writing because . . .

2. In future writings, I would like to . . .

3. My suggestions for improving our writing program . . .

If students see their teacher responding to their suggestions (let's admit how rarely this occurs!), they will take increasing responsibility for the program and, one hopes, for their own work. This is not a grade-specific matter: Students of any age can offer good advice. Deciding whether to color-code portfolios and how to store them, debating access policies, even describing the contents and criteria of a program, will generate a sense of ownership. These are not the school's portfolios, nor do they belong to the teacher. Only one portfolio in the bunch is "the teacher's portfolio"!

The students will obviously work harder and dig deeper if they sense a teacher's excitement than if they are given assignments in which the teacher has long ago lost interest. I find that some writing prompts work over and over, with each new group of students, but at least half the time I'm inventing a fresh writing assignment either because it covers something I want to write or because I think it offers a slant on whatever lesson I'm trying to impart. I might create a 180-day curriculum from such ideas, but I would rather work from a set of nine interests or "teaching goals" — one goal for each month of the school year — and allow daily writing assignments to emerge from spontaneous classroom and real-world situations.

Nine such goals, by month, might be:

September: humor
October: revision
November: dialogue
December: plot/organization
January: metaphor
February: sentence variety
March: the elegant phrase
April: word play
May: rule breaking
June: review

Another teacher might have a very different set of goals.

I would probably start with humor. Use September as a month to read and write material that is relaxed and funny. Do students like a certain stand-up comedian? Do the students tell stories that rely on humor? What are the strategies of the stand-up comic, or of the storyteller? I'd introduce written examples of humor, from Shel Silverstein to Howard Frank Mosher, and ask students how humor can be used to enhance a serious message. Can we think of topics that will allow us to write poems in Silverstein's "voice"? Should we read Edward Lear and Ogden Nash? Can we write limericks?

In October I would focus on revision, providing models and encouraging students to describe, during class discussion, their techniques for revising. Where is your favorite place to revise? Do you eat while revising? How do you decide what to change or cut? (Barry Lane's *After THE END* (1993) is an excellent reference on revision and teaching revision.)

November would be dialogue month, with some review of humor from September. I'd encourage the students to listen carefully to a variety of conversations and to re-create patterns of dialogue and the rhythms of speech, both casual speech and formal, spoken presentations.

I would spend December on plot and strategies for organizing nonfiction, with emphasis on revision.

In January I'd emphasize metaphor, revisiting humor and dialogue. The students and I would keep running lists of metaphors we've overheard or invented, and we'd give detailed consideration to the various types of metaphor, not only the technically termed *metaphors* we find in good writing, but the metaphors for life we observe in all art and during our everyday activities.

In February I'd ask each student to revise one piece or start and revise something new, giving special consideration to sentence variety.

March would be spent on the elegant phrase, with some emphasis on dialogue/theatre or radio plays. As in metaphor month, I'd ask students to keep a list of language they've overheard or invented that displays the qualities of "the elegant phrase." Great political orations might provide a model or two — fair game, perhaps, for parody.

April would be reserved for word play and to revisit humor and metaphor. In considering word play, I'd ask students to explain the rules of any word play they might currently use, including Pig Latin, and any other less-known, or locally invented "alternative languages." I'd also hope to involve students in discussing special codes and coded language. I'd want to be sure that every student recognizes the irony that *embargo* backwards is "o grab me," that *revolution* backwards (phonetically) is "no shoe lover," and that *catatonic* is "cannot attack." I'd want the students to compile and use lists of spoonerisms, especially those where a certain justice arises from related meanings of the phrases that emerge: *Grilled cheese* is "chilled grease," *flat head* is "hat fled." Believe me, the lists of ironic spoonerisms and backwards words can be surprising in their length!

I'd devote May to rule breaking. Faulkner might provide examples.

In June I'd celebrate, reviewing each of the nine goals, and asking the students to help decide which have been most useful in their development as writers.

The contents of a writing portfolio kept with such goals in mind might include science papers, original jokes, a history report, memories of something that evoked laughter, songs, a comic strip, instructions for a new game, limericks, overheard conversations, interviews, a letter to the editor, scripts, short stories, an explanation of the solution to a mathematics problem, poems, research papers, opinions, and any other original work a student might want to include.

I wouldn't tell the students my goals because I'd want the assignments, guided (not driven!) by the month's focus, to seem (if not be) spontaneous — less exercises than valid writing assignments. I'd be sure that review is incorporated daily, integrating past lessons with the current month's goal. Metaphor, for instance, cannot be taught in a single month; it requires repeated observation and metaphor making. The discussion of abstract definitions should be as brief as possible; through practice, students should recognize metaphor at various levels and should invent their own metaphors as a matter of course. "A list of twenty original metaphors: you have seven minutes. Pencils up . . . .

"Tomorrow we'll do similes. Looks like a lot of you wrote some similes *today*."

The students may get glimpses of this nine-goal scaffolding or even recognize that "This must be revision month." That's fine. I'm not trying to keep the goals a secret; I simply prefer not to announce the focus of each new month, but to let the class evolve. Many good teachers have the magician's ability to force a card on an audience whose members believe *they* are choosing the curriculum. Plan it out too far ahead and you're not allowing sufficient spontaneity. Announcing goals locks you in and suggests that once a goal has been covered it can be forgotten.

"Kids these days just can't write," a local executive complains. "We have to train them specially, even the ones with a high school diploma." I'd love to see a sample of that executive's writing before it's cleaned up by a secretary! But the pressure is on, from corporate presidents to citizen members of local school boards, to produce students who write well (although "write well" means *spell* and *punctuate* to some, *express complex thought and feelings* to others).

Educators accept this challenge, knowing that success depends on factors seemingly beyond their control. Do the students come from homes where literacy is practiced on a daily basis? Do they see their parents writing letters? Do family members read aloud to one another? Are books not just displayed but used? Does the family listen to radio productions or attend public readings? In short, are the students members of a literate community?

Public libraries, coffee houses, small bookstores, nonprofit galleries, local newspapers, and an occasional arts council can all serve as loci for the building of such community. A teacher who spends time in the public library or attends or participates in other local arts events is an enormous asset to the community. That teacher models essential activities outside the school day and knows the workings of institutions that can be important to the students. Good rapport with a librarian and a local editor might make all the difference in a teacher's efforts to encourage literacy beyond the classroom. Working with the local arts council, perhaps in cooperation with the public library, teachers can bring professional writers to their communities and classrooms for readings and workshops.

In any case, whoever's complaining should be invited into the existing literate community, whether it be the classroom or a library presentation by some of the students, and encouraged to participate. In this way the complainer contributes to the solution and gains a deeper understanding of the community of learners that, on the surface, served as the target of complaint.

So our corporate president gets hot under the collar one day when her son brings home the school newspaper and she sees two articles in a row with conspicuous grammatical or punctuation errors. She decides to do something about it and phones her district's state senator, who happens to head an education committee. "Listen to this!" she says, and reads from the newspaper. "Published work! That's what our school is turning out. And if it's this bad in *our* district, think how much worse it must be in the poorer communities. Can't you do something?"

Well, the senator has had a few other calls like this in addition to several recent complaints about property taxes and how the schools should be supported without penalizing homeowners. ("Hell, I'm paying property taxes for overblown salaries to a bunch of 180-day-a-year teachers and I don't even have kids!") The senator rarely stops to wonder why no parent has yet called to cite something "really impressive" from the school paper, or to say, "You know, property taxes aren't so bad this year."

So the senator calls the commissioner of education and asks how can we improve writing instruction in our state. The commissioner says what we test is what we value — if you want to improve writing in our state, you have to test writing. And the senator says I have an idea, get a statewide writing test going; and the commissioner says we can set up a committee to devise a system . . . .

And thus is born: Writing Assessment.

Any committee set up to study a proposal is likely to deem the proposal a good idea. How many committees report back to their funding source that "the idea we've been reviewing these past eight months is a lousy idea"? More likely the committee reports: "The idea merits further study and possible implementation. Here are three scenarios . . . ." Thus, committees perpetuate themselves: people who have grown accustomed to working with one another on something they care about want continued opportunity to meet and discuss their dreams.

Meanwhile, the unsuspecting teacher is writing up next year's lesson plans as committees continue to meet and legislators fend off complaints: "The commissioner is working on that." This is a hypothetical case, but it's not far from portraying what's been happening locally and on the national level where, back in 1989, the nation's governors established six national education goals that were later approved by President Bush.

The goals set 2000 as the year when all American youngsters arrive at school ready to learn; students exhibit proficiency in mathematics, science, history, and other subjects; American students lead the world in mathematics and science; schools are free of violence and drugs; and all Americans are literate and possess the skills to compete in a global economy.

A bipartisan governing board now seeks to ensure that national standards are set and that students are measured against these standards. The New Standards Project, a joint venture of the National Center on Education and the Economy and the Learning and Research Development Center of the University of Pittsburgh, already involves partner states and school districts with more than half the nation's student population. With New Standards Project support, teachers (usually assisted by their students!) are devising tasks, inventing portfolio systems, and debating assessment measures in preparation for a national assessment system that highlights literacy, mathematics, science, and, soon, other curriculum areas. If you want to improve something, you have to test it!

Combine this philosophy with the growing notion that buying an off-the-shelf test from a distant, mail-order testing service fails to ensure that what is locally valued will be tested and that what is tested will be valued by the local community. To what local uses are these expensive, multiple-choice tests put? Do they have any effect on classroom practices, or do they simply define students in isolated moments when they are given a number two pencil and asked to fill in a bunch of bubbles on a scannable sheet?

So an enlightened approach to even large-scale testing has emerged. Teachers should design and administer these measures. In that way, the assessment is directly linked to instruction. The teacher is constantly measuring student performance against published standards. "You have to get to work designing your own reliable system or someone's going to invent one for you . . ." has served as many educators' explanation of why they're participating in one or more assessment projects in their districts, states, or nationally, where large groups of teachers exchange and assess students' portfolios.

No matter what the scale of a program, the logic of performance-based assessment translates to the smallest, most "local" unit of all, the classroom.

1. The student understands the assessment, is familiar with the standards, and may well have formulated an independent assessment of the work.

2. The teacher/reader's response is applied consistently to all students' work. The reported response is linked to standards that are published (with examples) well in advance of the actual assessment.

3. *Assessment*, Latin root *assidere*, "to sit beside," implies an ongoing conversation, not a series of pop quizzes. Assessment comprises a variety of approaches through which students show what they know and can do. The next time you hear a test publisher use the word *assessment* as a euphemism for *test*, mention *assessment's* Latin root.

4. If the assessment has high stakes attached, students have repeated opportunities to show that they can meet or exceed the standard.

One might look at all the hours spent on these assessments. Teachers learning to teach and to assess their students' work in a consistent fashion need time, lots of time, to accommodate a performance-based assessment system. Administrators should recognize the energy required to sustain a shift in old habits; the whole community, in fact, may be asked to hold its breath while a new system is built and set running. Five years, to be honest; give it, at the least, five years. After all, how many years and billions of dollars have been spent devising multiple-choice tests?

In the sense that I am as much editor as author of this book, I gratefully acknowledge the contributions and ideas, credited wherever possible, that have informed my work as a writer and as a teacher of writing. Students, teachers, and my fellow writers everywhere are the sources of every idea herein. For Janet, for Vermont's writing network leaders, for Vermont's teachers and for Vermont's students: credit where credit is due. And heartfelt thanks to Dawn Boyer, Linda Hamilton, William E. Varner, Richard Korey, Cannon Labrie, Barry Lane, and Sue Biggam — who read various drafts of this book and helped me make it readable.

A word on conventions for this book: When I say *pencil* or *pen*, I mean any writing implement!

A Practical History of Vermont's Portfolio-Based, Statewide Writing Assessment Program

At the heart of this chapter is the inevitable tension in assessment programs between measurement and professional development for improved instruction. Advocates of assessment programs insist that a testing program is an essential tool in motivating improved instruction. "What you value is what you assess," they say. "Therefore, what is assessed will become part of the curriculum."

So in Vermont, long ago in 1988, the new education commissioner, Richard P. Mills, appointed committees of educators, challenging them to devise statewide assessments in writing and mathematics. The commissioner wanted an assessment system that would measure more than students' capacity to memorize bits of information. Standardized objective tests would only perpetuate teaching to a very limited test. Portfolios would show what students know *and* what they can do, on a day-to-day basis. Such an assessment might be supplemented with a uniform task (for example, a prompted, on-demand, timed-writing sample) to confirm the validity of the portfolio assessments.

At the time this was happening, I was unemployed, unaware of the program that was brewing. But for the previous twenty years I had been writing and teaching writing in a variety of writing residencies in schools and colleges across the country, always a little frustrated that my impact on a school seemed limited to the relatively brief time I had with its students. I wanted something more permanent; perhaps working directly with the teachers would ensure greater longevity for my ideas. So when I saw an ad in the local paper for a writing/secondary English consultant at the State Department of Education, I interviewed for the position and bluffed my way through the question that asked about my experiences in writing assessment. I knew little about testing and had always been skeptical of the notion that one could devise a system that would fairly judge students' writing samples or measure the improvement of groups of students. Somehow, I wormed my way into the position.

Getting Started

My first look at "assessment" came at a conference on writing assessment sponsored by the National Testing Network. I learned that *assessment* is part of an ongoing conversation, not just a periodic score obtained through testing. I learned that in a fair assessment program, the rules and criteria are known to all participants well in advance of any formal evaluation. It was a revelation to me that both fair assessment and fair testing offer the student the precise standards by which a judgment will be made.

I have to admit this new focus sounded, if suspect, good to me. I was distressed that it had not prevailed in the 1950s, a time that still haunts me in a nightmare. There, among hundreds of classmates sitting in rows in a stuffy gymnasium, I finally break my pencil in frustration and march from the examination with a strange sense of triumph, telling the teacher in charge, "Take this test and shove it!" Except for this occasional nightmare, I have not unduly suffered for my lack of skill as a taker of tests. But it tickles me that in a contemporary, portfolio-based assessment system I might have been considered a good student, maybe even a pretty good student!

So as little as I knew about testing, I was happy to place myself among those who say, "If we don't design a useful and humane performance-based assessment, someone else will come along with a test!" And, "If a teacher is going to teach to the test, we might as well design a test that is worth teaching to."

Sometimes arrogantly called "*authentic assessment*," performance-based assessment looks at what students can do, letting them know in advance what the standards are. The Girl Scouts and Boy Scouts, organizations that award merit badges upon completion of specific, well-defined tasks, provide an example of this form of assessment.

Vermont's announced purpose in assessing student writing is to identify the strengths and weaknesses of each school's *writing program*. The state has no interest in collecting data on individual students, so portfolios of the actual writing that a student does during the school year make better sense than a test; but as a means of ensuring some link with "traditional" testing, each fourth- and eighth-grade student also submits a piece of timed writing in response to a uniform "prompt" — a single writing topic that all students address. Parallel efforts have also brought portfolio-based mathematics assessment to Vermont's fourth- and eighth-grade classrooms.

The Vermont State Legislature is paying for this program. When the Department of Education first proposed assessment by portfolio, the legislators told department officials that the plan was too hazy, possibly unrealistic. The department responded with a detailed plan for a portfolio-based assessment system that would be piloted in 1990–91 and implemented statewide in 1991–92. The legislature awarded the funds.

I had arrived at my new job in the fall of 1988. The following spring the commissioner of education asked me to assemble a team of the state's teachers who would design Vermont's portfolio-based writing assessment program. The commissioner and his deputy in the project promised to listen carefully to the recommendations of the design committee, but the program would have to be created with certain commitments in mind regarding data delivery. And we'd need to have a credible plan no later than the fall so that Vermont educators could be apprised of the proposal while it was still in its design stage.

Skeptical though I was of any means of assessing writing, I wanted to assemble a committee that would accept the challenge enthusiastically. A small committee would ensure each member an opportunity to make meaningful contributions, but we needed participants who represented the diverse groups of teachers who would be affected by our program. So I asked seven teachers with varied specialties — but a common interest in writing — to volunteer their time for three meetings. I was sure we could put together a credible recommendation after two or three meetings and promised the committee members that we would adjourn well before the end of the school year. But by the end of my second meeting with the Writing Assessment Leadership Committee, I saw that beating the deadlines would be a challenge. The seven members, all teachers, were just getting to know and to like each other: They talked a lot!

I was slowly recognizing how important social interaction is. A stiff committee isn't going to dream very much. I was lucky to be working with people who wanted to meet more often than I thought was necessary. In June we had met five times, and I announced that we could resume our work in early September. "No," came the unanimous response, "we need to meet throughout the summer — every three weeks." And these people were volunteering their time!

In the process of developing the program, the committee participated in several battles with the department's program development officer, who supervised the planning of assessment initiatives. I was surprised by the first of these disputes because I had thought that the department's intention had been clear that the portfolios would be part of the assessment. "What do you mean these portfolios will be assessed?" asked the committee in mid-July. "Assess a uniform, prompted-writing sample, assess the best piece, but leave the portfolio for instruction purposes only!" At the time, I was swayed by the persuasive skills of my fellow committee members and tried hard to represent their argument to the commissioner, who replied that he'd made a commitment to Vermont's legislature: portfolios would be a major component of the assessment. Two years later the enormous value of assessing the portfolios became clear to me: Students and teachers who consistently view their own and one another's writing through a common lens begin to develop a common language and common expectations; and, because of the assessment, teachers have an opportunity to glimpse what is happening in one another's classrooms.

Key to most policy debates was the committee's ultimate commitment to professional development and an arguable view that the administration's principal interest lay in delivering data. We have a budget of approximately $400,000 (one-tenth of 1 percent of total Vermont expenditures on all public schools), which is shared by the writing and mathematics assessment programs. Measurement and results remain a driving force behind the program, which sometimes frustrates me, but I have repeatedly seen the ongoing commitment of our funding sources to vigorous professional development: Half our budget is reserved to provide teachers with access to one another as resources. Without the "measurement process," our professional development efforts, the program component that most engages teachers in isolation-breaking, face-to-face meetings, would be without focus.

The committee's summer meetings were often combative, but they were a joy for their intensity and frequent, necessary moments of levity. By summer's end, we had outlined a program: Fourteen criteria would be suggested for application to a portfolio of either fourth- or eighth-grade writing. Each portfolio would contain, at the least, a student-designated "best piece" of writing, a letter about the choice and composition of that piece, a piece of creative writing, a report on a public event or a response to some social or scientific phenomenon, and writing from outside the language arts curriculum.

The First Draft

In September, 1989, the committee published a twenty-page draft of its proposal, a neatly calligraphed booklet (Figure 1–1). It included a list of the types of writing that would comprise a portfolio and the fourteen criteria by which this writing would be assessed. The booklet made several requests for responses and allowed generous space for teachers to enter their comments (Figure 1–2).

In other words, the proposal also acted as a questionnaire. We mailed twenty-two hundred copies to Vermont's fourth- and eighth-grade teachers, their principals and superintendents, and to professional colleagues around the country. One hundred and seven responses (some coming from committees of teachers or even from entire faculties) helped us to redesign the program. "Too many criteria!" most responses said. "Keep it simple!" The committee started whittling and refining. Among criteria that were discarded or combined:

- awareness of different audiences
- logical thought sequence
- understanding of prose or poetic structure
- sentence/paragraph revision
- editing for spelling and syntax
- use of prewriting strategies
- use of conferences

and a series of other considerations that focused ever more intently on the writing program.

Five criteria, currently in place, emerged from our deliberations: purpose, organizaton, detail, voice/tone, and grammar/usage/mechanics. As frustrating to some Vermont teachers as our constantly changing guidelines may have been, the committee's position was that the program needs to demonstrate enormous flexibility by responding to the experience of the educators and students who work with it.

When the Vermont State Legislature awarded funds for the 1991 fiscal year, the Department of Education invited six hundred representatives of our 144 pilot schools (approximately half the schools that would eventually participate) to Vermont's only suitable-for-six-hundred, central indoor gathering spot. As teachers entered this cavernous room, they received heavy notebooks containing what we thought was all they needed to know about Vermont's assessment program. Teachers were talked at all morning, and the afternoon wasn't much better. The meeting could not have been judged a success by any criterion other than attendance.

FIGURE 1-1

PORTFOLIOS AND INSTRUCTION

We'd like to suggest a few ways the writing portfolio can lead to improved teaching and learning. The teacher, as a "writing coach," may cite each student's portfolio as an individual record of achievement. The portfolio contains all drafts of any piece the student wants included, and because the portfolio spans at least one school year, it can become quite thick: students who have never kept portfolios are often surprised when they see how much work they have completed.

The portfolio provides a body of work for private conferences. Some teachers like to thumb back through previous assignments to show students how much their writing has improved.

Perhaps as important as anything is that teachers join their students in keeping portfolios, while exploring the several challenges a writer faces. In this venture, the teacher's role as "teacher-researcher" is enhanced, because the teacher becomes personally aware of the pleasures and the pains a writer faces. Seeing the teacher's involvement, the students are most likely to take seriously their own work as writers. (*See Bibliography*).

GOOD WRITING, GRAMMAR AND "THE PROCESS"

After our many meetings and discussions, it has become clear that the word "assessment" means different things to different people. No surprise. But one idea seems to be a constant among variables: that there <u>is</u> something we may call good writing.

Over and over, researchers, teachers, students and readers insist that the best writing is expressed in a "voice" that is natural to the writer, not forced or made "formal." Because Vermont teachers will serve as evaluators, we should work toward a common understanding of what good writing is. Good writing is deeply rooted in the culture, a part of our very means for survival; but it's elusive and fragile, too. Assessment meets the challenge of finding good writing and keeping it off the endangered species list.

"Writing involves organizing one's thoughts, feelings and knowledge, usually with a specific purpose and audience in mind. But it can also involve the active discovery of one's thoughts, feelings and knowledge." (Writing Assessment Committee).

Figure 1–2

"Writing is the process of constructing meaning through the dynamic interaction of the writer's knowledge, the language available to the writer, and the audience for whom that writer is writing." (Writing Assessment Committee).

"The comprehensive question is whether the writer exhibits power to inform and move an audience through control of a large range of the English language." (National Council of Teachers of English: "Achievement Awards in Writing—Procedures for Judging").

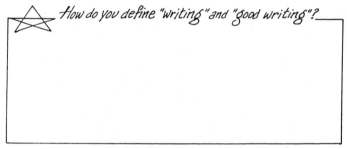

How do you define "writing" and "good writing"?

"Write, write, write" is the advice of writing researchers. It's important to become aware of grammar and to learn proper spelling, but these skills cannot be learned in isolation from the act of writing. As grammar and spelling problems arise, they should be solved on an individual basis, within the context of the student's own writing.

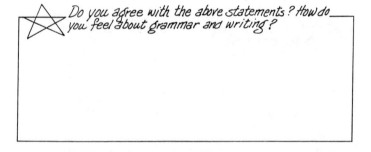

Do you agree with the above statements? How do you feel about grammar and writing?

As a committee of educators we know there are many ways of teaching writing. "Process Writing" or "The Writing Process" has gained a broad following in Vermont, and we support it as a valuable strategy for helping people develop as writers. But we also recognize that it is not the only way to foster good writing.

We learned our lesson and, as the year unfolded, the department planned smaller, regional meetings for teachers who were piloting the program. These teachers soon realized that our announced intention of inventing the program as it progressed was sincere; their experience in the classroom would continue to inform the development of criteria and guidelines that would form the 1991–1992 statewide assessment. As teachers from neighboring school districts gathered to discuss the teaching of writing, the same sort of social dynamic was building across the state that I'd witnessed in our tiny writing assessment committee. "Teaching is the world's most isolated profession," someone had told me when I first came on the job. I had no idea what that meant until I saw the enthusiasm with which teachers share ideas, sentiments, and classroom strategies. I quickly learned that my services as an administrator were most valuable when they were invisible during the actual hours they had helped to shape. Get the teachers together, set up the overhead projector or the newsprint, then get out of the way. And take good notes.

More tension surfaced between the teacher-designers of the program and the people whose main concerns centered around data gathering when an independent contractor was hired in early 1991. The contractor would oversee the administration and assessment of the uniform, prompted-writing task and would help design the system by which Vermont teachers would assess their own students' portfolios. The contractor would also assemble and report the resulting data. Some members of the committee distrusted these hired guns from out of state who seemed more comfortable with numbers than with the committee's insisted-upon language that would be used to describe (not measure!) each student's writing. Does the writing exhibit and maintain a sense of purpose? "Rarely," "Sometimes," "Frequently," "Extensively." These four levels, indicating degree of accomplishment in each of the five criteria, would create a profile of each student's writing skills. A school's report would essentially be a chart showing the percentage of students who were assessed at each level of the five criteria. Using words instead of numbers to describe the levels of achievement would prevent newspapers' ranking schools on the basis of numerical averages. (The headline I'm dying to see: "Local School Ranks Highest in Voice!") Using adverbs instead of adjectives would help keep students from feeling that their portfolios (or they, themselves) were "unacceptable," or "good," or "excellent," and would keep the focus on the act of writing.

Throughout the program's development, we had neglected the design of the uniform, prompted-writing sample. As late as March, we had not decided what prompt to use or what the format of the prompt would be. Anxious teachers had been asking, "How can I tell my students to write to an external prompt in a timed situation when all year I've been teaching them 'the writing process'?" I don't know how much of this argument would have been defused if, at the time, I had been able to describe the prompt, at least in general terms. When the committee finally met to discuss the prompt, a two-hour debate erupted over whether the prompt would be scored holistically or with the same analytic system we had designed for the portfolio and best piece. The program development officer argued in favor of holistic scoring. It would be simpler and less expensive than our five-feature analytic system. Here's a dispute the committee won, then quickly moved through the process of accepting a prompt suggested by the contractor: "Tell about a time when you felt happy, scared, surprised, or proud." This prompt had been successful in other states and would work for both fourth- and eighth-grade students. Students would be allowed up to ninety minutes to draft, revise, and edit their writing. Knowing these details might not have assuaged all teachers' reservations about the "writing test" that was brewing, but the plan for its administration (allowing access to thesauri and dictionaries) replicated the "real-world" situations under which people are usually asked to write. I have argued this point unsuccessfully with some teachers who won't admit that externally dictated topics and deadlines are often at odds, outside the classroom, with the principles by which some people identify "the writing process."

In any case, a prompted, uniform writing task had been deemed essential in establishing the credibility of Vermont's portfolio-based assessment system. It would provide a "standardized" component to the whole program, a task common to all participating students. And, to ensure objectivity, it would be scored by readers from outside Vermont. The legislature and the public would regard the prompted task as a trusted, established way to assess writing, and the results could be used to verify the portfolio assessment.

When writing researcher Donald Graves visited one of our committee meetings, he mentioned a study Jay Simmons had conducted that showed a high correlation between the scores of students' portfolios and their scores on timed-writing activities. I asked Graves what I thought was a loaded question, "Given this high level of correlation, is the prompted-writing sample even necessary?"

"Keep the prompt," Graves replied. "Keep it for just as long as it takes to prove itself redundant. Otherwise, you're going to have people screaming for a prompted piece or other standardized test to demonstrate reliability."

What I haven't decided yet is whether we may one day face a situation exactly opposite from what Graves described: people screaming to get rid of the portfolio assessment because the prompted piece gives an accurate enough assessment of how our students write. This suggests the same tension between the competing interests of professional development and data collection, interests that compete all the more fiercely when the budget is tight. Our premise that portfolios are a test worth teaching to has, so far, kept portfolio assessment in place.

But the weakness of such a program, especially noticeable during lean times, is that portfolio-based assessment is not especially efficient. It is time-consuming and, on a large scale, requires the acceptance of a common standard by the many people who will act as readers. Yet within the "small-scale" classroom, a teacher assesses each student's writing as the portfolio develops, sharing observations with the student and, ideally, encouraging the student also to assess the work on an ongoing basis. These practices, *in place of* the traditional "correct-and-give-a-grade" strategy, can reduce the extra time involved in portfolio assessment. The extra burden of such a program applies more to assessments that involve reporting outside the classroom than to small-scale efforts, in which the assessment of portfolios is restricted to the classroom or school.

Partially in anticipation of the criticism that statewide portfolio assessment is "too messy, too complicated," our independent assessment contractor suggested that Vermont's teacher-designed writing assessment borrow from the British and Australian models: the classroom teacher assesses each student's writing portfolio, then brings a random sample of portfolios, with the assessment results, to central meetings where teachers' assessments are "moderated," (a process sometimes labeled in the United States as "calibrated to a common standard"). This would train Vermont's teachers to use a common standard in assessing their own students' work, rather than having Vermont teachers go into one another's schools to assess the writing of children they had never met. It would also ensure that each student's work was assessed within the context of the classroom, effectively linking instruction with assessment as parallel, if not synonymous, ongoing activities.

At this point, our contractor introduced the committee to an analytic "rubric" (see page 85), a scoring grid that explains, with brief "descriptors," each level of accomplishment for each of the program's criteria. Our next task would be to bring large numbers of student writing portfolios to a central place so that teacher committees could select "benchmark" pieces of writing to serve as exemplars of the four levels of accomplishment in each of the five criteria. Publication of these benchmarks would provide tangible evidence of, say, a "Rarely" in Purpose that might incidentally be assessed as a "Frequently" in Detail, and so on.

Once we had selected and printed the benchmark pieces, we were ready to invite teachers bearing portfolios to a central site where they would assess one another's students' portfolios and best pieces, in a gigantic portfolio swap. Then, without knowing the scores given to the portfolios of their own students, the teachers would carry the portfolios back to the classroom and assess them independently. The classroom teacher's assessment would be compared to the central-site assessments in an effort to learn how "reliable" his or her own assessment might be. We would probably not need this type of central assessment again, our contractor advised. Once we had used such a meeting to obtain baseline data that would then be compared to teachers' "at home" assessments, we'd know what level of reliability to expect in future years.

Fifty fourth-grade teachers gathered, each carrying approximately twenty writing portfolios. After four hours of training, they spent the remaining day and a half assessing one another's students' portfolios. At the end of the same week, fifty eighth-grade teachers spent two days doing the same thing. In groups of six or seven, each group with a designated table leader, teachers pored over stacks of portfolios. Two teachers assessed each portfolio independently, reporting their findings on spreadsheets that were then compared for discrepancies. If, under any criterion, two teachers' responses to a student's work varied by more than a single level, the table leader invited the discrepant readers outside the room for a brief conference, where their responses were discussed and moderated to the point where they were, at least, "adjacent." Reporting such results produced what is effectively a seven-point scale: Rarely, Rarely/Sometimes, Sometimes, Sometimes/Frequently, Frequently, Frequently/Extensively, Extensively.

What did we see when we collected fourteen hundred writing portfolios for random perusal in search of benchmark pieces, then, six weeks later, assessed nearly two thousand portfolios at our central assessment session? Well, it's probably fair to say we saw the whole imaginable range of fourth- and eighth-grade writing. In classrooms where the program had clearly not been welcomed by the teacher, portfolios contained a grudging minimum of student writing, if any at all. What we found in these portfolios, typically, was a sheaf of worksheets and short-answer quizzes photocopied from workbooks. Fortunately, such portfolios comprised no more than 15 percent of those we reviewed, but they served as a nagging reminder that, in spite of our emphasis on professional development, our message had not reached every teacher who participated in the pilot year's activities. We do not yet fully understand the effect on these teachers of reading portfolios from classrooms where writing is valued more highly than short-answer worksheet drills, but several teachers did tell me: "I had no idea students this age were capable of such advanced work" as they saw in the portfolios from schools other than their own. And, in the following year's review of portfolios, we observed a dramatic decrease (to close to zero) in the number of worksheets and short-answer quizzes. The professional development resulting from such an exchange is, I think, more important than the "assessment results" for which our legislature is asking; we'd be smart to devise a reliable way to measure and report the instructional changes initiated and nurtured by the program.

In a healthy majority of portfolios, we found the program's "suggested minimum contents." Not as many portfolios, but still a majority, contained more work than was requested, and a good number of these contained work that vastly exceeded the minimum contents. Probably 250 of the portfolios that were lugged to the central assessment session contained so much work that a fair assessment of everything in them would have been impossible in the fifteen minutes-per-reader-per-portfolio-on-average we had budgeted. In such cases, table leaders told the readers to review the minimum contents, and then randomly to sample as many other works as time allowed.

At first, assessing the portfolios was laborious, because most readers would score each piece in the portfolio on each of the five criteria, and then seek to determine averages for the final profile. But once they gained confidence, through experience, in their abilities to score reliably, most readers ceased recording scores on a piece-by-piece basis and essentially derived a holistic sense of each portfolio for each of the five dimensions. Having allowed thirty person-minutes (fifteen minutes per reader times two readers) for each portfolio, we were pleased and a little surprised when we were able to adjourn the fourth-grade, two-day marathon an hour earlier than expected, then ran only ten minutes over schedule with the eighth-grade assessment session.

A look at the reports from Vermont's pilot year of writing assessment showed amazing consistency in the strengths and needs of fourth- and eighth-grade writers (Figures 1–3 and 1–4). In both grades, the prompted writing samples, which were assessed by a team of professional readers assembled by our contractor, and the best pieces (assessed by Vermont teachers, who also assessed the portfolios), were found to be stronger than the portfolios as a whole. In both grades, no more than 5 percent of the students were found to write at the "Rarely" level under any of the criteria. More fourth- and eighth-grade students' writing was assessed above the midpoint on our analytic scale than below it.

In almost all criteria, whether they were judged by the uniform piece, the best piece, or the portfolio, eighth-grade students were assessed at a higher level than fourth-grade students. Because these assessments were based on benchmark pieces that are specific to grade level, we cannot expect that eighth-grade students will always be assessed at a higher level than fourth-grade students! Nor should we claim that such results show how much our students improve as writers between grades four and eight!

FIGURE 1–3

Pilot Year Report: Writing Assessment

Two teachers independently assessed each portfolio and best piece; professional readers, hired by an independent contractor, assessed each uniform piece (prompted writing sample).

In reviewing these tables remember that they represent a *pilot year* assessment, when inter-rater agreement among the teachers who assessed the portfolios and best pieces was achieved through moderation if the two readers' scores differed by more than one point.

In Figure 1–3, each table covers one type of submission — Portfolio, Best Piece or Uniform Assessment. The vertical columns show the percentage of students whose work was assessed at the "Rarely," "Sometimes," "Frequently," and "Extensively" levels in each criterion: Purpose, Organization, Details, Voice/Tone, and Grammar/Usage/Mechanics.

There are, also, asterisks marking "in-between" levels of achievement — between, for example, "Sometimes" and "Frequently." These show the percentage of students whose work received adjacent assessments, with one reader assigning the lower level and the other reader assigning the higher level.

P — Purpose
O — Organization
D — Details
V — Voice/Tone
G — Usage, Mechanics, Grammar

Grade 4

	Best Piece					Portfolio					Uniform Assessment				
	P	O	D	V	G	P	O	D	V	G	P	O	D	V	G
Extensively	9	6	4	5	8	4	3	2	2	3	5	3	4	4	5
•	17	17	14	13	19	9	10	5	7	10	8	7	6	5	8
Frequently	28	28	21	19	32	28	26	18	17	32	32	29	22	25	39
•	25	26	31	28	20	30	31	35	29	25	22	23	24	27	23
Sometimes	16	15	23	23	14	23	23	34	36	21	22	27	36	29	15
•	5	7	6	11	6	4	7	5	8	8	6	7	5	7	5
Rarely	1	2	1	2	2	-	1	1	1	2	5	5	5	4	5

Because percentages have been rounded, totals do not always equal 100.

Grade 8

	Best Piece					Portfolio					Uniform Assessment				
	P	O	D	V	G	P	O	D	V	G	P	O	D	V	G
Extensively	16	10	10	13	12	6	6	5	7	6	17	16	19	14	20
•	23	24	22	22	17	15	12	11	14	11	16	16	17	14	17
Frequently	34	29	22	22	33	35	34	28	23	30	38	39	37	34	40
•	14	23	22	22	20	24	24	22	26	26	15	16	14	18	13
Sometimes	12	12	18	15	14	17	22	28	23	23	12	10	11	16	7
•	1	2	4	6	2	2	3	5	6	4	2	2	2	2	2
Rarely	-	-	1	-	1	-	-	1	-	-	1	2	-	-	1

FIGURE 1–4

The graphs in Figure 1–4 group the pilot year's moderated results by criterion — showing, for example, how eighth-grade students performed on Purpose in the Portfolio, Best Piece, and Uniform Assessment. Here, the results are simplified: the graphs show the percentage of students whose work was assessed in the low range (from "Rarely" through "Sometimes"); those whose work was assessed at the midpoint (the asterisk between "Sometimes" and "Frequently"); and those whose work was assessed in the high range ("Frequently" through "Extensively").

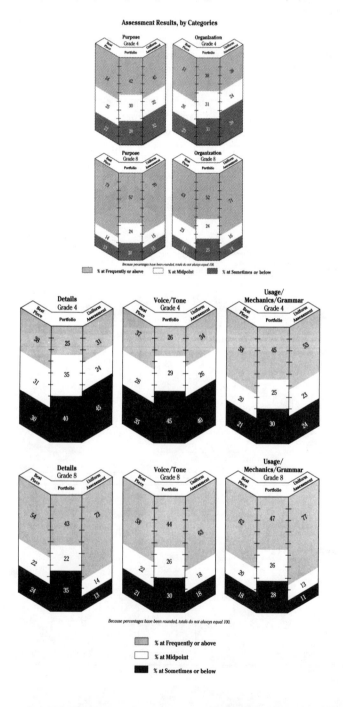

Vermont's project supervisor hopes that eventually we will be able to move from the central-site, portfolio-swapping assessment model to obtaining reliable data directly from the classroom teacher. If that system is implemented, I worry that we will lose some of the marvelous camaraderie that develops during these gatherings. Many teachers arrived at our pilot year's two-day sessions skeptical, some with their arms folded across their chests, some even scowling. But halfway through the first afternoon, they were enjoying one another and were obviously engrossed in the portfolios. The opportunity to peer into another teacher's classroom was exhilarating. Bursts of laughter permeated the assessment sessions, and an occasional group of teachers could be seen blinking away tears as a piece of student writing was passed around the table. At the fourth-grade portfolio assessment session, a teacher on the writing committee who had vigorously and unsuccessfully opposed the "process piece" because he thought fourth-grade students are too young to write about the process of writing, came over to my table at lunch and said "Was I ever wrong! These letters about the composition and choice of their best piece are usually the best writing in the portfolios!" The value of teachers' seeing what other teachers' students write cannot be overstated.

Perhaps the most common observation among teachers at these central assessment sessions was that the most lively portfolios were those in which the student had been encouraged to explore the writing assignments without excessive teacher guidance. These exhibited the greatest sense of student ownership. Portfolios where the teachers had been so conscientious as to dot every *i* and point out every comma splice tended to have an assembly-line feel; because we were assessing portfolios in piles by classroom, it wasn't hard to gain a sense of rote subservience to the teacher, writing as exercise, as opposed to writing for self-expression or discovery. Although such portfolios were in the minority, they certainly ran in batches, by classroom. The fault was not always the teacher's insistence on crossing every *t*. About half the time it seemed to derive from assignments that were too prescriptive, insisting too rigorously on following instructions, so that the student seemed afraid to write anything different from what the other students were writing. All the lecturing in the world, all the professional development sessions that have ever been held on earth, could never be as effective, I believe, as those teachers' seeing the work that was happening in classes where the teacher took a more relaxed stance, possibly even writing with the students, possibly keeping a writing portfolio, too.

The week following these assessment sessions, the assistant superintendent from one district called me for some information. "By the way," she said, "three of my teachers came back from last week's assessment meeting and told me it was the most valuable professional development activity they've ever had!"

The results of our experiment, when teachers returned home to assess their own students' portfolios — not knowing the assessments derived at the central site — were heartening for a pilot year. The rate of *exact* correlation between the central site assessments and those reported by the classroom teachers was 55 percent, "not great — but a good start," according to the contractor, who tabulated the results. Better news was that, allowing adjacency as we had at the central assessment, classroom teachers were in near 100 percent agreement with the results of the large-group exercise. Detractors will point out that on a four-point scale, this unanimity is impressive, but not earthshaking. It was certainly encouraging enough that we felt confident in planning for a statewide implementation the following year that did not require assembling all participating teachers for another portfolio swap. We could check their reliability by asking them to bring a small sample of portfolios they'd already assessed to a regional meeting for assessment by second readers.

Our critics challenged the supposition that adjacent scores on a four-point scale constitute reliable scoring. They pointed out that pure chance will bring this level of "agreement" 62.5 percent of the time. So in our first year of statewide writing assessment, 1991–1992, we asked teachers to meet a much higher level of agreement. A teacher's reported scores would be accepted if second readers corroborated the scores of five randomly sampled portfolios with fewer than eight points of difference. In the pilot year, a teacher whose required one hundred decisions (five criteria times five portfolios times four levels of achievement) were all adjacent to those of second readers would have been accepted as "in 100-percent agreement." By the new rules, this teacher (assuming the second readers themselves were found to be accurate) would be judged "in agreement" 0 percent of the time. Only eight adjacent scores would be allowed!

It didn't work. Teachers' scores were so frequently discrepant that we could not determine whether the discrepancy lay with the first or the second reader. A front-page headline of the December 16, 1992, *Education Week* announced "Serious Problems in Vt. Portfolio Program." The portfolio data we had hoped to send back to the schools, essentially a verification of what the classroom teachers had told us about their students' portfolios, could not be delivered with confidence, and we had to limit our report to statewide data.

In 1992–1993, we tried to sort out the widely varied possible points of weakness in our system. Did we need more and better training? More time (three or four years?) for teachers to internalize the standards? Was there a lack of consistency in our instructions to teachers? Was our rubric flawed? Did we need to lighten the load on teachers? Is such strictly defined teacher agreement possible in the first place?

Throughout the year, we worked on all the areas where improved procedures might make a difference. Professional development was provided through seventeen geographical networks, each with one or two classroom teachers serving as network leaders. Every other month, each network offered a standard set of scoring exercises and seminars on various aspects of writing and writing instruction. A study committee reviewed our rubric, and recommended that it be overhauled, simplified. And we held a five-day summer session where a highly trained group of forty fourth-grade and forty eighth-grade teachers scored a sample of portfolios from each school. Through this rigidly controlled exercise, we were able to observe teachers making these hair-splitting decisions, and could ask them on the spot, "What assists and what impedes the process?"

This summer session preceded the development of a revised rubric and new benchmark pieces to accompany that rubric, which may explain why our new, improved system delivered data that was only marginally more reliable than we'd gathered the year before. But, in our parallel mathematics assessment, reliability figures jumped dramatically; it was in mathematics that a refined rubric had been devised in time for the summer scoring session.

As we continue to refine the system in search of greater reliability, we continue to ask classroom teachers to assess all their students' portfolios and to exchange a sample of those portfolios with other teachers in their network. We encourage these teachers to share the results of their assessments locally, but we will report, as official data, only the results derived at our summer session, and take the lessons learned from that session into account as we refine the program for ensuing years. Our goal is to enable fourth- and eighth-grade teachers across the state to report reliable assessments for every child in their writing classes.

Some teachers complain that insistence on "teacher agreement" is taking the place of sharing student work; our recent professional development sessions have focused heavily on scoring. At the same time, the commissioner and our state board believe that, as much as anything, this is an effort to foster equity across the state. Student work at one school should be assessed with the same standards as student work at another school. Almost daily, teachers make decisions and judgments that will affect their students' lives forever; it seems only fair that an "A" in Bennington should mean the same thing as an "A" in Canaan, and that diplomas from every school in the state be regarded with equal respect.

Our hope is that, within a few years, we'll be able to repeat — this time sucessfully — the assessment procedures we attempted in 1991–92. At the same time, I am doing whatever I can to learn about new ways to measure teacher agreement, and the "reliability" of the ensuing data. How much agreement is enough, and how do we measure and report that agreement? Is it fair to hold performance-based assessment methods to standards of reliability that were developed for objective tests? Does the computer-scoring efficiency of multiple-choice tests forever lock performance-based assessments and multiple-choice tests into a wasteful competition for limited funds?

People from other states mention to me that Vermont's portfolio-based assessment program has a chance of success because Vermont is a relatively small state, with only 100,000 students. Perhaps larger states would face greater challenges in making such a system work, but Australia and Great Britain have used performance-based writing assessments successfully, and in the United States the New Standards Project has been devising a national system for reviewing student portfolios. Arguably, size can be overcome by thoughtful organization. The issues of reader training and reader agreement, however, are likely to loom larger in programs involving multiple rooms full of readers than in assessments where only one or two schools are involved.

Vermont's assessment results, over the next few years, may answer some questions we have not yet addressed: Are we holding our students (and ourselves) to a high enough standard? (The benchmark selections provide a subjective answer to that question.) Is our scale sufficiently discriminating to keep assessors from lumping their responses in categories that are too general? Does our system take sufficient care to ensure that teachers will be objective in assessing their own students' work? What will we do, if we return to our original plan of seeking reliable statewide data from teachers' reports on the portfolios of their own students, when a teacher's assessments are way out of line with those of other teachers?

And what is next, once we have worked out the glitches and created a useful and reliable system? First, I continually remind myself, we should never "lock up" our system by chiselling its guidelines in stone. For the program to be useful, it must be forever responsive to the experiences of those who are asked to make it happen. The day we decide that we have the perfect assessment system is the day the program starts to die.

Writing is only one part of the academic picture. Will we be able to take the lessons learned from our infant experiences assessing writing and apply them to other disciplines, or at least to other areas of "the language arts"? This approach can certainly be applied to reading, and possibly to speaking and listening as well. To reflect the growth and depth of a student's understanding of literature, a portfolio might contain student papers that respond to selected works. Such writing, collected at strategic intervals in an academic career, would surely show more about the student's progress as a reader, an *interpreter* of literature, than content-based, objective tests.

A strength of Vermont's system has nothing to do with the details or with the assessment itself: Vermont's teachers built the program from scratch. An increasing sense of involvement grew from teachers' responsibility for developing the guidelines, nominating the criteria, and fighting the policy battles. Members of the design committee consulted their colleagues at every stage of the program's development and they continue to listen to what their fellow teachers and students have to say. It makes me wonder: Can there ever again be an off-the-shelf test that Vermont teachers and administrators welcome?

Yet, as I write this, I am painfully aware that patience is wearing thin in high places. What further changes must we make to keep our funding intact? Even as we wrestle with the questions raised by our ongoing experiment, what are we getting from the program already in place? Teachers are becoming more and more intimately involved in the teaching and assessing of writing, their students are coming to understand what is expected of them and their peers across the state, and a statewide conversation has begun: What is good writing and how does one produce it?

◆ 2 ◆

Music
and
White Noise

B rows furrowed, eyes scanning the page, Timmy presented his paragraph, an extraordinary description of clouds that included the startling image of a "soft lawnchair in the heavens." I asked him to read it again. First-, second-, and third-grade students, so many sardines compressed on the library's carpet, had fallen silent. It was one of those rare moments when everyone — children and teachers — recognized unusual achievement. Brows furrowing again, Timmy focused on the page and recited his paragraph. Its power was confirmed in this repeat performance.

A loud bell proclaimed the end of our session, and as the students were filing out of that tiny school library, I caught up with the second-grade author and asked if I might make a photocopy of his paragraph to take home. He seemed pleased and showed me his page: a confusion of lines and house-shaped objects covered the paper. "Here's my paragraph," he said with pride.

When I mentioned this later to Timmy's teacher, expressing awe at his seeming word-for-word and unstumbling repeat delivery of the paragraph, she laughed: "Oh, you don't know Timmy!"

As I write this, I am chagrined that I did not take Timmy's page and photocopy it. What a lost opportunity, in every way. Photocopying the page would have affirmed the author's sense that his writing is important, and — even though I had only a memory of Timmy's voice to decode the message — I would have the artifact, access to the mystery of his symbology. My definition of "writing" was so narrow that I missed the opportunity to save a great paragraph!

But my point in telling this story is to acknowledge from the start that every student is an individual with unique promise of idiosyncratic expression. That expression is not evoked equally from all, nor is it equally inspired by any single approach to teaching. In spite of my belief that no one can teach writing, I strongly advocate an environment in which students can learn to write. A variety of approaches, from near independence for highly motivated writers to heavily assisted communication for people without the skill to create words on paper, constitutes what I call "writing instruction." For a few students, the story exists only in the telling of it, and a tape recorder and subsequent transcript may be necessary to unlock the special literacy that, for whatever reason, they just can't get on paper.

Students who learn to trust their spoken language are far ahead of those who are taught that writing is a special form of communication, reserved only for formal occasions requiring proper English.

The Writing Habit

I learned to write by writing, sometimes under the tight supervision of cranky grammarians, sometimes guided by teachers who cared more about what I had to say than about where I placed my commas. Lucky for me that I found a way to be interested in what both types of teacher imparted, and I quickly developed a love for the act of writing. I love to talk, and writing has always been a way for me to see all those words. I also love the sensation of running the right kind of pen over the right kind of paper, and as long as my back doesn't start to ache, I am an enthusiastic typist who satisfies a variety of macho fantasies by typing fast, boldly, recklessly, and (often as not) "wrecklessly." These pleasures occupy a large space in my identity and often gang up like bubbles in an empty stomach, creating a hunger for at least a few minutes of daily indulgence.

So writing has become as much a habit as anything else in my adult life. I like music in the background, whether I'm writing in longhand in my notebook or sitting at a computer or typewriter, transcribing revisions from a hand-edited second draft. Music becomes a kind of white noise, some fairly constant source of varied rhythmic structures. I tune in a favorite FM station because I like to be surprised by the sequence of songs, but I'm almost as happy with a stack of recordings.

A Writers' Community

I've been writing and teaching since 1967, but I have never taught the 180-day school year which, for most teachers, defines a "teacher." When I work in the public schools, the assignment involves a writer's residency, averaging five days; I am almost always treated as a guest, with proper deference from even the most aggressive or restless students. This magic usually lasts the full five days, by which time my residency conveniently folds its tent and slips out of town.

As a writer, I have certain reservations about the use of portfolios for assessment purposes. The "assessment" can be casual and natural when the student simply rereads the work over the years. But when a formal assessment is planned, the contents of the portfolio may assume artificial significance — inflated language and essays written to satisfy a particular formula. If purposes of assessment drive its creation, the portfolio may become another layer of veneer, which is an excellent reason for the teacher to keep a portfolio, too: to emphasize that student assessment is not the sole purpose of portfolios!

As a writer I know what works for me and am eager to share my techniques and quirks. I'm equally interested in the techniques and quirks of others, especially children's techniques and quirks, for children, often surprised by their own flashes of creativity/brilliance, come closer than adults to expressing their delight, their wonder, and their strategies. I believe in the social dynamic of a writing community, which I define as a classroom where students and teacher(s) write together and read their work to each other, freely discussing strategies, problems, and solutions, and describing their responses to one another's work.

While I respect the precepts of whole language, the writing process, cooperative learning, etc., no single big-name set of strategies works for every student. A writing community covers more of the bases of these laudable education movements than rigidly adhering to the latest dogma. Each student is respected and challenged. The writing sessions are almost always fun. (If I am not looking forward to it, something has to be changed.) If it's fun for the students, it will be fun for me and vice versa. We *are* a community. And there is rarely a good excuse for me, as a member of this community, not to write every time the students write.

The "Writer's Muscle"

For one thing, I am a fast writer. I do not allow myself or students to chew on the end of the implement. The pen is almost always moving, exploring the physical sensation of skating fresh tracks on virgin ice. The desire to revise and polish these unplanned journeys comes only when the trail produced by the pen is engaging. Often a matter of topic selection, engagement is hard to engineer simultaneously in a room of ten or more people.

So . . . because I myself am a fast writer, my goal is to create a room full of fast writers while providing a wide range of possibilities for engagement. If I only allow a few minutes for each writing assignment, the assignments that fail to engage students will be over too quickly for them to become disheartened. My goal is to get the students writing and to give them time, if they want it, to read that writing to one another. My opinions, I am learning, are less important than the fact that the students are writing and discussing that writing with each other. It's a little like sports. Students improve their skills and stay in shape by practicing. In sports, this will probably require at least an hour a day. In writing, all that's needed is ten minutes.

"Ten minutes a day — that's all you need," I tell students, "to develop a writer's muscle." The writer's muscle, I explain, develops as a callus on whichever finger (usually the middle finger) absorbs the pressure applied by the thumb to hold the pen or pencil in place. (I'm not quite convinced this "muscle" is really a callus; perhaps it's the mountain it seems to be only because all that thumb pressure creates a permanent crater!) Walking around the room, feeling each student's hand, I use the writer's muscle as a way to make physical contact with a group of writers who are new to me. The bolder the student, the more emphatically the muscle is displayed.

In spite of my insistence that most people write best when they write fast, I recognize that some students may be determined outliners, ponderers, or pencil-chewers. I have to tolerate occasional "rule-breakers," including those who stop to reread, erase, and pencil over, etc., trying to revise as they compose. It's important for the students to discuss their feelings about my "fastwrite" assignments and their strategies for those sessions. Although I discourage outlining and erasures, I eventually accept *any* solution to the challenge of having to write fast for a few minutes, as long as the student completes one final draft for every five or ten "starts."

Getting Pens and Pencils Moving

I walk into the classroom and see twenty-six eighth-grade faces and the top halves of those few students who aren't slouched nearly out of sight behind their desks. Some of them are chewing gum and many of the boys wear baseball caps, the bills of which keep most light from their faces. My patter goes something like this.

"Today we're going to write fast and as much as we can. We're trying to throw as many words on the page in the next eight minutes as we've ever thrown into an eight-minute conversation. Does everyone have paper and a pencil or pen?" (I use the five-minute commotion that generally follows to chat with one or two of the students who, because they came prepared, are not scrounging up materials. I am forever amazed by the irony that, in almost every writers' workshop I offer, even those for adults, I can count on a three- to five-minute break when I ask participants to gather paper and pen!) Whether I'm working with children or adults, I seek to maintain a rapid pace and hope to come up with enough variety in my "starters" to engage every participant.

"In the next eight minutes I want you to write as fast as you can. Here's the situation:

"a) Two people are walking down the street. From the dialogue you write for them, the reader will understand that they are friends, not 'I really am glad you're my friend,' but something more intimate, like, 'Then I told her to get a life! Do you think I was wrong?' They both see the same twenty-dollar bill on the sidewalk at the same time. Describe, using dialogue and narrative, what happens.

"b) You are writing from the point of view of a janitor who is sweeping out the bank-president's office. He notices that the top left drawer of her desk is open, and that it contains a fancy leather book with gold lettering: 'My Diary.' Write what he thinks and what he does as the scene unfolds.

"c) If you would prefer to create your own situation and your own characters, please feel free to do so.

"Remember that we'll write as fast as we can.

"**Pencils up!** . . . Spelling and neatness don't count. As long as you can read it, that's all that matters.

"**Get set!** . . . Prize goes to the longest piece, don't think, just write. We've only got eight minutes.

"**Write!**"

My pen slams down to my notebook and I'm scribbling away, almost always driven by the sound of fifteen or twenty pencils around the room doing the same. I don't look up. The sound becomes louder as more students see and hear that "everyone else" is involved. I continue writing. When I am about one paragraph short of completion, I announce: "Two minutes to go!" I give a twenty-two-second warning when I really have an ending in sight, and I announce the completion of the exercise when I feel the room's energy let up, which is sometimes a minute or more after the twenty-two-second warning.

"Not everyone will have completed the assignment. That's fine. You can take it home tonight and work on it if you want to. Does anybody want to read his or her response?" At this point, if I see that some students are still furtively scribbling, I know the assignment has worked.

Of course I'd quickly tire of teaching if in every class I asked students to write about two friends and the twenty-dollar bill, etc. Each teacher needs to evaluate planned-writing assignments to be sure they are likely to deliver work regarded as important. Developing such assignments, in collaboration with the students, is the topic of a later section.

In classes where students are reluctant to read their work aloud, I simply move on to another writing assignment, using the same format but varying the challenge — a radio play, for instance. I explain that this is just a dialogue between two people, say, on a bus, and one of them is an aristocratic fancy lady from Great Britain, and the other is a tough guy from the Bronx and, having just boarded the bus, he approaches the seat next to her and starts a conversation.

"Hey lady, dis seat taken?"

"See how much you can communicate about these two people through their dialogue," I say. "Be sure to pay special attention to their distinct 'accents' and word choice, and see if you can create a complete radio play in the next eight minutes. Everyone ready? Pencils up! Neatness and spelling don't count. Get Set! Write as fast as you can. Write!"

A Flow of Events

Only when I am halfway through this second writing assignment will I start to look up from my page to see if some students are chewing their pencils. I need to learn why they aren't writing and will approach their desks slowly. Half the time my very approach gets a student to writing — am I inspiration or feared intruder in these cases? And half the time I need to talk with the student. "I can't think of anything," "I don't like to write," and a few variations of such remarks I treat as a challenge to win this child over to writing. The ideas I come up with on the spot are all predicated on the search for a short-term solution: just get the kid writing so I can move on to the next reluctant writer, another pencil-chewer.

"What do *you* want to write about?"

"Nothing."

"Do you like to draw?"

"Better than I like to write."

"Good! Make a cartoon or cartoon strip of two people on a bus . . . ."

"I don't want to."

"All right. Then I have to insist that, for the next five minutes, you write as fast as you can a speech that warns people about the dangers of writing about people on a bus or the dangers of riding on a bus! Don't be afraid to make the speech funny, or silly, or serious, or sad."

Sometimes I ask the students to read their work to one another, but no one volunteers. This rarely happens in elementary schools, but older students can be resistant, or seemingly hostile. When no student volunteers to read I feel I'm in trouble. Something's wrong with the class and I'd better figure it out, and fast. Meanwhile, some student has to break the ice so I can further test the atmosphere. The first student I can make eye contact with is the one I'll gamble on.

I do not allow my eyes to drift from complete eye contact with that student. "Will you read yours, please?" I ask in a tone that is a little commanding, but not demanding. I maintain eye contact until I have my answer. Nine times out of ten it's "Okay, but it isn't very good . . . ." The next day I'll remember to explain how apologies only waste time, but today, grateful to have someone breaking the silence, I let the student grumble about the piece's failings.

If, after all that eye contact, the student declines to accommodate my wishes, I try very hard not to become anxious. Excusing the student in a friendly, offhand-as-possible manner, I search for a new victim for my never-fail eye-contact technique. If the second attempt bombs, I know I'm in deep trouble and buy time with a fresh eight-minute assignment. If I show anger or frustration at this point, the students may feel this next assignment is a punishment, and I have been wholly opposed to writing as a punishment ever since my fourth-grade year when Miss Clough, about twice a week, invited me to remain after school and write, "I shall practice behaving myself" one hundred times on the blackboard.

Another way to break the ice when it's more than an inch or two thick is to provide an easier point of entry for the students. "How many people chose to write about two friends and the twenty-dollar bill?" (show of hands) "How many people chose to write about the janitor?" (show of hands). Then, having made eye contact with one of the students who raised a hand with some enthusiasm, "Good! Will you read yours first, please?"

If I am still without a reader, I sometimes read my own response and lead a discussion of ways it might be improved, both the reading of it and the writing. I thank each student who offers help, but I do not waste time responding to the suggestions, reminding myself: Author, just absorb!

Other strategies for coping with "read-aloud reluctance" include asking follow-up questions of a student who refuses to read. "Don't want to read it aloud? How about describing it?" Or, as a last resort, "May I ask another student to read it for you?" "A last resort" because handwriting and decoding problems often result in a choppy, time-eating reading.

My final option is simply to collect the papers and read them back to the students, with some likelihood that I'll encounter handwriting and decoding problems myself. This is my least satisfactory solution to the challenge of putting students in direct contact with one another's writing.

Adapting Fastwrites to the 180-Day Classroom

My writing rituals require a regular schedule, a "habit." And because I find it hard to start or break a habit midstream, I would initiate this program at the beginning of the school year, at the start of a marking period, or just after a vacation.

Students arrive in class prepared to write for eight to ten minutes at the beginning of each session, ideally at the same time each day. Writing then becomes, at least for the days the class meets, part of life's daily rhythm, a survival activity like eating. Regardless of the students' conscious perceptions of the activity, their systems are becoming habituated to finger and hand movements — *frantic* finger and hand movements if I have my way — daily at ___ A.M. or ___ P.M.

Starting a Cycle of Writing Challenges

The teacher's responsibility is simply to ensure that every student has a topic and to be also engaged in a writing project. The teacher should suggest a new range of writing ideas every day.

Monday: A list of items in a bachelor's refrigerator. A scene where he cooks dinner for a boss he's in love with. Factors to consider — from his point of view, from hers, or third person? Present or past tense? Personal quirks of speech or habit?

Any other scene you want to create that involves two or more people and uses dialogue.

Tuesday: A letter to the president of the United States, explaining why you missed the appointment where he had planned to interview you for a special cabinet position that pays a million dollars a year.

Wednesday: Go back to Monday or Tuesday and rewrite the piece of your choice as a telegram, where you have to pay a dollar per word. See how cheaply you can tell the story or convey your message. Does it help to change point of view or tense? Should it be like a brief letter?

Or: Review Monday or Tuesday's work, taking a section of it to "explode." Provide even the smallest detail or action with moment-by-moment description, using vivid language to hold the reader's interest.

Or: Revise or expand one of the pieces you started on Monday or Tuesday.

For Thursday I would encourage the students to brainstorm a long list of possible topics, leaving them on the board for continual reference, additions, and deletions, for the rest of the semester.

For Friday, the conclusion of the first week, the class should be ready to embark on a recurring two-week writing cycle. A description of that cycle follows the next two sections.

Writing Starters, Audience, and "The Research Paper"

A history teacher told me how unenthusiastically his students wrote research papers on the Civil War and how bored he was reading them. The class brainstormed a new form of term project and decided to create a newspaper that would capture the essence of a fictional, 1850s New England community — its commerce, church news, entertainment, editorials, and advertisements.

When the teacher showed me the newspaper, I could see the obvious care given to a design that looked old-fashioned, with heavy black type for headlines. Smelling the newsprint and ink, I could tell I was going to enjoy the whole paper, including the ads, many of which were illustrated with printer's dingbats from the period. The teacher may or may not have suggested a political bias for the newspaper's editor and publisher, but the students had taken care to reflect, in the editorials and elsewhere, strong Yankee sentiments.

This teacher simultaneously allowed his class to solve the audience and writing-starter conundrum: Research papers often assume only a one-person audience, the teacher. The subjects/topics of such papers are almost always ill-chosen, too broad or too narrow, and their information is usually paraphrased from stilted secondary sources, the voiceless wonders that are our reference and text books. It may be that students learn the art of paraphrase from concocting such research papers and it's likely that, for a given moment, they know the facts presented in those anguished pages. My question is, does the teacher look forward to reading these research papers? Where the language is declarative, stiff, and factual, the teacher might want to consider whether the student has work in the portfolio that is more natural, and challenge the student to experiment by applying that "voice" to the research paper. It's usually a matter of *assimilating* the information, using direct quotes where necessary, and contesting or substantiating assertions found in the primary and secondary sources. But, as often, fundamental limitations in conceiving audience may have straitjacketed the student's language and thought, inhibiting the injection of a little personality, some personal belief, into the work.

Challenge the student to rewrite the biography of Abe Lincoln as a campaign speech. Better yet, make the original assignment a campaign speech where the necessary biographical information is presented in the context of an effort to win political office! Or ask each student to write an Abe Lincoln rap song.

Other possibilities include: an epistolary story; a piece where the narrator is from a specific time period or has a particular bias or experience to express; the students' own projections of themselves into a contemporary world news situation; their "on the scene" reports for a radio commentary.

Students should be taught proper sequencing skills and should be able to write clear instructions. They should be able to conduct and write up an interview. But these skills are frequently emphasized too early in the game or at the expense of *personal* response or imaginative treatment of the assignment, the very qualities that spark a writer's investment. John McPhee's work provides teachers with a good model for writing on a wide range of topics — from geology to tennis to oranges to truck gardening, all investigated by a single writer — and the sense of investment that infuses the work when the author feels ownership of the material, a clear concept of audience, and the attending compulsion to get it all down on paper.

The trick to delivering these elements of ownership lies in *challenging* the student, not inventing some cute way of wrapping the assignment in cotton candy. And the best check to ensure that an assignment contains sufficient challenge is whether the teacher looks forward to seeing the student's response and to writing a response too. Be specific about the challenge; if you have them, provide examples of work that successfully meets that challenge. And, in seeking to meet that challenge yourself, become conversant with the stumbling blocks you face and share your approaches with the students just as you ask them to share theirs.

Factual Lapses, Streamlining, and Deception

Once students have learned to employ the personality of a selected persona, they may feel more comfortable exploring their own voices, experimenting with the full range of devices a narrator may choose for a variety of writing activities. It sometimes helps to remind students that even "nonfiction" must often take shortcuts that result in factual lapses. Sometimes, for instance, it's just too com-plicated to explain that so-and-so, who is incidental to an essay, is one's cousin by marriage and not by birth, so calling that person a "cousin" may be accurate

Assignment: 5–6 pages, double-spaced, clean copy. Choose one:

1. From Mary Lincoln's point of view, an essay or letter about the Civil War, using anecdotes to supplement her personal observations.

2. Re-create the scene, as it might be described in a newspaper of that time, where John Wilkes Booth assassinates President Lincoln and is apprehended.

3. A eulogy for Lincoln, as presented by a windbag like Wendell Berry's seminary student, Brother Wingfare, in *The Memory of Old Jack* (1974).

Challenge: To create a well-organized sequence of events, presented in a lively narrative, where the reader is able to follow the history being presented.

Papers will be assessed for their success in establishing a clear sequence, for appropriateness of tone, and for mechanical/technical conventions. Students are asked, before they turn in their papers, to write one or two paragraphs assessing the paper's success in these three areas.

enough. Or, to clarify a sequence, certain details may be omitted or invented. Here is an excellent opportunity to discuss ethics and truth in writing!

Do we sometimes need to obscure the identity of a subject?

How does one tell the truth without slander or hurt feelings?

When does "streamlining" a narrative become whitewashing it?

What is the relationship of audience to these questions? What, for instance, is the difference between a personal letter and a letter to the editor?

How do these questions relate to writing that is not autobiographical but purports to represent historical fact?

What are the tricks of deception? Can we spot them in our texts and newspapers? Can we create assertions without actually lying? I recently attended a reading where novelist Don Mitchell presented a piece of nonfiction that involved his ten-year-old daughter, whom he had invited onstage to tug his shirt every time his narrative swerved from "the truth." The audience quickly saw how frequently "nonfiction," often for very good reason, alters historical fact. In *The Silent Woman* (1994), Janet Malcolm describes the difficulties biographers often encounter obtaining reliable information about their subjects, and the question is raised whether, conceivably, truth can be found only in fiction, for only in the fictional world is there only one true set of circumstances, the author's.

Generating Ideas

The track coach who uses the afternoon to lecture athletes about stride is less likely to help them win meets than the coach who asks the athletes to run laps. Writers need to stay in shape; they do this by writing.

So how does a teacher come up with all these topics that will offer each student some hope of engagement? The best source is the students themselves.

Sharon Brown, a teacher in Brasher Falls, N.Y., devised a group of headings, and regularly asks students to brainstorm topics that will fit them:

- something that makes you angry
- something you wonder about
- a topic that seems to be of wide concern
- relations that are special
- things that make people come to life after a dull day
- things to soothe a person
- things that you know that others should know
- an emotional issue, either personal or general
- people of interest
- events of interest
- a look into the future
- a look into the past
- a recurring dream
- a problem that needs addressing
- your favorite period of history
- a place you've always wanted to visit
- making a fantasy come to life
- explanation of how to do something
- school issues that teachers should be aware of

The list of topics brainstormed under "something that makes you angry" is two-and-a-half pages, single-spaced. Here are the first entries on that list:

- people
- recycling
- rumors
- bad drivers
- speed limits
- speeding tickets
- flat tires
- when people are two-faced
- Middle East
- when people use people
- a cold
- rude people
- guys
- child abuse
- sexual abuse
- family members (my brother)
- JV basketball players
- referees
- teachers
- tests
- homework
- ex-boyfriends

Reading these lists, one can see the common and divergent trains of thought brainstormed by a roomful of young people, and the endless ideas of which students, guided by a simple list of headings, are capable. Certainly expository-, narrative-, persuasive-, and imaginative-writing assignments could be specifically devised from such a list.

Another way to generate an almost endless realm of writing starters is to create an "idea wheel." Students are asked to brainstorm a list of possible characters, providing for each character one or two words, at most, of elaboration. So, instead of "a doctor," the students are encouraged to be specific: "a shaky brain surgeon." Each of these characters is listed around the perimeter of a circle drawn on the chalkboard. Next, students are asked to suggest human action: "wins the lottery" or "sails a raft to Europe." These ideas are listed on the perimeter of a second circle that encompasses the first circle. A third, larger circle may be created that suggests specific technical challenges: "historical present," "persona piece," "nothing but dialogue," etc. Replicas of the circles that are on the chalkboard can be cut out of construction paper, and students can copy onto each resulting "wheel" the information from its chalkboard prototype. The wheels are then joined at the center by a single thumbtack so the smaller wheel(s) can be spun, as in roulette. The resulting correspondence of character with action (and technical challenge, if such a wheel was created) provides grist for an eight-minute fastwrite. If only two wheels are used, and each wheel contains but twelve ideas, 144 starters are available. Add twelve technical elements, and you have 1,728 potential writing challenges!

Sustaining a Cycle of Writing Challenges

Once the students have established a list of possible topics for exploration, start each writing session, until Friday of the second week, by inviting the students to explore an item from that list. More than just suggesting topics from this student-authored list, I would seek to create dynamic situations around each topic: for example, "bad driving makes some people angry." Create a scene where a student driver has just backed into an executive's limousine, and the executive is climbing out of the limousine to talk to the student driver. Or write a letter to the editor about bad driving . . . .

On Friday of the second week, I would say: "Good news! Today we have a full forty-five minutes for writing. Look back over the pieces you started during the past two weeks and choose one to work on." I would hold conferences for writers during these every-other-Friday sessions, the only time in the two weeks I, too, would not be writing.

With necessary adjustments to accommodate class size and school schedules, this pattern will provide, every two weeks, a piece of writing that has received enough attention from the student to be a candidate for the portfolio. Assuming the teacher can squeeze in eight to ten conferences every other Friday, each student in a group of thirty can have a conference once every six weeks.

Advocates of "the writing process" sometimes smother a student's enjoyment of writing by insisting that every piece the student starts should be taken through all the steps of the process. In the next chapter, we'll revisit the writing process, and consider strategies for keeping students motivated to do their best work, in their own way.

♦ 3 ♦

Portfolios and the Writing Process

It was Joan Simmons, eighth-grade English teacher at Vermont's tiny Craftsbury Academy, who clarified for me that the keeping of portfolios and their subsequent assessment are two critical stages that have been missing from the so-called writing process.

"At one time teaching writing was easy," says Joan. "The teacher assigned the topic, corrected responses (preferably with red pen), required students to recopy their themes correctly, and recorded the grades. Frustration reigned because there was so little improvement in student writing while the experts explained that not everyone was meant to be a writer.

"Writing-process training created drastic changes. Teachers began to write with their students. They revised, held conferences, and published the results. Students were no longer writing for the instructor, but for a larger audience. Teachers and students became partners in writing workshops, the entire classroom atmosphere changed, and teachers began to see improvement in student writing.

"The experts now suggested that students keep writing folders, and suddenly the pieces of writing had a home other than the wastebasket, on the refrigerator door, or under the bed. Some schools asked their students to keep folders each year and presented their graduating seniors with samples from each year's work. All of this was wonderful, but one serious problem remained: how did one assess student writing?

"With the birth of our statewide assessment program, the final stumbling block was removed. At last there was agreement on the qualities of good writing and how to assess student work. Teachers and students could successfully chart student growth."

The Writing Process

Even with her strong feelings about the use of portfolios as part of the writing process, Simmons agrees that references to "*The* Process," as if there were only one way to write, can be alienating. As "the process" is defined, it involves the steps professional writers supposedly follow. In my estimation, this process works for a majority of young (and old) writers, but to require that a writer observe all the stages of the process, excluding other methods of composition and revision, is to make rigid an activity that insists on obeying an individual's idiosyncracies.

In "the process," a writer first lists ideas, brainstorms, webs, or freewrites. (For an example of webbing, see Steven's fourth-grade portfolio in Chapter 6.) In the old days, students were asked to make an outline before they started their compositions. The outline became a kind of straitjacket for students to don before they could begin "writing." Many children of the forties, fifties, and sixties remember completing the outline only *after* the piece had been written. Once a list, web, or freewrite has been completed, the author writes a first draft. Often, the freewrite will serve as a first draft.

Next, the author revises the piece, providing focus by cutting digressions, expanding the main points as necessary, and polishing sentences. A conference can precede or follow the revision, or a conference can both precede and follow the revision; further revisions may also be interspersed with conferences.

After revision comes editing, where the author pays special attention to punctuation, sentence structure, and spelling before preparing the final draft.

The final step in the process is publication, which is properly defined in its broadest terms: to make public. A single, hand-written copy, placed on the bulletin board, is made public, therefore "published," as is a piece that is typeset and printed in multiple copies. The function of publication might also be satisfied by presenting the piece in a public reading, or selecting a completed piece for inclusion in the portfolio.

This sequence of events describes logical steps for drafting, revising, and polishing a piece of writing, whether it be a poem, a letter to the editor, or a lab report. But too often "*the* writing process" is imposed on students as a formula or checklist to be used with *every* writing assignment. Some students, knowing they will be required to revise whatever they write, will write only to suit the minimum length requirement, or will refuse to "let go" during the freewriting, trying to generate a perfect first draft, one that needs no revision.

That's why I suggest that only a few pieces a month be taken through several or all steps of the writing process. It's hard to sustain the enthusiasm of young people through prolonged activities. The more choice the students have, the greater their ownership of the work, the more likely they'll catch fire and put real energy into the project.

Along the way, students might be asked to discuss or write about their pleasures and challenges in the various writing stages. Just as the students may be asked to assess their portfolios in a completed state, they might keep a diary or journal for any piece of writing they take beyond a first draft. Here is an example.

1. I chose this piece because . . .
2. My first revision improved the piece in the following ways:
3. Revising was fun or boring because . . .
4. I had a conference on this piece with: (check all that apply) ___ another student; ___ the teacher; ___ a parent; other: _____. We discussed the following ways to improve the piece:
5. After the conference I made the following improvements:
6. I consider (do not consider) the attached copy my final draft.
7. I will/will not seek to publish it. How?

Brainstorming or Webbing

In brainstorming, no one is allowed to groan or make negative comments about another participant's suggestion, but using another person's idea in a new way ("building") is encouraged. A successful list on "frogs" from an elementary classroom might start like this:

> slimy
> where they live
> green
> what they eat
> as pets
> how big they get
> bullfrogs
> how bullfrogs make such noise

Older students might come up with a more sophisticated list of concerns:

> physical characteristics
> habitat
> species and families
> reproductive habits
> commercial uses
> natural contributions to habitat
> a world without frogs

A science class might generate the lists just described, while a language arts class might come up with another set of ideas:

> a poem or story from a frog's point of view
> slimy
> the biggest frog in the world
> the frog who became president
> frogs in literature

I like to limit each brainstorm or webbing suggestion to a short phrase, preferably no more than three words. Especially with younger students, this is sometimes difficult. An enthusiastic child may want to tell a whole story at the brainstorming stage. Of course this interferes with other students' opportunities to participate; it also may diminish the originating student's subsequent interest in writing the piece — once the story's been told, why bother to write it? Disclosure of the whole story is like describing a baby before it's conceived: It preempts the discovery and for most writers locks into place their idea of what the piece will be. In effect, it becomes an outline. The time for such discovery is while the pen is moving, because the act of discovery is usually what keeps the pen moving.

Does this explain why so many students resist traditional reports and "research" papers, where the very format of "research and then write" puts discovery first — not simultaneous to the act of writing? In recognition of the value of letting the pen get ahead of the brain, I sometimes offer a writers' workshop entitled "Write Before You Think," and I often hear myself telling high school students, only half in jest, to write their term papers first, *then* do the research.

Having said this, I want to acknowledge that some writers do like to tell their stories before they write them, and for a few students, an opportunity to "talk through" their piece may be very important. The time for this, however, is during the freewriting stage, not during brainstorming, which should be fast-paced and focused on generating single words or very short phrases.

Freewriting

Some teachers define "freewriting" as "you choose the topic," but since I've never had much success turning a whole class loose to unguided choice (see the next chapter for a story about the class where I started to discover that unguided choice rarely works), I prefer to define freewriting as a preliminary stage in writing where the author writes quickly and with little or no concern for accuracy, neatness, organization, or other conventions.

As a group leader, working with students of any age, I often overlook the brainstorming/webbing activities, relying instead on offering a choice of writing starters, usually digging into my own interests and technical obsessions as a writer. A few years ago I was wrestling with a poem about space travel, where the narrator has exceeded the speed of light and thus, in accordance with the theory of relativity, is growing younger because time is running backwards. "How many tense shifts can a piece endure before it falls apart?" is the question I was asking myself. Groups of fifth- and sixth-grade students wrestled with this question that year, as well as some students I visited at a nearby high school where the discussion evolved into more general experiments in rule breaking.

Many good writing teachers argue that offering students a prompt or writing starter makes them dependent on outside guidance for topic selection. I agree that there is some danger here, but I also trust students to write independently of the writing starters I suggest. Further, I encourage students to break, at any time, the rules suggested by the assignment. And finally, I almost always say, "If you don't like any of these ideas, write whatever you want."

As I mentioned in Chapter 2, rather than settle on a simple topic, I like to present a dynamic situation that helps bring action, conflict, or urgency to that topic. So, instead of asking students to write about an injury, I might ask them to "imagine that you are building a fence and have just crushed your thumb with the hammer when a neighbor you don't like stops for a chat. What is the conversation that follows?

"Or write about two people at the opera. One hates the show and wants to leave, the other wants to stay. They have to whisper or they'll disturb other members of the audience. What are they saying to each other, and what happens? Could this be a funny story? Can the words you choose for the whispering have lots of hissing sounds or otherwise make a lot of noise, even when whispered?

"Or write anything else you want that captures a conversation and a sequence of events. Any questions?" (Asking for questions is important at the beginning, but if you learn to answer yes to every question, the students will soon come to understand that just about anything goes, as long as it reflects their own, original ideas.) I often respond to the questions that seem born of anxiety: "Yes, the answer to all of your questions is yes, unless you want the answer to be no, in which case the answer is no.

"So . . . you are either building a fence and bang your thumb just before an obnoxious neighbor stops by for a chat, or two people at the opera are arguing whether to leave or stay, or you are writing any other conversation with a sequence of events, involving two or more people. We only have eight minutes to write, spelling and neatness don't count, pencils up . . . ."

The Advantages of Fast Writing

Fast writing is the equivalent of a potter's heaving a whole bunch of clay up onto the wheel. All that clay probably doesn't have much form, but unless there's clay on the wheel, the potter has nothing to shape. Asking students to write without undue concern for quality or content helps them put something on the wheel. Further, if a student subsequently balks at the notion that the writing might benefit from revision, the teacher can always ask, "How could this be your finished draft? You've only had eight minutes to work on it!"

It's a good idea to remind students that not everything they write is going to be worth further work. Professional writers generally estimate that no more than 10 to 20 percent of their first drafts ever make it into published form, but our classes are often set up in a way that implies that everything the student writes will, eventually, be of publishable quality. In those classes where students are told that their grade will be based on five papers, for instance, the presumption is that each of these five efforts will represent the student's best work. Acknowledging that people learn to write by writing, a more productive approach might be to invite students to write as many extra papers as they wish, until they have the five grades they want.

"Intentionally Poor Writing"

Sometimes, especially in secondary school settings, I run into a group of students who are so intimidated by the fear of looking foolish in their writing that they make only minimal efforts, or refuse to read their work to the rest of the class. In these situations, I often rely on the subversive, "Okay, for the next eight minutes, I want you to write the sappiest love poem you can come up with. You may choose to use cliches, a soupy rhythm-and-rhyme scheme, inappropriate detail, poor grammar, or outright rule breaking to come up with something that is truly atrocious!"

The exaggeration, parody, purple prose, and hearts-and-daggers imagery that emerge from such an assignment usually provide rich opportunities for laughter. Even students who are normally reluctant to read their work aloud generally participate after such a writing exercise. And, surprisingly, on occasion the results are better than where the effort has been to create a masterpiece. Credit the shifted sense of expectation. The author is suddenly relieved of the pressure to come up with something "good," and a whole new kind of energy infuses the effort!

Students usually take great pleasure in explaining where their "bad" pieces deviate from the traditional standards of good writing.

Notebooks, Not Journals

If a writer approaches a freewriting activity with an open mind, knowing that it can be abandoned at any time, the piece can become a discursive exploration of any subject or situation where the author is not afraid to take risks, to try explorations that might never have been ventured, except in daydreams. I like to use a notebook for such freewrites. This notebook is private. It is the intellectual equivalent of a diary and may indeed contain equally private observations. Some teachers use the term *journal*, which I find intimidating and confining.

Students can be encouraged to develop their own coding systems for entries they worry may someday be read without their permission. The point is that the notebook should receive largely uncensored feelings and thoughts, a record of where the mind and heart have been, not pieces specially prepared for the consumption of others.

The notebook is sacred. I don't ask students to let me read it. If I need to be sure that everyone in the class is writing day by day, I ask the students to stand at the back of the classroom and hold up their notebooks, open to the page on which they are currently working. I can see at a glance whether the notebooks are being filled. A student who wants to discuss a given piece in the notebook can copy it or direct a reader's attention to the appropriate pages.

Read Alouds and Public Speaking

Because I believe some (if not all) students learn more from each other than from their teacher, I cannot imagine productive writing classes without frequent opportunities for students to read their work to one another. With secondary-level students, "read alouds" are enhanced by providing copies or an overhead projection of the work being read. At all grade levels, I want the read aloud to be an anticipated moment — it has everything to do with fostering an atmosphere that is conducive to the comfortable exchange of thoughts and ideas. From such a secure base, students can develop a love for public speaking, which recently made headlines as the one event many adults in this country fear more than death!

A danger in expecting students to read aloud everything they write is that no room is left for private writing. Understanding that I will not be required to read or show my work to others allows me to take risks as I write, to decide later whether others should have access to the results.

Giving students an opportunity to read their freewriting to one another may provide the ideal venue for group discussions and instant response, but read alouds can grow stale, expected, and possibly dreaded. One goal of a writing program might be to help each student discover preferred speaking or read-aloud situations, and the confidence to look for or create such situations. To keep read alouds an eagerly awaited event:

1. Don't offer a read aloud every time the students write. Consider offering students an opportunity, every three or four days, to select a freewrite or finished piece to read aloud.

2. Avoid the word *share*! Instead of asking "Who will share his or her piece?" ask "Who will read his or her piece?" *Share* is a loaded, saccharin, term: *read* is more honest. The student who doesn't want to read aloud

may not be at all greedy; the student who will not "share," it might be inferred, lacks generosity.

3. Insist on three rules: no apologies (apologies take too much time); no racial or ethnic slurs; no piece may be intended to embarrass or hurt the feelings of a schoolmate or other member of the community. Note that these rules apply only to work selected for a read aloud. Students may want to explore negative feelings in writing that is kept private.

The read aloud is an excellent time to teach public speaking and listening skills. In practice, these two skills are braided. A good speaker can "hold" an audience, a good audience can inspire a speaker. In less ideal circumstances, still tolerated in otherwise exemplary classrooms, the student, paper jammed in face, mumbles from behind a desk, while dozens of classmates slouch at their seats, rolling their eyes and fidgeting. The teacher is straining to hear in the hope of offering *some* response to the student's effort beyond "Good job, a little louder next time."

The teacher must insist that the student project, enunciate each syllable, and speak slowly. The teacher must also insist that the other members of the writing community listen attentively. When the reader lapses from clear, apprehensible articulation, and this may happen frequently during the first two or three read alouds, the teacher intervenes. This should be a game, not an ordeal. "Anyone who cannot hear the words make a deep and loud buzzing sound." Instant feedback without verbal interference can give the reader a chance to adjust the presentation. Just as a theater director offers nonverbal cues to the actors, or a baseball coach sends signals that don't interfere with the flow of the game, a teacher or entire class can help the student read *with pride*, an attitude that is miraculously infectious and can create positive audience response regardless of content: witness TV commercials and political oratory. A good reader is a good salesperson for the script.

Only in exceptional cases would I allow a student labeled "shy" to get off the hook before making a step, even a tiny step, in the right direction:

1. Stand behind desk.
2. Sit behind desk and tell title of your piece.
3. Stand behind desk and tell title.
4. Sit behind desk and tell title clearly and audibly.
5. Stand behind desk and tell title clearly and audibly.

Et cetera, until the student can stand and read the entire piece to the rest of the group. At any point the student may skip forward one or more steps. By "exceptional cases" I mean those where an Individualized Education Plan (I.E.P.) stipulates that the student should not be asked to participate in public speaking, or those where a child's fear of reading aloud is obviously inhibiting the writing.

Of course all this needs to be tailored to the student's personality and unique circumstances or physical challenges. The more that members of the writing community are involved in the coaching process, the better. Support, not patiently waiting one's turn, is the atmosphere a teacher should strive to create. Once this happens, all the year's lesson plans, the day-to-day activities, can become a working document instead of a coercive maze to be negotiated. What are the skills and bits of content you need to teach? The list should be cumulative, and what's imparted in the fall needs to be *maintained* throughout the year.

Fastwrites and Read Alouds: Physical Attitude

Just as students deserve a rich variety of writing assignments, they should also be offered diverse physical circumstances for writing and read alouds. Find out what works best for the individual student and encourage that physical attitude, with occasional experiments in other positions. Remember that the primary goal here is serving the writers' community, with conditions slanted in any way possible to give each student the greatest chance for success. It isn't a matter of "allowing" students to read aloud from behind their desks, but finding what works best for each of them. Bringing each student to the head of the class takes time, and requiring such a formality might be saved for the big events. "Some of you may want to try reading while sitting down. It's harder to project that way and it's harder to hold your audience's attention. Most of you may want to stand at your desks, but you may certainly come to the front of the room if you'd like to give your piece a little extra impact."

The same holds true for the act of writing. Some people like to write standing up, some like the confines of the kneehole of their desk for knee and leg (and sometimes whole body!) insertion. Some like to lie on the floor, head propped by the hand that isn't writing. The more the teacher can accommodate these individual preferences, the better the students' mental attitudes toward writing will be!

Writing Implements and Read-Aloud Boosters

Some professional speakers prefer a platform and podium, some like to address an audience while sitting on a desk with their legs dangling. Some writers cannot work in pencil, some can't use a fountain pen. Discussion of personal preferences is an essential, often-neglected stage of building a writers' community. With these discussions should come an aura of mutual exploration. "*That* worked for you? Maybe I'll try it with tomorrow's assignment!"

For me, a biggie is the width of the pen and the feel of the ink as it flows. I don't like pencil. It's too hard, too noisy, too impermanent (given my ego), though I love the sound of the pencils moved by fifth-grade students scraping words onto the hard surfaces of cheap paper on flat, plastic-laminate desk tops. Some students work best with a pen or pencil that's been "fattened" with adhesive tape or other adaptive device. Some need low-impact implements, even felt-tip markers, and some students need a keyboard or a tape recorder. I get a certain degree of legibility from a medium-point ballpoint pen, I prefer blue ink (though black photocopies better), and I want a BIC round stic more than anything, bleeding beneath my blazing hand into a college or university composition book that is sewn through the middle, eighty sheets, 10" x 7⅞", green cover with white webbing, about three dollars. The sewn binding keeps it permanent (it's durable and stands up to "foldback" and insertion of extra sheets, etc.). As I mentioned earlier, it is *not* a "journal." It's a "notebook." For all practical purposes, it's expendable, and it doesn't draw attention to itself as a journal or diary does. Thus, my attitude toward it is low key, low expectation. I write in it as messy or neat as I want and sometimes regret the decision.

Given my notebook's permanence, I use a variety of strategies to encode any material that might hurt the unintended reader. If I want to write something unkind about someone who might snoop, I can always use a persona, recording the subject's stupidity as if he or she were the narrator of the story. I can write "fiction." I can break up the text and scatter it throughout the notebook. Using pseudonyms, changing the setting, falsifying certain details, or otherwise inventing fictional environments can create a safe context for work that might hurt someone's feelings.

Being physically comfortable, with just the right atmosphere and the proper implements, can serve as a powerful boost to the writer's attitude. From time to time, a formal writing assessment might be used to gather information on what conditions work best for each student.

The Potential of Theater

A community of performers and audience can dramatically advance the teacher's goal of creating a community of writers and readers. Enormous variations immediately develop when we recognize the potential of theater applied to a writing community. Suddenly, the boxes next to "Speaking" and "Listening" can be checked on that troublesome list of competencies embedded in most schools' language arts curricula. But more important, theater fuels students' writing efforts. The revised concept of audience and character when one writes for the stage, the need to create and maintain setting, the awareness of dialogue and speech patterns, narrative sequencing, the effects of lighting and sound, the potential for music, physical characteristics, and gesture, all play important roles in theater and can inform a writer's subsequent work in other genres.

When a student lapses during a read aloud, I am not shy about asking whether I may borrow the piece to demonstrate the qualities of oral reading that I'm hoping to find. This works best with a student who is talkative and energetic, an extrovert. Having borrowed the piece, I explain to its author the quality my reading will demonstrate. "Listen to how *slowly* I read this piece," I may say. "I'm going to ask you to read it as a parody of how slowly *I* read it. So listen carefully." A good wiseacre will listen with mock attentiveness to the teacher's reading and then go for broke with an acceptable parody, which is a lot closer to the way the piece should have been read in the first place. Call that a big step and hope the lesson sticks with the student and the other members of your class. It usually does. But don't hold any child on the hook beyond the point of making a step or becoming uncomfortable, whichever comes first. Move on. Keep the activity lively. If you are calling on students instead of asking for volunteers, don't let the students know who will be called on next, because that may encourage some of them to relax their concentration.

And, of course, don't insist that everyone read at every read-aloud session. Some sessions will engender so much classroom response that only a handful of students will have time to read. In other sessions, a goal might be to have every student read a short piece. Keep track of any student who is not volunteering to read from time to time. Make such observations a part of your conference with the student. "I notice that you're an excellent listener, but you don't often

IMPROVISED DRAMA

Several summers ago playwright David Schein and I devised this exercise as we were team-teaching Schein's improvisational theater workshop at the Governor's Institute on the Arts. This activity will keep everyone in the class writing at full speed, except for the two students who are improvising the dialogue and action.

First, the class brainstorms a list of characters, including a one- or two-word elaboration for each character — for example, "an Olympic swimmer with a broken leg." To foster creativity, encourage generic characters; that is, instead of "President Clinton," select "a president" or "a national leader."

You'll need to brainstorm at least as many characters as there are students in the class. Write each suggestion on a scrap of paper. Possibilities: mother with newborn; marine recruit; bum who just won the lottery; concert pianist about to perform. Drop these scraps of paper into a hat and have each class member draw one. Ask each student to consider, for a minute, how to portray the character. Then, without knowing which characters they have drawn, quickly pair up the students at random.

Two paired characters at a time improvise dialogue and action; encourage student actors to match dialogue, body language, and actions to their character. The rest of the class, everyone with pencil and paper, is divided into three groups.

The students in group one are stenographers. Stenographers rarely get to see the action; they are too busy capturing language. They write as fast as they can to keep up with the dialogue that unfolds, using abbreviations, messy writing, anything to keep up with everything that comes from the actors' mouths, including coughs, repeated words, pauses, etc. (A more sophisticated system rotates the stenographers so they are not all trying to keep up with the *whole* play that is unfolding. They take turns capturing the dialogue, writing alternate sentences, or capturing the words of alternate characters.)

The students in group two are choreographers/directors. They write down every action, gesture, and facial expression made by the actors, entering only enough dialogue to indicate where the actions, gestures, and expressions occur.

The students in group three are critics. They report what happened and how it could have been improved, much as a professional critic might review a production on Broadway. (It helps to have the students read a few theatre reviews from a local or city newspaper ahead of time and consider a parody of the form as their response to this assignment.)

Have the students read their versions of what happened. Improvisations generating the most enthusiasm are then scripted and rehearsed.

Limit the improvisations to five minutes or less. Rotate the chores so that the stenographers of group one become the choreographers, then the critics, and so on, until each student participates in all three writing activities.

(by Geof Hewitt, Reprinted from *Ideas Plus*, Book Eight, (c) 1990 by The National Council of Teachers of English: Urbana, IL.)

raise your hand when I ask for volunteers to read their work to the rest of the group. Why is that?"

There are times when students tire as listeners, or don't seem to pay the exacting attention one expects of a thoughtful writing community. At such times I often suggest a new writing prompt with a request for a certain kind of response. "A man is walking up the stairs of a two-story boarding house. He sneaks into an apartment that is not his. What does he find and what happens? I hope you will fill this piece with lots of specific detail. Pencils up, get set, write!"

Eight minutes. Now, "Okay, I want each of you to read your response. The rest of you, listen carefully and write in your notebook any detail you hear that you wish you'd come up with. At the end, we'll go around the class and each of us will read from our list." In this way, student authors receive instant recognition for the details they've loaded into their responses. Student listeners learn to focus their critical attention, and everyone gets a list in the notebook of ideas that might be worth borrowing.

Envisioning Audience

Given the writer's satisfaction with those physical elements that can be easily accommodated (teacher allows students to sprawl on the floor when they write, but refuses to play hard rock or rap on the school's P.A. system for *every* writing assignment), a specific description of the audience for the piece can be very helpful. Is the piece intended to be a children's story, a business letter, a letter to the editor, an academic research report, a campaign speech, a personal plea intended only for the teacher to read?

Trust

The teacher needs to be sensitive to the writer's sense of audience. Students who worry that they will be required to read their work aloud may be reluctant to write honestly. A sense of the "private audience" is legitimate and, for some writers, a necessary assurance. To accommodate such students, teachers might occasionally assign challenges that involve public communication so the students who usually consider their work too personal to read aloud or show to others will be obliged to address a general or specific outside audience. Students who habitually participate in read alouds should play a smaller role in any read alouds arising from these "public" assignments, which are designed to provide opportunity for private writers to generate material for their portfolios and to read to their classmates.

Revision

Revise: "to see anew." For most writers, the seeing anew is enhanced by a long period of separation from the original piece. Sometimes I suggest that students not even reread the fastwrite they have just scribbled into their notebooks. "Stay away from it until next week, when I'll ask you to go back in your notebook to look for it."

Let's take a look at a high-school student's final draft, (Figure 3–1) some personal writing in which the flow of the narrative and a sense of the narrator's involvement ("We have a tree in our yard and twice a year it sheds helicopters. He would always complain and sweep them up. That day, he said, 'Well look, Meliss'a home. I missed you.'") pull the reader through to its chilling, final sentence.

FIGURE 3–1

```
                         FINAL  DRAFT
```

I lived in Winooski, Vermont, for five years before we met
the Myers. Mrs. Myers wanted us kids to call her "Glenna",
but my mom said it wasn't right. So we called her Mrs.
Myers.

Mr. Myers called my mother Mona. He could remember my
little sister's name because she had played with his grandson,
but he could never remember my other sister's name.

And he could never remember my name.

Michelle to him was always, "J.J.'s sister". I was always,
"Mona's daughter". He never called me Melissa in the five
years we lived here.

One day, when we had gotten home from Morrisville, I was
the first one that Mr. Myers saw. He was sweeping his
driveway. We have a tree in our yard and twice a year it
sheds helicopters. He would always complain and sweep them up.
That day, he said, "Well look, Melissa's home. I missed you."

I started joking with him. He told my parents, "Come on
over, party on the Myers." So we got into our bathing suits and
went over. We had a lot of fun. We always go over there now.

It was time for dinner. Mr. Myers was cooking and I was
helping bring things out. Mrs. Myers told me, "Here, bring
these things out to your Uncle Kenny."

I said, "He isn't my uncle."

She said, "Bring it to your Uncle Kenny."

So I when out and said, "Here, Uncle Kenny."

He just looked up and smiled.

He was joking with us like he always did. We ate and went
swimming. Then, about six-thirty, Mr. Myers said to us, "Time
for church." He told us that we could stay because J.J. was
still in the pool. "Just look after J.J. and lock up
afterwards", and he went into the house to get ready for
church.

He passed out in the bathroom. His brother Pat brought
him back and carried him to the living room. There he
started to vomit. Everyone was going crazy. The ambulance
came. When they carried him out of the house, he was purple.

Mrs. Myers came out of the house yelling, "It's Kenny, it's
Kenny."

My mom and I grabbed him grandchildren and went to our
house so that they wouldn't get upset just yet.

Mr. Myers died in the ambulance. His son Jeff was gone
that day. When he got home, his father was dead. Pat's wife
had to tell him. I say she could have been a little better
at it.

Jeff made a dent with his fist in the car.

FIGURE 3–2

```
                        FIRST DRAFT

I had a very good summer. I went to some dances in
Morrisville. Went to my uncles parents house met a nice guy.
But he was taken. My parents went to Maine once and took us
kids once.

    My aunt had a baby. A baby girl her name is Morgan. I have
one more aunt how is going to have a baby in Oct. I can't
wait.

    My neibors has a pool and thay just got it heated. I
haven't been in it yet, but I will next year. My neibor is
like a grandmother to me and my sisters, since her husband
dies two years ago. Her name is Miss Myers, and she is really
nice she is always looking out for me.

    Her son graduated last year from here. You should know him,
Jeff Myers.

    Well thats about it. I wanted to tell about my summer.
```

Compare that final draft to a first-draft, high-school personal piece (Figure 3–2), in which the narrator is merely going through the motions of responding, apparently, to that famous all-purpose September assignment, "My Summer Vacation."

What amazes me is that the final draft emerged from that first draft. What magical coincidence of trust, caring, and craft went into that transformation? (Unfortunately, I do not have any handwritten drafts that may have contributed to this startling evolution; what I'm presenting here are facsimiles of the three-page handout a high-school teacher gave me several years ago.)

Some clue to the piece's growth is provided by the paragraphs entitled, somewhat mysteriously, "Second, Third Drafts" (Figure 3–3).

Reading this draft, one sees that the real breakthrough occurred between the first and "second, third" drafts. Maybe the teacher reviewed the first draft and suggested that the real story might be hidden in its third paragraph (where the writer introduces the Myers family and their pool), challenging the student to write a whole piece focused on that paragraph. Whatever happened, the student suddenly came afire with purpose and narrative energy. Compare the opening sentence of the first draft with the opening sentence of ensuing drafts: "I had a very good summer" becomes "I lived in Winooski Vermont for five years when we first met the Myers." This sentence is so direct that the reader is eager to know more, and each sentence that follows grows from what precedes it; the narrative is well-organized, details almost always contribute to the reader's understanding, and the piece delivers a strong, emotional jolt without the narrator's intrusion with the kinds of asides most young writers might feel are essential, like, "I felt awful," "it was terrible," etc.

The transition to a final draft has been largely cosmetic, a careful editing job that may or may not represent the student's response to the teacher's markings on an earlier draft. I am fascinated by my suspicion that the power of the second draft

FIGURE 3–3

SECOND, THIRD DRAFTS

I lived in Winooski Vermont for five years when we first
met the Myers's. Miss Myers want us kids to call her Glenna
but my mom said it wasn't right. So we had to call her
Miss Myers. Mr. Myers called my mother Mona.. he could
remember my little sister name because she had played with
his grandson. but he could never rember my middle sister or
my name. Michele to him was always J.J.'s sister and I was
Mona's daughter but he never call me Melissa within the five
years we lived here. but one day when we got homeform
Morisville. I was the first one Mr Myers saw. he was
swipping his drive way. see we have a tree in our yard and
twise a year it would shed helacopters. he would always come
plain and he said "Well look Melissa home I missed you."
then I started joken with him and he told my parent come on
over party on the Myers. so we got in our bathing suits and
went over. We had a lot of fun. he was joken with us like
always did. Mr. Myers was cooken and I was helping bring
out and Miss Myers told me to bring this to uncle Kenny. I
said he was not my uncle. she said bring it to your uncle
Kenny. so I went out and said here uncle Kenny he just
looked and smiled.

Than about 6:30 Mr Myers said to us time for church he told
my family we could stay because JJ was still in the pool.
Just lock up and he went in the house.

to get ready for church he past out in the bath room. his
brother pat brought him back and carryed him to the living
room. there he started to vomet every one was going craze.
the albalance came when they carryed him out he was purple.
When Miss Myers came running out yelling its Kenny. My mom
and me grabed his grandchildren and went to our house, so
the wouldn't get upset just yet.

Mr Myers dies in the amblance.

Jeff was gone that day on his bike when he got home his
father was died. Pat wife had to tell him. I say she could
have been a little better at it. he all most made a dent with
his fust in the car.

grew from the writer's lack of concern for mechanical and grammatical conventions:
a lacklustre, gum-chewing recapitulation of seventy school-free days (first draft)
becomes a dynamic, grammatically flawed narrative, an opening of the fountain.

When revision is understood to be an option always available and rarely
required, writers are freed to write the sloppiest, most discursive freewrites/first
drafts imaginable. They know, as they write it, that they'll never have to look at
it again unless, as they are writing it, they start to fall in love with at least some
of its parts. Instead of being the dreaded next step in the writing process, revision
is reserved only for those pieces that engage the writer or when the assignment,
itself, stipulates revision.

Because we sometimes neglect to show models of revision (often they are too sloppy to be decipherable except to the author), students confuse revision with editing or what amounts to recopying. I like to think of revision as when I casually read through a piece, pen in hand, cutting out all (I tell myself) the boring stuff, filling out the details, and providing necessary facts while tightening the language. Once my pages become too full of marks or as soon as I feel "I've got it!" I go to the typewriter or computer and create a new draft, taking the newly revised pages away for more revision by hand.

I never revise on the computer, but enter the changes on the screen only after I have made them on hard copy in longhand. I have three reasons for this practice. The first is that having hard copy protects me from computer breakdown. The second is that revising by hand allows me to sprawl wherever I want, indoors or out. And the third is that revision does not always improve a piece! Sometimes the freewrite contains paragraphs or sentences in which a spontaneous quality, for instance, is lost in revision. Having each draft in hard copy is critical, and for me, having the original in my notebook is equally important. The notebook is where I can go if the computer crashes or if I lose my only typewritten copy.

At the beginning of the year, it's important to demonstrate revising on the chalkboard or on an overhead projector, and to give students copies of a page that demonstrates thoughtful revision. Little tricks and ideas for revision should be shared on an almost daily basis. Overhead-projected or chalkboard pieces can be revised as a group activity. Students who revise enthusiastically can be asked to explain their process in a brief chalk talk where they demonstrate the decisions they made along the way.

Just as it is important to provide some sort of focus for each freewriting assignment, it's a good idea to provide specific technical challenges to be considered as students make revisions. These challenges can be articulated in a variety of ways: double the length, change the narrative into the historical present; cut out half the participles — any way the teacher chooses to help the students build an awareness of the alternatives that a writer may command.

After THE END, Barry Lane's popular book on teaching revision, suggests that a writer should look for the "potato," the important idea or significant detail that's often buried in a first draft, and make that the lead and the focus of ensuing drafts. This is the sort of "broad stroke" revision that usually distinguishes revision from editing or recopying. Working with students at Vermont College's Adult Degree Program, I have adapted Lane's "potato" suggestion, encouraging students to look for the first place in their formal book annotations where personal opinion starts to emerge. "Experiment with a draft that *begins* with this opinion," I suggest.

Note that the freewrite assignment itself can be phrased in a way that invites a second version. "Using only passive voice, write a brief report on butterflies." The revised version might require only active voice. A third revision might invite the student to make individual decisions between passive and active voice.

Write a personal letter. Revise it into a speech.

Write in the past tense. Revise into historical present.

Write a third-person account. Revise into first person or with a persona as the narrator.

Write a set of instructions (imperative mood). Revise into questions and declarative statements. Revise again to suit your preference.

Write a brief, one paragraph business note. Revise into expanded, fluffy, meaningless language.

Grammar, Punctuation, and "The Process"

"Oh, I don't teach grammar," one teacher told me recently, "we do the process." However "*the* process" is defined, it should include within that definition a moment — or several moments, throughout the compositon and editing of a piece of writing — when the author is concerned with grammar and punctuation. But a definition of the process for an eight-year-old might be different from that for a fifteen-year-old. Getting good grammar into the writing has more to do with fostering a desire for good expression than learning rules. The abdication of concern for grammar, punctuation, and spelling is irresponsible and foolhardy. It's a matter of valuing the variety of elements that comprise good writing, being honest with children, and letting them let us know when they are ready to learn.

The trouble with the traditional approach to teaching grammar is that everyone is expected to learn it at the same time, and people living in homes where parents read and speak well have an enormous advantage over people from families that do not read or use the dominant language properly. And, as I've already mentioned, many language arts programs emphasize "correctness" over expression, intimidating young students and often implying that there is only one way to be "right" as a writer.

Richard Lederer, known as the "Grammar Grappler" for *Writer's Digest*, and a widely read linguist, often gives talks in the guise of "Conan the Grammarian." "Which is correct," he sometimes asks an audience, " 'nine and seven is fifteen' or 'nine and seven are fifteen'?" Audience members raise their hands, and when the vote has been tallied, Lederer points out that the sum of nine and seven is *sixteen*, and that neither statement was correct. "We spend so much effort on correctness," he says, "that we often miss the meaning."

Once again, it's a matter of balance. We don't want to frighten the daylights out of children who are just learning to express themselves in writing, but we need to instill some particle of respect for conventions in their older siblings. Connie Didier, a teacher in Lafayette, La., presents her middle-school students with the following radical statement, written on the chalkboard: "A woman without her man is nothing." After the girls in the room have tried to extinguish the source of the smoke that's been pouring from their ears, Didier asks the class if punctuation might change the meaning of the sentence. Students quickly see the importance of careful punctuation when she adds a colon and a comma. "A woman: without her, man is nothing."

A person who senses that a piece of writing has promise can develop parental feelings toward that piece of writing; the piece must be "raised right" to reflect well on the parent. This is a natural consequence of ownership, perhaps not universal, but common and contagious.

QUICK EXERCISE
(A Collaborative Poem?)

1. Students are not told what the product will be.

2. "Write a phrase — not a complete sentence, just a phrase — for some observation you experienced between waking this morning and arriving at school. You have twenty-two seconds. Pencils up!"

3. At random, call on students to read their phrases. An option to calling on students is collecting the written phrases.

4. Write the phrases on the board as you receive them, each phrase on its own line, asking the students to enter the same lines in their notebooks. Stop when you have ten to twelve lines. Don't hesitate to include your phrase!

Here is the response a group of middle-school students generated. As I took dictation from the students, I modeled my own, homemade form of shorthand:

> The sprgs on the seat r obliterated
>
> Oatmeal again
>
> Cloudy rainy atmosp w/ colors all arnd
>
> Beauty fds truth, truth fds beauty
>
> A steamg hot egg sandwich
>
> T sun radiatg thru t clouds
>
> T wd was haulg
>
> Run t car up on t sidewalk to park
>
> I saw the leaves expressg themselves. Again.
>
> Didn't know we had class
>
> Dilettante's gaze
>
> A sesame seed bagel tht tasted like chicken broth
>
> Cold wind
>
> Freezg while waitg for t bus
>
> Red ashy coals fadg away in t wdstove
>
> T trees flew by like a blur as t sweat dripped off my brow

I write exactly what the students have dictated, to the point of asking about punctuation and being sure the student reads exactly what is on the page (there's often a difference, albeit sometimes subtle, between what is written and what the author *says* is written). I then read the responses aloud, carefully and slowly, using my voice to smooth over the rough spots. "Okay, what have we got here?" Students will often respond, "A poem!" "Alright, maybe so. But what makes it a poem?" "The way you read it made it sound like a poem." "Plus, it's all pretty much about the same thing — you know, morning images." I hope that the students are coming to see that good speaking skills enhance the audience's response to a piece of writing, and that even the random ideas of a group of diverse students — the equivalent of a bunch of random impulses from a writer's brain — can be made to sound like a unified piece.

(continued)

"Be sure you have copied these lines into your notebooks. I'm going to ask you to use this as your first draft and, for homework, to revise it into a poem or story that you've changed so much you can call it your own. Here are ways I might consider revising the piece . . . ." Spontaneously, now, I want to show as many strategies for revision as I can, announcing my biases as I go.

> The springs on the seat are obliterated,
>
> Oatmeal again! (**Exclamation point adds a little zip.**)
>
> Cloudy, rainy atmosphere with colors all around:
>
> Does beauty find truth, truth find beauty? (**Question mark adds variety.**)
>
> The sun radiates through the clouds (**Participles are really emasculated verbs — they've been robbed of tense!**)
>
> Like steam rising from my breakfast, my lame toe! (**Nonsense, perhaps, but a later revision may clarify this expansion on the original response, with "lame toe" added because it is almost the same as "oatmeal," only backwards — a little nod to word play. Later, we come to "sidewalk" and I point out that backwards it is "clawed ice."**)
>
> The wind was hauling
>
> as I ran the car up on the sidewalk to park.
>
> I saw the leaves express themselves. Again. (**I really admire this use of a fragment for emphasis. Omitting the ensuing three lines sacrifices some excellent details, but seems necessary for continuity: Maybe the lost lines can be worked back into a later draft.**)
>
> Cold wind knifed my jacket as I waited.
>
> Trying to stay warm I thought of red coals
>
> In the woodstove, then boarded the overheated bus: (**Adding "overheated" justifies the poem's final image.**)
>
> Trees blurred as sweat dripped off my brow.

"Needless to say, this was a fast, almost thoughtless revision, just to show you the kinds of changes you might want to consider. I'll certainly go over the revisions I just made so hastily and reconsider each one because I know that, although revision often leads to improvement, it doesn't always make things better!"

Here are suggestions for students who may feel stuck in their approach to revision:

> Review with an eye toward eliminating as many adjectives and adverbs as possible, strengthening as necessary the nouns, verbs, adjectives, and adverbs they modify.
>
> Counting syllables in each line, create a "syllabic poem," in which each line has the same number of syllables, or in which a syllabic pattern is established.
>
> Rewrite the piece as if it were being told by the Queen of England, from her point of view. Try to capture royal British speech patterns.
>
> Review the piece and determine whether the imagery is primarily visual, tactile, aural, olefactory, or cerebral. Create a second draft that makes use of *all* the senses.

RULES FOR REVISING OUR CONCEPT OF REVISION

1. Be more interested in what is NOT on the paper.

2. Ask questions that make the writer want to tell and write more.

3. Understand that one method of revision is to write a new paper.

4. Develop strategies that fit your students' individual and personal needs.

5. Pay attention to your students' revising process and find methods, such as interviews, to make them aware of it.

6. Don't make your students revise everything they write. Rather, teach them that writing *is* revision.

7. Never be afraid to be critical. Know when to be a tough editor and when to be a nurturing teacher. Remember that too much unqualified praise can be as damaging as flat rejection. Focus your criticism on one or two points.

8. Never tell a student a paper is finished. Always point out more suggestions for revision. Remember Flaubert's assertion, "A work of art is never finished, only abandoned."

9. Find methods to put students in charge of grammar and spelling problems. Better to have an imperfect paper where the students have done their own correcting than a perfect paper where the teacher has done it for them.

10. Encourage the peer group revision process where possible. Let the students be their OWN best critics, but give students critical guidelines to follow.

Reprinted from *The Portfolio Source Book,* edited by Andrew Green and Barry Lane, (c) 1994 by Vermont Portfolio Institute.

What if we told our third graders, "You're not ready for the rules yet" and then relented, teaching only one? "How many of you want to write stories that break this rule?" Breaking a rule is a good way for children to show that they understand it.

When I work with students at the junior-high or high-school level, I seek not so much to teach the avoidance of errors as control over the language. So, if a student habitually writes run-on sentences, I ask that student to write a paper that is a single, run-on sentence, and then to give a minilesson to the rest of the class on run-ons. The student who writes frequent sentence fragments might be challenged to write a paper with nothing but fragments, and to give a lesson on the fragment. "The King of the Run-on" and "The Fragment Queen" might then be challenged each to write a piece where half the sentences are fragments, half are run-ons, thus learning and practicing another kind of technical "error." Control, not fear, is what I'm trying to impart.

The Conference

Keep it brief! Three minutes or so. For many students, this is a time to make personal contact with the teacher in a private discussion. If the sessions are known to be prolonged, students may be anxious before the sessions begin. A student who knows that the session will be brief will probably use the time to let the teacher know what is needed. Anticipating this brief interval with the teacher every six weeks or so, the student may even begin to "plan" for the conference, being sure the time is used well.

I start such conferences only having found something positive in the student's work, and I use it to open a conversation. For instance, "I'm really glad you're using exclamation points to add zest to your dialogue; is this a conscious choice on your part?" Or, "That's a scary character you've created in the Halloween story. I'd hate to run into her in a dark alley! What does she look like, and what are some things she does that really scare people the most?"

Such focus on open-ended questions, not judgments, is essential for successful conferences. The conference should end as soon as the teacher has briefly surveyed the student's progress from the previous conference and posed one special challenge from this conference, such as "more judicious use of exclamation points and increased use of question marks," or "a rewrite of the Halloween story that is rich in detail."

In almost every case, I try to remember to address "the narrator" of the piece instead of the student, asking "what did the narrator intend here?" instead of "what are you trying to say here?" This allows a comfortable buffer between the student and the voice of the writing.

A simple record on the portfolio's inside back cover provides the teacher and the student a convenient reminder of what has happened in these conferences.

Conference Record: _____
(Student's name)
Date of conference: _____.
Commendations:

Goal for next conference:

Date of conference: _____.
Commendations:

Goal for next conference:

Date of conference: _____.
Commendations:

Goal for next conference:

Date of conference: _____.
Commendations:

Goal for next conference:

My suggestions for conferences with students are pretty close to my ideas for marking on student papers: Stay focused on content and only one or two technical matters. Ask questions or tell what you get from reading the piece, e.g.,

"Here the narrator's observation about what his business colleagues wear tells me he's style conscious." Or, more generally, "This piece expresses a strong view on abortion. I am pretty sure that the narrator, although trying to remain objective, is in favor of allowing women the choice of legal abortion."

Ask questions. "Did you intend for the narrator to come across as pro-abortion?" Listen carefully and try to guide the student toward a new piece of writing or a revision that addresses the challenges noted during the conference. If the students says, "I can't seem to get dialogue that sounds realistic!" suggest taking notes on overheard conversations (lunchroom, schoolbus, etc.); the writer can then alter the content, but not the flow of these eavesdroppings, allowing them to provide the form of a conversation. Thus:

> "My grandmother died last week" becomes
> "My cousins are coming to visit."
> "I'm sorry. Was she very . . ." becomes
> "That sounds like fun. How long . . ."
> "Just 64. But she was getting mean because . . ." becomes
> "Six weeks. Their father lost his job and they need . . ."
> "*My* grandmother got mean just before she died!" becomes
> "Seems like everyone's losing their job these days!"

Conferences don't always need to involve the teacher. Once the teacher has modeled good conferencing skills, students can work with one another. As long as the focus of the discussion is on the work and not the student, conferences are generally positive. Remind students to refer to "the narrator," rather than "you, the writer" to help ensure that the focus remains on the work itself.

At one elementary school in Barre, Vermont, a visionary principal has come up with a daily ritual: Students take turns, day by day, visiting his office and reading a piece to him. Each student receives a badge after the reading that says, "I read my writing to the principal!" This is not a conference, per se, but it does provide the students with a sense of occasion for the formal presentation of their work.

Teachers' Biases

Perhaps my most successful writing class was a two-week, two-hours-per-day, six-days-per-week session in 1990 when I worked with a dozen high-school students who arrived at our first meeting already blessed with what I consider the essential ingredients for a good writers' community. I needed only a bare minimum of time to review ground rules and get the class running. In addition to the fact that all members of the class enjoyed writing, one or two of them were willing to speak their minds, to be wiseacres when they felt like it, to take risks. This inspired a teacher who is more often accustomed to classroom wide compliance with the demands of "Mr. Authority."

In describing the content of our writers' workshop, I had set as a possible goal the writing of a collaborative novel, something I had never done. "If enough students are willing, we may, during the second week of our meetings, create a short novel, each participant taking responsibility for one chapter."

The students quickly made clear that they were interested in accepting this challenge (see Chapter 4). I made clear that, before I agreed to launch such a difficult project, they would have to recognize my biases. I did not ask the students to *accommodate* my biases but simply to recognize them. They include:

1. I can't stand handwriting that uses circles or hearts to dot the letters *i* and *j*.

2. Adjectives are often a sign of weak nouns, and adverbs sometimes indicate weak verbs, adjectives, and adverbs. Use sparingly!

3. Most fiction needs a lot of dialogue, a variety of sentence types, and *action*.

The students were especially troubled by my cranky attitude toward adjectives and adverbs, and the wiseacres immediately set to writing little stories and poems that were intentionally overloaded with modifiers. Revealing my biases had given some members of the class an opportunity to exercise their natural, satirical (and possibly, until then, repressed) inclinations. They were unquestionably seeking to drive poor Mr. Hewitt around the bend, but I reveled in pretending to be shocked and disappointed by their persistence in employing such "easy detail," and slowly convinced one or two of them how much more powerful their work generally was with all but the most essential modifiers eliminated.

If nothing else, participants in that workshop learned that to allow unnecessary adjectives and adverbs to stand was to invite a repetitive diatribe from a teacher obsessed with a certain point of view. If nothing else, students in that session gained a lifelong awareness of two parts of speech. Had I been able to work another two weeks with this marvelous group, I'd have discovered, or if necessary invented, another set of biases to guide their considerations in further writings. Over the course of a year, then, I might have been able to review my entire, idiosyncratic canon, and imparted to my students if not the need for obedience to its sometimes crackpot tenets, some knowledge of those niceties. Establishing temporary biases can force students to attempt variations of language and approach, and thus to develop an awareness of a variety of strategies.

Such biases can extend beyond matters of style and presentation to content choice (I hate blood-and-guts stories or stories whose characters are borrowed from television or other niches of pop culture) and need not always be expressed as negative sentiments. For instance, I love poems in which the narrator considers the feelings of the "other" in the poem: That's one of my positive biases!

The point is to be clear in distinguishing one's biases from the rules of proper usage and to handle these biases with a sense of humor. They are, after all, what makes the teacher human.

Further, students should be encouraged to discuss their own biases (both of content and style), to provide examples of work that touches on those biases, and to explore why they hold such biases. This is really an approach to establishing criteria, but because "bias" tends to have negative connotations, it's a way of getting at criteria from a different perspective than that usually used to select standards.

Giving students permission to enumerate their biases also gives them a position from which to critique their own and others' work. It's much easier for me, and for my students, to deliver what might be considered harsh criticism by prefacing it with an acknowledgment that the response about to be offered comes from someone who acknowledges he's a crank on the subject, so take it for what it's worth. Again, the effort here isn't so much to dictate a way in which the piece must be revised as to inculcate an awareness of certain technical matters. The effect of suggesting specific revisions may not become apparent in the piece being revised, but emerge in later work.

Editing

Editing can be a part of revision or remain a special focus of one final step in "the process," whether it involves just a careful proofreading or extensive research on spelling and punctuation. I like to edit as I revise, simply because I'm always thinking, "This will be the final draft," and because I don't like to read my misspelled words over and over, draft to draft.

Many teachers who are enthusiastic about peer conferences also extol the virtues of group editing. This can be organized in a variety of ways, from a simple one-on-one swap of nearly final drafts to more intricate arrangements in which each student is assigned a specific editorial function and signs off, for instance, on a paper's focus, mechanics, grammar, or tone.

Regardless of whether the author receives editing assistance in a group process or not, it is the author who must take responsibility for the final draft. I encourage students to read their final draft aloud to themselves or a partner very slowly and carefully to be sure it sounds right. And finally, I suggest they give the piece one last proofreading, asking themselves if *this* is exactly what they would want to have made public as their work.

Publishing

As I've mentioned, to publish is simply to make public. Just as the decision on what goes into the portfolio should remain with the student, the decision whether to seek publication also should rest with the author. Only after the author has decided to seek publication does an editor accept or reject the work.

That's in the real world. And, in the real world, there are lots of authors receiving almost-daily rejection slips. In school, the situation can be tipped sufficiently so that every student has an opportunity to publish.

In many schools, students create their own books, complete with cover, title page, biographical notes, and illustrations. Some teachers even ask their students to equip their books with library cards and place them on the shelves of the school library.

Another form of publishing occurs when students write stories and poems for students in a lower grade. I've been told of programs where the older students first visit and interview the younger students, returning to their classrooms to write pieces that are individually tailored to the interests of the students they've interviewed. Once the custom-made stories and poems have reached final-draft stage, the students again visit the younger classroom, this time to present their work.

Most schools publish a literary magazine, usually on an annual basis. The problem with this sort of effort is that it is often the province of just those few students who sign up for "Lit Mag" as an extracurricular activity, and the students whose work is published sometimes comprise only the school's literary elite.

Teachers might survey the national small-press scene to reassure themselves that a literary magazine does not have to be the standard, 5" x 8 ½", perfect-bound, white-paper, overloaded-with-tiny-type production that everyone buys but no one reads. More important than an annual, comprehensive school magazine is the informal publication that every class can produce on a regular basis, using imagination and a photocopy machine.

Original plays also offer an intriguing avenue for publication. Such plays can be as ambitious as a three-act opera, complete with period costumes and sets, or as casual as an hour of staged readings of one-act plays the students have written.

Uncluttered displays on bulletin boards or within the library's display cases should be posted for no more than two weeks so that the work is always fresh. School newsletters can announce the changing of such exhibits. Students might take responsibility for choosing and posting the work.

Readings and celebrations also offer an excellent opportunity for students to publish. Consider staging such events as literary tea parties, beatniklike performances, school assemblies, or multimedia presentations. Such presentations can be tailored to fit relatively intimate or large-scale formats. Ask members of the community to bring their own short pieces, to read as part of an open reading where everyone is encouraged to participate. Local radio and television stations may be interested in broadcasting these events.

Student readings can also be incorporated into other types of gatherings. Wherever a potential audience exists, students will usually find an enthusiastic reception and opportunity to publish.

◆ 4 ◆

Teacher Experimentation, The Writer's Attitude, and Student Ownership

I thought I'd learned everything there is to know about teaching writing from my writer's residency in 1972 at Hardwick Elementary School. There I invited the fifth and sixth graders to write an anonymous piece and received the best writing I've ever seen from that age group. But I am still making discoveries about what happened when I told the students, during our third of five meetings, that I was depressed about their lack of involvement in the poems and stories they were automatically churning out to satisfy me. I had been adhering to an erroneous interpretation of "freewriting" — allow the students to come up with their own topics ("anything goes").

The trouble was that "anything" turned out to be what the students guessed a teacher might want: tepid poetic imitations of Dr. Seuss, almost inevitably finding opportunity to rhyme *hat*, *rat* and *cat*, and stiff, predictable stories whose heroes were the same characters that, in 1972, were featured on the Saturday morning, action-television cartoon shows, such luminaries as Wonderwoman and Spiderman. I was depressed and I showed it. I felt that we had wasted the first three of our five precious sessions. "Go home and write something honest," I implored, "something true to your real or imagined experience. And, because I want you to be honest or daring, you may not sign your name."

It was a spontaneous, desperate invitation, and when I returned to the school for our fourth session, at least half the dozen-or-so responses were unlike any fifth- or sixth-grade writing I had ever seen, and I later included them in *Living in Whales* (1972), an anthology of student writing I edited for the Vermont Council on the Arts.

I am interested in the obvious accomplishment of these student authors and marvel at the almost instantaneous (overnight) transition they made from mediocrity to excellence. It's as if they suddenly saw that I could be trusted. At the same time, I am aware of the risk a teacher takes, inviting students to convey personal information. I am not sure how, today, I would respond to the frightening imagery of "Untitled." Is it a piece that would require the attention of a guidance counselor? In 1972, I merely acknowledged the power of the anonymous writing without reading it to the group or seeking to learn the author's identity.

Something Honest
Movies

I've gone to the movies twice now. Twice with my boy friend. The first time as if we were brothers & sisters. We did nothing. Next time he was going to sit on the other side of the theatre. My girlfriend went to get him. Another girlfriend also sat with her boyfriend. We held hands part way until the scary part. He put his arm around me and so did my girlfriend's boyfriend. I moved closer to him and put my head on his shoulder. He kissed me many a time and put his arm on my shoulder. My little sister was there and every couple of minutes (either when we were kissing or talking) she would come and ask me if she could get a drink. No matter what happened that was a wonderful evening.

Untitled

One day this boy I knew came up to me. He was older than me and went to a public school. I went to a Catholic school. He said to me "Come here Penny, I have something really neat to show you."

Being only in second grade, I didn't expect anything so I followed him. He took me to an alley and led me to an empty garage. He asked me if I had started my period and I said I didn't know what it was, and that they didn't teach that in school. He seemed to think that was funny and it was okay. He pulled down his pants and told me to do the same. I hadn't the slightest idea what was happening. He started getting closer to me. Then his sexual innercords went to work. Suddenly I got real scared. I ran and ran, and ran. Whenever I saw him I quickly went inside.

Reprinted from *Living in Whales*, 1972. Geof Hewitt, ed. Vermont Council on the Arts, Montpelier, VT, pages 39, 41.

The Power of Persona

The magic of having written well stayed with this group of children when I lifted the restriction of anonymity for their final session. In "A Schoolteacher's Story," student Carol F. gave me a fresh perspective on the capabilities of young writers and the amazing potential of persona. I will forever be impressed by how skillfully the author shifts the syntax in the piece to reflect the stuffy pronunciations of adults in a formal hearing. The voice of the narrator also captures adult diction, but at a level with which a young reader can identify.

Finally, and this occurred to me after nearly twenty years of reading "A Schoolteacher's Story" to groups of writers and educators, the last three lines of the piece, its final paragraph, prove the power of persona to unmask the unwitting author. Only half in jest I ask who else but a child with six or seven more years of institutional education would write: "I am sentenced to life in prison . . . . I am innocent."

A Schoolteacher's Story

I am a schoolteacher. My name is R.C. Clements. This is the story of my
school-teaching. Since I have nothing left to do with my time I am writing it.

My first week was trying — for me at least. As I walked into the new classroom, I heard
a murmur of voices. I walked over to my desk, set my things down, and called
everyone's attention.

"My name is Miss Clements," I said, putting it on the board.

"Goody for you" said a boy.

"One thing I can't put up with is rudeness," I said sternly. "Now, let's not start the day
off like this."

The whole year I had three trouble-makers and one proved to be real trouble.

Each year the sixth grade I got seemed to be more mature than the last sixth grade.

On my third year, I was really interested in the goings on with the kids. Two were in
love, and had a fight. Other kids were showoffs.

I'm not supposed to be interested in things like that, but every chance I got I would
look for notes or eavesdrop.

The girl that was in love had supposedly taken another girl's boyfriend away. The
situation was a mess.

Once I found a negative note about me saying I was a bitch and that I stuck my nose
into everything I could. I decided to improve.

Soon I got so that I was more interested in out of school life than I was in teaching. I
had several embarrassing moments. Like once when we were having math,
Istopped to listen to what two lovers were saying. Luckily no one noticed. I
grew out of that, though.

On my sixth year of teaching I got many pupils. Once they wouldn't shut up and I
hollered "Why can't you kids keep your god damn mouths shut?"

Of course that was brought home to the parents and they brought it up at a P.T.A.
meeting.

The superintendent came to the stand. He said "Miss Clements you know that it is
strictly against all rules to swear in the classroom. It may influence the children
to do the same. Since you know this, I presume you did this intentionally. You
are therefore relieved of your job."

I was infuriated. All the kids swore anyway. I went mad. I pushed down chairs and tables
and I spilled refreshments.

I was brought home yelling, screaming, my teeth gnashing together and they locked
me in.

That night, a man was killed in the apartment building where I lived. There was blood on
my door knob and it trailed to the dead man's apartment. I had been framed . . . .

Nobody would listen though. They figured I had to have done it since I had gone
mad.

Children were told to avoid me when I came out of the building, guarded.

In one month I was tried and I was found guilty because the jury had already decided
before the case was opened.

I am sentenced to life in prison. The truth lies between God and me. The one thing I
want the world to know — I am innocent.

Armed with part of my lesson from Hardwick Elementary School, I accepted another writer's residency and, after two sessions of encouraging the students to "freewrite," I saw that, again, the students were mired in predictable rhyme and stock characters. During our third session, I pulled the old "Hardwick Routine," lowering my head and admitting that something was wrong. "And so for next time," I concluded, "as an experiment, I want you to write something that is true to your real or imagined experience, and because I want you to feel free to be honest, you may not sign your name!" The students filed out of the classroom, and I went home, anticipating my next visit and the marvelous student work that would pour in.

Well, I was disappointed. The students arrived for our fourth session with their new pieces, all anonymous, and none especially distinguished from the preceding work.

Although I'll never know for sure, my sense is that because my plea at Hardwick Elementary School was spontaneous, it caught the students' attention, inspired their trust. In its second playing, my announcement was little more than a performance. Something in my demeanor gave it away as a trick of sorts. The difference is the same as the difference between *reading* a speech to an audience and *delivering* the speech from notes. At least for me, all appropriate conversational tone vanishes from my voice when I read, or memorize, a speech.

Now that I understand that most students need guidance from the start in developing writing topics, I no longer need to dream up some histrionic device to get them on track. What is important is that I be committed to the challenge I'm asking the students to undertake. It helps if I am forthright in expressing any reservations I may have, admitting, "I've never tried this before, so I'm not sure it will work, but let's give it a whirl!" If a particular exercise has worked well with other students and I cannot resist trying it again, I do not announce, "Another class tried this and responded brilliantly," which, in my experience, kills any sense of pioneer effort the students might feel in tackling the assignment.

An Experiment

Almost twenty years after my taste of success with the students at Hardwick Elementary School, I had an opportunity to work for two weeks at the Governor's Institute on the Arts, an intensive, residential summer gathering that brings high-school students and practicing artists together. For my writing class, I announced at the orientation meeting our goal would be an experiment: Could we write a collaborative novel?

I was blessed with twelve daily, two-hour sessions and a dozen ninth- through eleventh-grade students who loved to write and were not afraid to disagree with their teacher. The first night's homework was for each student to create two characters and a theme that would place the characters on an airline journey, then to write a brief in-flight dialogue.

The next day I asked the students to read their brief pieces to one another, then arbitrarily assigned them to writing teams of two, asking each team, for homework, to bring the four (total) characters they now had to the airliner's destination and to introduce some new action-filled element at that destination. The following day I asked each team to join with another team, so we'd have a total of eight characters in the next team-generated piece of writing. This didn't work; the four-member teams had a difficult time compromising.

But the students' progress was stunning. We were getting some very funny and some very sad episodes. Technically, most of the writing was close to flawless. Within their group-writing efforts, the students were apparently acting as excellent group editors. Each night I battled the temptation to outline the rest of the two-week course, wanting to plot out how it would go. But I resisted that urge, feeling that spontaneity was at the heart of our evolving success.

We started to explore our characters and themes, revised what was working, borrowed freely from one another's pieces, and discussed style, aesthetics, and the need for our novel to be filled with character and action. After Saturday's class, I realized that everything we had written to date was only a "warm-up," and that we should start from scratch on Monday.

On Monday, I arrived with a twelve-chapter outline, borrowing themes from the first week's writing and from our group experience as participants at the institute: Famous young male writer meets young woman at residential artists' colony, where they are dorm counselors. Returning to their real lives as college students in different states, they correspond, visit one another and young man badly misbehaves at a party to which he's invited young woman. They reconcile and plan to marry. Their parents are aghast because of religious differences, and the wedding turns into a brawl. On their honeymoon flight to London, the bride foils a highjacking and suddenly their roles are reversed — she becomes famous.

That Monday, I offered participants an opportunity to volunteer for chapters and to make any changes in the plot they wished. We selected names and physical descriptions for our major characters and agreed to use third person, past tense. The next day, each student had written a chapter and — *voila!* — we had a rough draft of our novel. Students read the chapters in sequence, keeping notes on others' chapters: What can you foreshadow as you revise, or what can you add to your chapter that is foreshadowed by an earlier chapter? We continued polishing, "fore- and post-shadowing" throughout the week and by Friday had a credible final draft of thirteen chapters (one student contributed two chapters). I invited the students to create and mail me alternate Chapter 14s, a variety of post-climactic episodes for our novel. The finished novel included three Chapter 14s, each a different ending.

Why did this project succeed? First, it was an experiment. I admitted I'd never before led a group novel collaboration and wasn't at all sure it would work. This seemed to inspire the students. Second, even though I proposed an outline, I imposed no restrictions on subject, theme, language, or style. When students did not like my suggestions, they were free to follow their own instincts, as long as they started and ended at reasonable "take-up points" for the surrounding chapters. Third, I had an exceptional group of young people, and we all benefited from the fact that we had only two weeks!

As I reread the novel, I am intrigued by the notion that the students may not so much have learned about syntax, detail, and voice (my hidden agenda for our two-week project) as they did about structure and working with others!

The Art of Change is no great novel, but for a collaborative, two-week high-school project, it's pretty good. It has its racy moments; Jesse Helms would hate it. Page 58 shows excerpts of the novel's climactic chapters with the authors' synopses, reprinted from *Our Own Horns*, the student-edited institute magazine of 1990. (I later published a limited edition of the entire novel.)

I never claimed that the novel is great literature, but it captures the youthful spirit, the energy, the fascinations, and concerns of adolescent students. Providing some outlet for these fascinations and concerns, the novel brought out a kind of writing some of these students had not known they could produce.

I tried a similar project at the institute a year later with another group of twelve students. It didn't work. My hunch is that in this second attempt, I telegraphed that old "Can do, because we did it last year" attitude that somehow reduced the students' sense of pioneering.

The Writer's Attitude

Sometimes young writers don't understand that their own point of view, their *attitude*, is what gives personality to the piece of writing and usually makes or breaks the writer's chance of holding the reader's attention. Attitude and persuasive writing are often seen as synonymous; in some educators' view, persuasive writing is the only time a student's attitude should surface. The author's point of view should neither be directly conveyed nor implied in expository work, nor should it surface in research papers or reports, goes the theory. Oh, attitude is also sometimes okay in creative writing, but it often gets in the way. More traditional blarney!

One of the great functions of poetry is that the form virtually invites attitude. Extending beyond mere appreciation, poems can demonstrate pleasure in word play, delight in the rhythms or sounds of language, horror or delight in specific human situations, personal joy, or sadness. When a poem fails to convey at least one of these components, it lacks attitude. "I want the gossip!" I tell students. "Not for you to tell the reader how to feel, but to re-create the scenes that evoke that feeling!" This is little more than a preference for detail over abstraction, and I expect the same kind of attention to detail in all types of writing.

By allowing or even encouraging attitude in expository and other narrative forms of writing, we suggest to student writers that they become involved with the material they are covering, not simply accept the role of parrots of the "research" paraphrase. Knowing that their attitudes can be an important part of their writing, students tend to "loosen up," and begin to present and examine *ideas*, not just facts. A student who feels comfortable expressing personal beliefs soon learns to use written language not only to present bits of research, but as a mathematician uses numbers — to arrive at a solution. Some people call this "discovery writing."

Discovering their attitude often helps writers who feel blocked. For me, sketching helps, and I've had some success encouraging recalcitrant writers to create comic strips, in which almost always the need for written language satisfies the "writing" requirement. Any student who is able to find attitude by beating on a drum, or composing a rap piece, or making a comic strip might then be asked to describe, in writing, the attitude that emerges from what has been, really, a brainstorming session. See Amanda Taylor's remarkable comic strip (Figure 4–1 on pages 62 and 63), created in Pam Benedetti's high-school English class, for an example of attitude conveyed at this level.

EXCERPTS FROM THE ART OF CHANGE

We join The Art of Change *at Chapter 11 for excerpted chapters leading to its climax and conclusion. Brad and Rachel have just barely caught the plane for their honeymoon to London; the only available seats are five aisles apart. Just before takeoff, Rachel uses the restroom and overhears talking in the aisle.*

Chapter 11

"When are we going to pull it off?"

"Soon as we are in the air."

"We won't kill anyone unless absolutely necessary."

"The guns. You are taking the ones in the bathroom and I the ones in the kitchen. And the copilot has the others."

Rachel hears this conversation in parts. She tries to understand the thick Irish accents and put it all together. Sounds like a hijacking.

Chapter 12

Rachel attempts to make sense of the conversation she overheard between the two stewardesses. She then begins to empty the weapons to hinder the hijacking attempt before it happens, but the terrorists still attempt to take over the plane with empty weapons, using only the ignorance of the passengers, and the psychological effect of the guns. Rachel then exposes the truth to the passengers which is the downfall of two of the terrorists.

"Hurry. Tie them up before the copilot gets out here," screamed Rachel. "His gun's still loaded." She leapt to the aisle and grabbed a tray from the kitchenette on her way toward the cockpit door. She poised beside the door with tray in hand. A broad man holding a pistol burst through, bellowing in an Irish accent, "Wot the bloody hell's goin on in ear?"

"Ponng," rang in Rachel's ears as she glanced the copilot in the face with the metal tray. The gun went spinning across the floor and was grabbed by a nearby passenger. "Don't move!" he yelled at the copilot, who was sprawled on the floor with his face buried in his hands. The copilot gazed up toward Rachel, blood oozing from his nose.

(continued)

I emphasize the importance of attitude, too, because I think it may hold the key to working with alienated students — those who say, in one way or another, "writing stinks." Just as a therapist may seek to have the patient reveal early moments of life, a teacher may need to give students access to their early tools of expression in finding language that will satisfy the day's writing requirement. "Why I Hate Science" is not the essay I'd be dying to see if I were the science teacher, but it just might provide a starting point for a conversation that steers a student toward a self-directed approach to scientific inquiry. By allowing students

---

"Bitch!" he gasped and pulled a knife from his jacket.

The "copilot" lunges at Rachel, a shot is heard, and he drops to the floor. Things return to a seminormal state as the plane prepares to land in London.

Chapter 13
Upon leaving the plane with celebrating passengers, Rachel is flocked by reporters, each trying to beat the others to the details of the hijacking.
A plethora of reporters hounded her as she took her last step down the stairs and onto the British ground.
"Excuse me, Mrs. Luther?"
"Mrs. Luther?"
"Rachel?"
"How do you . . . "
" . . . a hero?"

Rachel reacts calmly, making a simple statement. With Brad she walks into the airport. There they are greeted by a police officer who asks them to follow him. They do and soon are in a plush office overlooking the runway. Rachel and Brad watch as the hijackers are removed, and after, answer a lot of the questions asked by the officer. He thanks them, and declares Rachel a hero.

There is a time lapse, and the chapter reopens in Rachel and Brad's honeymoon suite. They start to undress, and the phone rings.

"Hello. Is this Rachel Luther?" the familiar voice asked.
"Yes. Who is this? You sound so familiar."
"Hi honey. This is Oprah!"
"Oprah?" Rachel repeated unbelieving.
"Yes honey. We in America are soooo proud of you. Usually I don't make my own phone calls, but I just couldn't help it. I said 'Oprah. Get off your butt,' and they told me your hotel, so I called there, and they said you'd asked for no calls. Oh, well, let's just say I've made a lot of calls. Rachel, I want you on my show. You're America's newest hero!"

---

to present their attitudes in writing, we open the door to writing that has a purpose beyond just proving that they have done the assignment.

Teacher Guidance vs. Student Ownership

The Governor's Institute on the Arts is held on the campus of Castleton State College, twelve miles west of Rutland, Vermont's second-largest city with a population of 18,230. In my first summer as writing teacher, my assignment included serving as advisor for the institute magazine. By tradition, the magazine publishes only material created during the two-week institute. Further, the finished magazine is distributed no later than the institute's closing ceremony, on Sunday afternoon of the second week.

Seven students signed up for Magazine Class, a two-hour afternoon slot where for our first four meetings we discussed editorial policy and looked at a variety of little magazines, debating their formats. By the fifth meeting I could see a certain disengagement among my student editors. A pair of girls, who had signed up apparently because they had nothing better to do, were so disruptive that Ariel — the five-year-old daughter of Mason Singer, a graphic designer who visited our sessions to help with layout and design — referred to them as "The Toys."

With eight days to go, we'd received only three student contributions (all of which, after long discussion, had been accepted); competing, immediately rewarding activities were sapping my editors' energies just when they were most needed.

My tendency, as a lifelong self-promoter and publisher, is to rush into the vacuum and fill the space with my own frantic activity. It was I who made arrangements with the campus copy center to print our rush job on the Thursday before our final Sunday. I was the one who, with Mason Singer and faculty spouse Chris Hart, stayed up way past midnight entering the text on a computer (the students had a 10 P.M. curfew). I was the one who insisted on being the final proofreader (I have degrees in English). I was the one . . . .

So it's no wonder that at noon on our final Thursday the copy center informed me that my own miscommunication (the manager had, indeed, agreed to print three hundred copies of sixteen sheets, but I'd never told her "back to back," and with the Fourth of July being Friday, they could only print what they had promised before closing for the holiday weekend) required that I find another printer for the half of the magazine I had neglected to disclose in my earlier negotiations.

I was immediately on the telephone to Rutland, combing the yellow pages under "Printers," repeatedly hearing that I "should have called a week earlier to schedule the work, sorry. Next year give us some advance notice and we'll do it in a day — as long as it isn't the Fourth of July!" When I finally reached a shop whose proprietor said, "If you bring the pages in before one o'clock, we'll have them copied by five," I was so happy I almost forgot to ask for a quote. The price was easily within my budget, but I had only thirty minutes to get to Rutland. "Just be here before one or we're going to start another job," the voice on the other end of the line sternly reminded me. I glanced back at the yellow pages and copied the address of Quikstop Printing, 123 North Street, and headed east the twelve miles toward Rutland, trusting that I'd cross a North Street when I pulled into town. Even if I had to stop for directions, I'd probably still make it by one.

Well, at 12:58 P.M. I pulled into the only parking space available on North Street and ran the two blocks back to the shop. Out of breath, sweating like a brass pig, I waited politely in the reception area's enormous black naugahyde chair while the receptionist, a woman wearing dark glasses at a dimly lit desk, concluded a prolonged and seemingly inconsequential discussion with a heavy, bespectacled man who alternately chewed and sucked on the stub of a dead cigar as he sat at an adding machine from which more than two miles of tape, I was sure, coiled off his desk to the floor. When the receptionist finally turned her attention to me it was 1:02 P.M. and I was standing at her desk, clearing my throat.

The bad news is that I wasted five minutes trying to convince the man (who spoke with an accent — the person I had talked with had an accent) that only half an hour earlier he'd agreed to print my magazine by 5 P.M. Finally he said, "We'll do the job, but not until Monday" and gave me a quote much higher than I'd heard over the phone. At this moment, 1:12 P.M., I realized that perhaps I was in the wrong shop! I had copied the wrong name and address from the yellow pages!

Glad to be ridding themselves of me, the receptionist and Mr. Cigar loaned me their phone book and telephone. I called down to Printquik on Elm Street and yes, he was expecting a job from the arts institute, but it was already after one . . . . Well, bring it down. We'll see what we can do.

"I can probably finish half tonight," the man at Printquik explained when I arrived at 1:27 P.M. "The other half you can photocopy on the machine you have at the college." It was better than nothing, so I left the job with him. He said, "There's no way I'm coming in on the Fourth — that's my only long weekend of the summer. Be here at 4:45 P.M. Don't come later because I close at five. I'll give you whatever I've done by then."

I drove back to the institute. The magazine students, as I pulled into the college's parking lot, were struggling to move a folding machine that the manager of the copy center had loaned them for the weekend. It must have weighed 150 pounds and had two bunches of fine copper wires streaming from its backside. I was sure this constituted electrical danger. In our little studio, "The Toys," whose disruptions had continued the entire two weeks, had set up a collating table and were trying to make sense of the stacks of completed pages that were still coming in from the print center. "This is page one, so why does it have page thirty-two facing it and page two faced by page thirty-one on the back?" I ran over to the institute office and reserved photocopier time for all day Friday, praying that the thing wouldn't jam or simply refuse to function in the humidity that had made it temperamental, at best, the entire two weeks.

As I started back to Rutland, double-checking the address and phone number of Printquik, I instructed the students to just keep checking to be sure they had the pages in sequence. "Don't mess with that folding machine. It'll only spoil copies and it looks unsafe with all those copper wires. Fold by hand, just be sure you make the folds in the right direction so facing pages actually are stapled in order. Make a mock-up to be sure you've got the folds and facing pages right."

I ran out the door, anticipating another forty-eight hours with no sleep. There was no way those students would have time or ambition to fold more than two or three of the copy center's eight groups of three hundred sheets, and half of them would probably be backwards. When I arrived at Printquik, the printer had completed less than half the job, but at least it was something. "I'm going to come in early tomorrow," he said, "finish the job, the whole job. I know the copier at your office — it won't work in this humidity." When I started a weak, pro forma protest of his decency, he cut me off. "It's *my* business. Please don't tell me how to run my business. Just be here at 10 A.M. tomorrow. No later."

When I arrived back on campus it was dinner time. I planned to take a few moments to clean up the studio and have some time to myself, but there was a strange noise coming from behind the door. A mechanical sound. I opened the door to discover, humming along, the borrowed folding machine, spitting perfectly folded sheets of our creation through its copper streamers. One of the

FIGURE 4–1

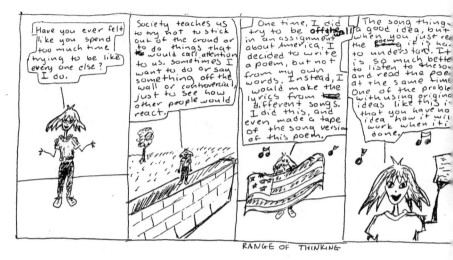

RANGE OF THINKING

LETTER OF

INTRODUCTION

Production Schedule
for a
Two-Week Magazine

Day 1. Create and distribute posters soliciting contributions.

Day 2. Produce and perform one-minute skit at all-group meeting to promote contributions.

Day 3. Put up "Name the Magazine" posters.

Day 4. Visit classes to announce solicitation and first call for manuscript/artwork pickup on Day 6.

Day 5. Have final call for manuscripts/artwork. Discuss format. Create dummy.

Day 6. Manuscript/artwork pickup. Conduct edit session 1. Begin data entry.

Day 7. Conduct edit session 2. Select title. Enter data.

Day 8. Conduct final edit. Proofread and lay out pages.

Day 9. Proof and lay out pages.

Day 10. Paste up pages.

Day 11. (Fourth of July)

Day 12. Place job at printer. Set up tables to fold, collate, staple, trim.

Day 13. Conduct production/assembly.

Day 14. Distribute printed magazine.

---

students showed me a mock-up and grinned, "My parents have a printing business. This machine's almost the same as the one they have. We haven't spoiled more than half a dozen sheets so far. The copper wires are there to keep static electricity from building up."

I slept nearly normal hours that Friday and Saturday, and on Sunday, as the institute's final ceremony was proceeding, back in our little studio, "The Toys" had, indeed, come to life, as if seeking eleventh-hour redemption. Their parents were not present for the closing day's activities, so they had volunteered to staple and trim the magazine. By the end of the day's final speech, the students in my magazine production class stood proudly outside the doors of the college's fine arts center, handing out copies of their magazine, not a moment too soon.

What did I learn from this nerve-jangling experience? Not enough. The following summer I agreed to try the class again. Again I had a handful of students — seven or eight — a workable number for the project, and again they seemed dispirited before the end of our first week. Again, and in spite of my vows the whole winter long, I tried to fill the vacuum, and again, at the eleventh hour, two or three of the students took over and saved the project.

Two weeks just isn't long enough to build a staff and produce a magazine from scratch, for sure, but it can be done (and subsequent teachers who've taken on the project have also seen it happen, with similar experiences). My theory is that the two-week deadline seems pressing only to the adult. It's *mañana* for the young people. Unfortunately, this means that, until the pages are ready to be collated, stapled, and trimmed on the day before the magazine must be distributed, the students don't really believe the magazine exists: Then the pages arrive like a gift from Santa in cardboard boxes. "It's pretty close to what I had in mind," the students are probably thinking as they thumb the first mock-up.

So if I *had* to do it again (not if I had it to do again!) I'd create a day-by-day set of deadlines, with a product at the end of four of the first five days, by which time the necessary tasks of editing and production would be evident. I'd reduce the philosophy and policy discussions to the bare minimum, erring on the side of telling the students what the magazine should contain and dictating the format to allow time for *activity* that results in tangible products.

If I were given a full semester for magazine production, or if I were to take on a magazine because the students requested such an activity, I'd allow six weeks, at the least, for the same fourteen-day wonder we were challenged to produce. And given a more relaxed deadline, I would try very hard to stay out of it as much as humanly possible — in other words, to follow the advice of teacher Steve Hudak, who says, "Accept that it will have flaws, sometimes major flaws, and let the students make the decisions and do the work."

Given a more relaxed production schedule, I would insist that the after-hours grunt work, including the organizing and scheduling, remain in the students' control. "If the magazine doesn't get done," is the attitude I could never quite master, "it doesn't get done."

If a teacher is timid, afraid to experiment, the students are unlikely to take risks. The same principle applies to portfolios. If the teacher dictates an official portfolio format, then tells the students which pieces of their writing to include, the students are likely to sit back and let the teacher manage their portfolios. Most teachers I know don't have that kind of time.

♦ 5 ♦

Creating
and
Using Portfolios

When I hear "portfoliossessment," a single word, I start to get nervous. Portfolios have existed since the cave people scratched shapes into the walls of their homes. The formal assessment of portfolios is a creation of the twentieth century and is still being explored. If the experiment in portfolio assessment fails, will some teachers say, "We tried portfolios and they didn't work"? It's important to remember the several benefits of keeping portfolios. Assessment efforts may be the driving (and complicating) force behind several portfolio programs, but what else does a portfolio have to offer?

1. ongoing, tangible record of accomplishment

2. constant evidence that the student's work is valued

3. opportunity for the student to reflect on his or her work

4. excellent tool for parent or faculty conferences, as well as for student conferences

It is hard to imagine keeping a portfolio without some form of assessment occurring; if "portfolio" means a *selection* of work, someone has to have done the selecting — which implies assessment of some type. So maybe "portfoliossessment" isn't such an aberration after all.

But some assessments are softer than others, and it is important to recognize that a formal portfolio assessment may not require developing a mountain of data, then worrying about its accuracy. Schoolwide assessment programs may present a healthy compromise between single-class assessments and the larger, more-compromised programs designed for districts and states. And let's also remember that the assessment does not always have to deliver scores. In Ypsilanti, Mich., third-grade teacher Joe Ann Allen participates in a portfolio program where the portfolio is used to observe each student's progress. "When you pass papers back it is not as easy to see growth, like an improvement in spelling, as it is when you have the work in front of you," she told the *New York Times* ("Education Life" August 1, 1993). Allen added that parents "liked coming in and having the materials right in front of them and talking about how the child was doing, and the children never felt like failures. The children were always so proud of their portfolios" (5). University of Michigan Professor Samuel Meisels, designer of the program, described the difference between his program and many others: "Unlike a professional portfolio, it is not a sample of the child's best work. The portfolio should capture or document the evolution of the child's work and the emergence of the child's skills. This way we know that if the child has not accomplished much, it is not because he had a bad day" (5).

Whatever the reason for keeping portfolios, the benefits just mentioned seem almost inevitable. Cultivate and enjoy them, whatever the official purpose of your program! Teachers who are burdened by externally imposed portfolio programs may find some relief by realizing that a portfolio is meant to show individuality; the teacher defeats the purpose of the portfolio by taking on each student's responsibility/opportunity for its creation.

The number one principle of managing portfolios is that the portfolio belongs to the student. Because reflection is so important in the growth of a writer, selections for the portfolio should be made by the student, possibly with advice from the teacher and classmates. As I mentioned in the Introduction, when teachers use portfolios as if they were the assignment ("Now let's all write a piece for the portfolio!"), they place the burden of judgment before the act of creation, a pressured situation not unlike a writing test.

In addition to making the selections, the student, no matter how young, should take responsibility for maintaining the portfolio. If a student loses the portfolio, let that student start a new one, not by re-creating the lost work, but filling it with new pieces! Student ownership and responsibility for the portfolio will save teachers work and time, in this case wasted time and wasted opportunity because the teacher learns little from managing a whole classroom of portfolios and the students learn so much from accepting this responsibility.

Being sure that students take ownership of their portfolios offers a second, gigantic benefit: If they make the selections for the portfolios, their writing will probably be better than if they have only limited choice over what goes in. In the words of Joan Simmons, my friend who teaches at Craftsbury Academy, "Over the years, it has been interesting to see the role of the teacher change from the commandant in charge of topic selection and judgment to that of writer and coach. When students select their best work for the portfolio, ownership shifts from the teacher's shoulders to the writer's. Now students and teachers alike know how to identify good writing, and this knowledge provides a blueprint for success."

A Generic Rubric for Reviewing Portfolios

In most assessment programs, the scoring guide, or *rubric*, presents discipline-specific criteria so that student work can be evaluated by subject area. In "A Guide for Judging Portfolios" (1994), Leon and Pearl Paulson present a rubric that focuses on the student's *relationship* to the portfolio more than the *quality* of the work. Use of such a rubric might precede the kinds of writing rubrics reviewed in Chapter 7. This sort of generic rubric is especially useful in the first few months of a portfolio program, as a means of helping students

---♦---

THE FOUR STAGES OF PORTFOLIO GROWTH
F. Leon and Pearl R. Paulson

An *Off-Track* Portfolio

An off-track portfolio is simply a container of student work or assessments, without an attempt on the part of the learner to provide organization. There is no attempt by the learner to make a coherent statement about what learning has taken place. The child's understanding of the task is minimal — the portfolio is about "collecting what the teacher asks for." For the student, the portfolio was built by following instructions. Self-reflective statements, if present, add little to clarify organization or explain learning.

An *Emerging* Portfolio

In an emerging portfolio there is a sense of intentionality controlling some of the student's choices. Students may not be able to verbalize the reasons, even as they reflect on their choices, but the reviewer may be able to recognize a relationship between some exhibits or infer the reasons. Or, there may be evidence that the student had some insight into the teacher's purposes. While evidence of self-reflection adds information to the presentation, at this point in the development of the portfolio there is insufficient information or organization to characterize the portfolio as either a story of learning or a portrait of the learner.

An *On-Track* Portfolio

An on-track portfolio is in the process of becoming a story of the student as an independent learner. There are relationships between one part of the portfolio and another. There is evidence of student ownership. The learner has a personal investment in selecting and explaining the content. It is possible to distinguish other stakeholders' goals from the student's or to recognize instances where they overlap. The portfolio may be created for others to assess, but there is also evidence of self-assessment. The student's voice is always audible.

An *Outstanding* Portfolio

An outstanding portfolio is a coherent story of the student as a reflective learner where all the parts of the portfolio bear a clear relationship to each other and to a central purpose. There is an awareness of the perspectives of other stakeholders, and the student's self-assessment has been enhanced by this knowledge. A reviewer can look at the portfolio and easily understand how the judgments about the learner came to be made and the degree to which different stakeholders would agree. When reviewing the portfolio, outsiders get the feeling they really know the person whose achievement is depicted there, and have a fair understanding of how the learning came about.

Reprinted from "A Guide for Judging Portfolios," F. Leon Paulson and Pearl R. Paulson, 1994, p. 4.

---♦---

understand the level of ownership they should establish and to give the teacher a gauge of how thoroughly the students are assuming that ownership.

Keeping Management Simple

In the first year of Vermont's statewide fourth- and eighth-grade portfolio assessment project, the Department of Education issued glossy folders with "Fourth-Grade Writing Portfolio" and "Eighth-Grade Writing Portfolio" printed in fancy type on the cover. Some teachers distributed these to their students; others did not. When, in the spring, it came time to assess a statewide collection of portfolios, teachers observed that the official folders generally contained the least work, and usually the least-thoughtful work. In the portfolios whose authors had created their own covers by drawing on the outside of a plain manila folder, the writing was livelier and there was more of it!

Once it is understood that the portfolios are supervised by the teacher but created by the students, the teacher can develop simple tools for keeping track of these sometimes cumbersome folders of student work. Start each student with a manila folder that's large enough to engulf one hundred sheets of 8 1/2" x 11" paper. Invite students to decorate front and back covers as they will. Encourage decorations/designs that identify the portfolio as the student's unique collection of work.

Some teachers color-code portfolios by class. The student's name on the portfolio tab is written in red if the student is in the day's first class; the names of students from the teacher's second class are written in blue, etc. Numbering the portfolios, once they've been arranged alphabetically, simplifies filing immeasurably.

Two sets of records can make up the inside covers of the portfolio. The first set, attached to the inside front cover, is an evolving table of contents, possibly listing criteria for the work that will fill the portfolio. On the inside back cover, a rolling record of student-teacher conferences can help students focus on goals they have individually set with the teacher.

Process, Product, and the Portfolio

Face it, we live in a society that values the product. Children see us swap our salaries for products, but only rarely do they see us studying the process by which those goods are produced. If the purpose of the portfolio is simply to represent the writer's accomplishment, final drafts may be all that's required. But with no focus on the process, the portfolio becomes a showcase, and the reader may be left with no contextual lens through which to view the crisp artifacts within.

For this reason, many portfolio programs ask the student to include multiple drafts of at least one of the portfolio's entries, and/or a letter of introduction ("Dear Reader, . . . ") in which the writer discusses the contents of the portfolio. This letter allows the student to create a sense of context for the portfolio; it is the "Introduction" most authors write only after the rest of the book is in its second or third draft.

Further, evidence of revision and letters about the work give the reader clues to the author's grasp of grammar and mechanics, clues as to whether final drafts in the portfolio are merely the result of recopying from a teacher-edited previous draft.

Time after time, in portfolio scoring sessions, I've seen this issue arise, "How can we trust that this final draft represents the student's work?" And, "This writing sounds as if it came straight from the encyclopedia; how do I score it?"

Only the classroom teacher really knows how much of the student's own work is reflected in final drafts. Policymakers, working with large samples, may not worry about occasional, undocumented abuses in which, for instance, over-zealous teaching may have contaminated the data. (Note that this is most likely to occur when high stakes are attached to the results of the assessment!) My concern with teacher editing is only half based on the student's lost opportunity to be the one who fixes the problem; I also worry that teacher editing often diminishes the student's voice in the work. With this loss of voice goes a sense of ownership. It's a delicate balance, correctness versus personality. Recopying teacher corrections may interfere with young writers' opportunities to express themselves artfully.

Back to "product." To the extent that a portfolio is used to display process, the writer's sense of formal presentation, showcasing, may be diminished. Especially in elementary classrooms, students can issue a monthly (or more frequent) literary magazine. What more is required than a simple newsletter format? Of course the students should be encouraged to design and actually produce the magazine, but keeping it simple ensures that even the teacher, alone, could publish it on a monthly basis!

What Does the Portfolio Look Like? What Goes into It?

The design and contents of a portfolio vary according to the portfolio's purpose and the personality of the person keeping it. Reading researcher and teacher Jane Hansen describes the portfolios she asks her students to keep as collections of evidence of who they are. Although they often contain examples of the students' writing, these are not necesssarily writing portfolios. Rather, they provide a picture of the student — a link between home and the classroom — that might otherwise never be seen by the teacher and the student's classmates. Within these portfolios may be photographs, certificates, physical mementoes, artifacts — whatever is important to the student.

Portfolios do not have to be limited by the shape of a folder but may, indeed, contain entire three-dimensional models, videotapes of experiments or performances, computer disks — anything deemed essential to the portfolio's purpose.

As for the portfolio's outside appearance, teacher Jane Kearns tells of a visit novelist Carolyn Chute made to her high school in Manchester, N.H. Chute arrived carrying her manuscript in a cereal box, a Kix box, as the story goes. The following day, nearly half of Kearns's students arrived at school with empty cereal boxes, into which they loaded the contents of their portfolios!

Two Portfolios!

The trouble with getting too definitive about the portfolio is that every portfolio should be designed by its keeper/creator, and this is where systems begin to interfere with individuality. In classrooms faced with the dual interests of ac-commodating assessment systems and fostering individual ownership, I strongly recommend that each student keep *two* portfolios. One portfolio is the "assessment portfolio"; it satisfies program requirements and can be used in parent-teacher conferences. The other portfolio is the student's working folder. I'd call this "the master portfolio."

The master portfolio contains the first drafts and all succeeding drafts of all writing, for all academic subjects. When a piece is developed that the student feels is suitable for the assessment portfolio, a copy of the final draft is added to that collection. This portfolio stays relatively thin; the master portfolio gets pretty fat, pretty fast.

Asking students to keep two portfolios helps solve the problem of an assessment program's stakes corrupting the portfolio. The master portfolio is where the student has ongoing responsibility and ownership, and where the real learning occurs. As a matter of fact, it is the "real" portfolio. The assessment portfolio, possibly assembled a week or two before it is due, contains material specifically chosen for outside scrutiny. Obviously, the more the student can be involved in the selection process, the better. If the student makes the selections, the assessment will have served a significant educational purpose, encouraging reflection.

In the classroom, I would habitually refer to the master portfolio as "the portfolio," acknowledging that "from time to time we'll comb through our portfolios to assemble an assessment portfolio, containing only the work we feel best meets the standards of the official assessment. We'll discuss those standards before we start making selections for that portfolio."

Weight Control/Reflection

Following this approach, portfolios can accommodate the focus of any assessment project, whether it be a formal, statewide program or the assessment that may happen during parent-teacher or student-teacher conferences. Weight control and reflection pertain much more to the master portfolio, which is where most student-teacher conferences should focus, with the implicit questions, "How can this piece be improved, made worthy of the assessment portfolio?" "What progress and continuing challenges are evident in this portfolio?" (Devotees of the writing process might see the assessment portfolio as fulfilling the function of publishing, the final step in the process.)

Every four weeks or so the students should spend an hour with their portfolios, looking for writing they want to work on, and sometimes thinning out pieces they want to abandon. Work that is too personal for the assessment portfolio can remain in the master portfolio or in yet another folder the student chooses to keep. Depending on space and the student's personality, portfolio discards might be stored until year's end, just in case the student wants to reconsider the work. (One of the great features of the paper recycling program at the office where I work is that I now accumulate in a green "Recycle!" folder paper that I'd otherwise toss daily into the trash can. More than once I've rescued information from that folder that I'd otherwise have lost forever.)

It's important to envision a portfolio program as an evolving system. The students should take responsibility for suggesting improvements and for maintaining the files, whether they be for the assessment or master portfolio, whether the portfolios consist of hand-copied originals or computer diskettes.

PORTFOLIO PURPOSES

To demonstrate growth: A portfolio kept for this purpose contains work from an extended period. It seems obvious to suggest that each piece in such a portfolio should be dated, but this critical detail is often overlooked! Typically, the student chooses a representative piece for this portfolio every six weeks or makes one or two selections from each semester's work. These samples become part of the cumulative school portfolio that progresses with the student from grade to grade. Although students have access to this portfolio, they may make additions or deletions only for the current year.

"Demonstrating growth" can be defined in a variety of ways. The growth might be that of a piece of writing instead of the student's overall growth. "Growth" might imply improvement in a very focused or limited way, spelling, for instance.

To encourage student goal-setting: Demonstrating growth implies some form of judgment or assessment, so when the purpose of a portfolio involves demonstrating growth, criteria should probably be established and applied consistently to every student's portfolio. Even without the impetus of an external assessment system, developing language for the standards of growth will give students the vocabulary by which to articulate their own development as writers.

Students thus develop the linguistic skills to make distinctions, to isolate the many qualities that contribute to a good piece of writing. In conferences, using these criteria, students can discuss their progress and set goals for future work.

To provide tangible evidence of a student's effort and a view into the writer's process: This portfolio may not be as heavily weeded as the growth portfolio; indeed, it may be kept for only a single semester or school year. Although its purpose need not be articulated as such, the "evidence" portfolio is a powerful convincer for some students who are tempted to drop out of school. The evidence portfolio, with its surprising bulk, is a reminder of how much effort the student has already invested.

Because the evidence portfolio contains all scraps of paper, notes, and early drafts, it provides an excellent source for observations on a writer's process.

(continued)

More than anything, the teacher is fostering an attitude: My work does matter. I'll save it and think about it, making decisions about the future of each piece of my writing. I won't be afraid to work on material that is too personal, or too idiosyncratic, or that otherwise will never make it into the assessment portfolio, because I recognize that the purposes for writing extend way beyond the demands of a system. I know that much of what I write will never have a reader other than myself. But only *after* I write a piece will I make decisions about what its future should be.

───────────── ♦ ─────────────

To showcase one's work: This is the purpose most often established, a common denominator, almost a given, of all portfolios. The performance demonstrated by such a portfolio has been in rehearsal over a period of time, with scenes being cut and added and the script often revised. This portfolio is polished!

To seek employment or entrance to college: The contents of this portfolio might be similar to those of the "showcase" portfolio. It's unlikely this portfolio will contain work from the distant past; usually, its contents will be chosen to provide the information and demonstrate the specific qualities the employer or college is looking for.

As a sort of scrapbook, to show a particular aspect of the student: In this case, the portfolio may be a collection of artifacts, containing little or none of the student's original work.

For faculty review: Most assessment programs require some faculty review of portfolios, but few formal programs exist to facilitate the discussion of individual students. This often-overlooked use of portfolios, a side benefit of portfolios kept for a different purpose, is generally reserved for the portfolios of those students about whom a teacher needs specific advice.

For teacher edification: As with portfolios kept for faculty review, teacher edification is usually a side effect of, not a declared purpose for, keeping portfolios. Glancing through a student's portfolio, a teacher quickly knows what has worked for the student and can focus instruction appropriately. Portfolios that are passed on, year after year, provide an excellent way for a teacher to come to know each incoming student.

In all these purposes for keeping portfolios, we see one common element: None of the avowed purposes is "assessment," but some form of judgment has to be made to meet these purposes.

As a tool for assessment: When the official purpose of keeping a portfolio *is* "assessment," several questions arise. What or who is being assessed — is it the student, a group of students, the teacher, the school? What consequences (high or low stakes) are attached to these results? How and to whom will results be reported?

───────────── ♦ ─────────────

In a community of writers, the teacher's keeping of a portfolio models the process, letting the students see how it's done rather than doing it for them or issuing repeated instructions and answers to individual questions. And, as I mentioned in an earlier chapter, the teacher who is not an especially good writer, the teacher who is embarrassed by stiff prose or weak spelling, can be the best model of all. "I'm working to improve my writing skills, I'm struggling with spelling," are excellent ways to acknowledge one's own status as a learner. Where improvement is noted, the teacher shouldn't be shy in acknowledging personal progress, made visible in (and perhaps thanks to!) the portfolio.

SCHOOL PORTFOLIO

Purpose: To give an adult reader, other than my own teacher, examples of my best writing. This reader will assess the portfolio to determine some of the strengths and weaknesses of my writing.

Required Contents: Multiple drafts of one piece, showing my strategies for revision

Final Drafts Only: Two pieces for a larger or different audience than the school community.

Two letters, one about the piece that is submitted in multiple drafts, the other about any other piece in the portfolio, or about the portfolio as a whole. (These letters should address why a piece has been selected, what qualities it demonstrates, and possibly give a detailed history of the piece.)

At least three pieces that show learning in at least three of the following areas: science; mathematics; literature; history; physical education; health and nutrition.

If students have been given ownership of the portfolio system early in the game, they won't need much coaching. Let them suggest the purpose of keeping portfolios, the required and optional contents, the criteria by which those portfolios will be assessed. Let them select the benchmark pieces for the highest levels of accomplishment, and (rather than hurting the feelings of a child whose writing may not meet the highest standards) challenge them to create pieces that intentionally demonstrate the lower levels of accomplishment. Sometimes a highly regarded benchmark has an early draft that can serve as an example of one of the lower levels of achievement.

The Electronic Portfolio

"But where am I going to store all these portfolios?" is one of the most common questions from teachers who are asked to shift to a portfolio-based classroom. Answers to this question will obviously vary widely according to the purpose of the portfolio, the school's available storage space, and the degree of accessibility to the portfolios that students and faculty need.

One solution to the space problem is storing the portfolio on a computer diskette. The biggest danger of electronic portfolios is that the work will be accidentally erased. But this danger is probably no greater than that of a student's portfolio being lost through student or teacher negligence (call it "misfiling").

A greater concern is that the portfolio, reduced to a mere electronic pulse, loses its immediacy. Surely some of the pieces on the disk will have been printed out as hard copy, but the physical reality of the portfolio is compromised by systems that rely on computers. At the same time, it is far easier to carry a file of computer diskettes to a scoring session than it is to lug milk crates filled with overstuffed folders!

Electronic portfolios should be understood as distinct from the use of a word-processing computer to generate drafts or camera-ready desktop publishing layouts of finished work. Given the use of word processing programs in the classroom, students may choose to keep electronic portfolios as a redundancy, in case the hard-copy portfolio is ever misplaced. Likewise, a hard-copy portfolio can serve as a safeguard against accidental loss of computer files. A good scanner allows artwork and the typewritten/hand-written pieces (as well as voice, music, and video — the whole shebang, given resources and imagination) to be stored and reproduced.

Whatever system you use, don't expect that electronic portfolios are a panacea. At a conference I attended last year, I heard a teacher complain that computer diskettes themselves create storage problems. While the hard-copy portfolio serves, at least, as its own label, computer diskettes have a funny way of escaping labels, of being copied over, of containing the work of more than one student in a single file. A glance through the hard-copy portfolio tells the reader with fair certainty whose work is represented (and this is done without needing a computer to translate); even if the work is not signed, an author's handwriting frequently provides the essential clue that electronic portfolios rarely offer.

None of this is to deny the computer's rightful place in a classroom that values writing. "The computer, more especially the word processor," writes James R. Squire in *Using Computers in Teaching English*, "demands cognitive processes and can help individuals become more systematic in their thinking. William Zinsser, for instance, has recently devoted a book to discussing the changes in writing made possible by use of word processors — ease in achieving unity, coherence, and emphasis; in eliminating clutter, in expanding and transforming sentences, in controlling decisions on diction and word choice. What the computer provides for Zinsser is refinement of strategies for effective writing that he earlier had to struggle to maintain. So may it be with all students" (1984).

Portfolios and Parents

"My teachers love portfolios and parents just eat them up" is how Robert Schackow, the founder of a private elementary school in Florida, expresses his feelings about writing portfolios. A teacher in a Manhattan public high school recently told me that parent phone calls about report-card grades had fallen from 20 percent to less than 1 percent after portfolios were incorporated into parent conferences. The portfolio provides tangible evidence of a child's progress. A parent conference is given focus when the portfolio is on the table and the parent becomes witness to the child's growth.

To the extent that grades are used to compare a student's progress to that of other students, the portfolio provides a unique opportunity to observe that student's progress in a noncompetitive context. Removing the competitive context accomplishes a subtle shift in the parent's expectation of the conference. There is no debate about a letter grade when the work itself provides the compelling evidence of a child's achievement. Just as parents typically support a sports team whether it's winning or losing, and just as they applaud both artful and awful student drama productions, they tend to support the performance represented by their child's writing portfolio.

At the same time that the portfolio should become a part of parent-teacher conferences, other aspects of the student's progress may require consideration. To the extent that the student retains ownership of the portfolio, and to the extent that it is defined strictly as a writing portfolio, it may not be the appropriate repository for teacher observations about speech, listening, and reading, and it may thus only be one component of the student's grade in a given class.

On the other hand, we might revisit the purpose of keeping portfolios and find that parent conferences are an appropriate reason, of themselves, to ask students to keep portfolios of their work. If parent conferences are a central purpose of keeping portfolios, the students may be especially receptive to the notion of keeping portfolios that track their progress, providing evidence of improving performance wherever possible. Such a portfolio may include videotapes or audiotapes, clippings from the school newspaper, work in mathematics, you name it, essentially a folder to which the student and teacher contribute for parent conferences. This sort of portfolio — call it a "learning record" or "learning portfolio" — may be quite separate, indeed, from the student's master or assessment portfolio.

Aside from their use in parent conferences, portfolios can be celebrated more publicly. At Wolcott Elementary School, Nioka Houston's fourth-grade class annually hosts a portfolio celebration, where parents and friends gather to hear readings and enjoy other presentations based on mathematics and writing portfolios. And a growing number of schools use portfolios as part of their graduation ceremonies. Portfolios are no longer the secret, slim files that are kept "on" a student, but open, living documents created by the students, sometimes as public evidence of their progress.

Portfolios and the Business Community

If parents like the use of portfolios in their conferences with teachers, it follows that eventually the business community will become interested in seeing such performance evidence before hiring decisions are made. Once again, the purpose of the portfolio should be revisited to see whether this is a consistent use of the portfolio or whether, yet again, we need to ask students to put a new set of labels on a new set of manila folders.

It might make a lot of sense to design a semester-long curriculum unit — call it "Junior Year English, Semester Two" — where the student identifies goals for the year following graduation, a job, or college, or the military, or whatever, and creates a portfolio that demonstrates the skills and knowledge necessary for opportunities related to those goals.

In Vermont, the business community, which had been clamoring for a statewide writing assessment, stepped forward with a dynamic approach intended to add significance to each school's portfolio program. More than 150 Vermont corporations signed a pledge that they would not hire a Vermont high school graduate without seeing, in addition to a transcript, a portfolio of that person's best work. This type of community support helps to make the keeping of portfolios a real-world activity, not just something one has to do for a certain teacher!

THE PORTFOLIO PARTY

by Nioka Houston, Wolcott Elementary School, Wolcott, VT

What Is It?

My students call it the portfolio party; I prefer to think of the event as a celebration of their minds. We hold minor parties throughout the year, publishing parties, Christmas parties, spelling bees, math counts, Valentine's Day parties, but this is the year's last party — the big one.

The celebration evolved naturally. We celebrate births, marriages, death, a baby's first tooth, first word, first step. We celebrate holidays, anniversaries, and job promotions. To celebrate an academic achievement seems right, seems logical. So began Ms. Houston's tradition, the portfolio party at Wolcott Elementary School.

Once we had the first party, the students in the following year's class just assumed that we'd celebrate their efforts too.

Planning

Teacher's Role: Minimal. Facilitate students' desires. Welcome the guests and then retire to the back of the room.

Students' Role: Major. Plan decorations, prepare refreshments, design programs, arrange for greeters, design and issue invitations, and script a public presentation that explains what a portfolio is and how one is put together. My students also explain the state's assessment criteria and scoring procedures.

The portfolio party is FOR the students. It's their time to shine, to strut their stuff. The teacher should be seen little and heard less during the party itself. The students should be given every opportunity to SHOW AND TELL about their learning.

We schedule our party for late May or early June. Once the portfolios meet the state program's minimum standards of content, once I have individually scored them, and after the students have had an opportunity to reflect, in writing, about their best work, only then are we ready for our party.

We invite parents, siblings, aunts, uncles, and grandparents. We invite the principal, school board members, superintendents and other interested district staff, as well as the teachers in our school, the education commissioner, everyone and anyone that the students want to ask and are willing to address

(continued)

Teacher-Teacher Conferences

Often overlooked is what the portfolio offers as a focal point when teachers meet to discuss their students. As described in *Teachers & Writers* magazine (1993), Arts PROPEL has created and used a faculty conference format that gives teachers useful insights into their students. This format can be adapted to suit almost any circumstance, whether the conferences are weekly, whole-faculty affairs, or an occasional, informal meeting between colleagues. Here is a simplifed format for faculty portfolio-focus groups.

in their presentation. And we invite the press, so the students can see the party and perhaps their faces in the local newspaper!

These parties usually run for two hours. We send out invitations. We decorate with flowers, balloons, streamers, and posters. We dress up. We serve punch and cookies.

The Party Itself

After the guests arrive, I give a brief welcome, and the students then make a whole-group presentation of approximately thirty minutes. Several students explain what we've been learning this year, how we put our portfolios together, and how we scored the work, using examples from the state benchmarks. Then for ninety minutes the students sit one-on-one with their guests, showing their own portfolios, talking about the contents, telling why they chose their "best pieces." Students tell what they feel is important and what they've gained during the year.

When portfolio parties spotlight the achievements of each student, with no student exempt from participation, student self-esteem grows. If the goal of education is to produce self-motivated learners, we as teachers need to give students a sense of satisfaction with their efforts. A portfolio party is not easy. It requires preparation, planning, and rehearsal. It may cause nervous stomachs, dry mouths, and shaky hands, but it ends with an aura of glory surrounding each student.

At my first portfolio party, the chair of our school board, a college professor, chose to go outside to talk with two I.E.P. students. I kept glancing out the window wondering what was going on. An hour later the outdoor conference ended and the professor returned to the classroom, saying: "This is incredible. Your students are amazing!"

Our superintendent has been to all the parties. Of course he already knows all about our portfolio program, but he continues to relish his one-on-one time with the students in their finest hour.

Soon after the party my class leaves me. The students head into the summer with their report cards certifying they're in the fifth grade now. They also carry a memory of a time when they could do all that their minds sought to do without threat or put-down. This memory stays with them. Portfolios bond students' learning with their egos, and they take pride in themselves as learners. Doing is learning.

◆

1. Teacher makes copies of portfolio work that illustrates a student's development.

2. Teacher distributes copies of the work, asking "What do you see here?"

3. Other teachers respond. They should make an effort to point out positive aspects of the student's work as well as to suggest teaching/interpersonal strategies. The teacher who brought the portfolio takes notes, but may not comment on what other teachers say.

4. After all teachers have had an opportunity to describe what they see in the portfolio, the student's teacher responds briefly, asking follow-up questions or pursuing specific ideas and strategies.

Such sessions typically focus on students with whom a teacher needs help; perhaps they should occasionally focus on a portfolio that demonstrates impressive progress, perhaps as a result of a teacher-teacher conference.

If such discussions focus on the work, rather than on a student's behavior or personal problems, the tone of the meeting is positive, helpful to the teacher, and beneficial to the student. Compare this to a faculty meeting where teachers can't wait to complain about a problem student and a group rite of eye rolling, breast-beating, and gossip ensues before everyone concludes, "But what can you do?"

Using the portfolio as a focal point, the entire faculty develops a common perspective on the student, which may help broaden that student's range of real contact points within the community. Faculty discussions around the portfolio should not be a hush-hush matter, but a chance to open doors: "By the way, Ms. Davis brought your portfolio to one of our recent portfolio review sessions; your science report on air bubbles is a gas!"

Portfolios Across the Curriculum!

Writing, a skill that is central to learning in a literate society, is not just "the English teacher's problem." Perhaps the English teacher is uniquely accountable for grammar instruction, but providing students the opportunity to write is every teacher's responsibility. "How else can I see whether my students understand the principles behind an operation?" Bob Kenney, a mathematics teacher and consultant, recently commented. "Of course writing is fundamental to good mathematics instruction."

It makes sense to extend Kenney's argument in all directions, straight through the school's entire curriculum. Students should write in their physical education classes and art classes, as well as in the classes in which writing is traditionally part of the curriculum. Remember that teachers who, because they are not English teachers, are reluctant to "correct" student writing, need not worry. Their focus can be on the content of a piece. When a sentence or passage is unclear, simply circle it. A teacher does not have to rewrite or explain why the passage is unclear: That should be the author's job!

In *A Language for Life*, Sir Alan Bullock's committee addresses secondary school teachers: "It is a common experience among English teachers to be constantly receiving criticism about the pupil's standards of writing in other subjects, and spelling is often the focal point of the censure. We believe that language production is a collective responsibility and that the subject teacher should be willing to co-operate by observing and recording in a way which will help his colleague" (1975, 168). To "help his colleague" does not mean that the content-area teacher has to be an ace speller or a confident grammarian.

Relieved of the expectation that they must act as English teachers, content-area educators should feel no hesitation to ask their students to write. If nothing else, the students' writing will tell that teacher whether the important lessons are

HELPING STUDENTS BUILD PORTFOLIOS
by Patricia McGonegal, Camel's Hump Middle School, Richmond, Vt.

A portfolio will be rich to the very degree that it contains artifacts a student cares deeply about. Can school produce such a portfolio? Can we create the environment where all students can write things we and they value? What would that take? Massive doses of committee meetings and courses? Sleight of hand?

Students who have real reasons to write have a universal edge over students who are constantly assigned topic, genre, length. At the start of the year I brainstorm with my students the kind of things they ought to know and be able to do as sixth-grade students. (They want computer opportunities, spelling help, publishing advice, or other specifics.) I post this list for a week or two, then put it away for a while, and focus on the first of our projects for the year. While engaged in this project (in our case a three-day environmental field trip to the coast of Maine), I nudge my students toward a variety of real writing they might do around the project. They write to get some work done, and as they write, they accomplish some of their goals.

Students write lots of letters around the trip. They solicit discounts on the groceries we will buy; they ask to borrow sleeping bags; they say thank you to the chaperones and donors of cottages we stay in; they introduce themselves and request interviews of local fishermen and environmentalists.

While we are in Maine we write free-form ideas in our journals. After the trip we brainstorm ideas for poems and stories about our recollections and experiences. We bind these poems and stories into a publication, and copies go to everyone involved in the trip.

I try to set up a workshop-style classroom and expect that students will write their letters, stories, and essays without too much teacher interference. Running this type of classroom challenges my resourcefulness. I try to assume the stance

(continued)

getting through. Asking students to write as part of their learning in every class is another way of saying: "This class counts. What you learn here matters, so you'll have to show your learning in writing."

The Use of Learning Logs
A simple learning log provides an easy way for teachers to invite their students to write. Each student keeps a notebook with the expectation that the teacher will, occasionally, peruse it. (Note that *this* notebook, unlike the notebook some teachers call a "journal," is kept with the expectation of regular teacher review.) Every day the student is asked to make an entry during class time, ranging from detailed notes to a simple question or two, possibly indicating ideas or information that aren't yet clear. At the end of a week, students should have ten minutes or so to review their logs and to write a summary of questions or comments they have about the week's learning. These summaries should go into a classroom portfolio for weekly review by the teacher.

suggested in Nancie Atwell's books: not "You are going to sit there until you write a thousand words or five paragraphs," but "Here is a safe place where you will have the time to write." I keep a daily checklist on each child's project. Who is in the computer room? Who needs special help? On which skills does everyone need a lesson? I circulate among the children, coaching, editing, suggesting, occasionally writing myself.

So goes the year. Students take on projects they invent, or act on suggestions I make around topics or genres, current local or nonlocal events. I like to be sure students have tried out a range of genres during the year, so I establish deadlines now and then. In the fall, I ask that they finish at least one letter. In November and December, I ask them to interview a relative or friend about celebrations or other customs. A thoughtful piece informed by an interview will serve many purposes: it is an engaging task, by nature individual and unique; it reaches beyond the classroom to family and community sources; it teaches students to use a powerful research tool.

Occasionally I ask students to read their pieces aloud. When we hear high-quality pieces, it elevates everyone's experience and expectations. We establish the standards for what is good. Later, we can measure with those standards, and revise our original list of what the class ought to be able to do. I am constantly on the lookout for engaging topics that have an authenticity behind them: real purposes for students to write, with real audiences. Real extensions into their writing lives beyond school. Each month or quarter we focus on one genre, but I let the students work at their own pace. I will often suggest a topic or an audience, with the option my teacher Ken Macrorie always gave: If you are burning to write something else right now, go to it.

In the winter, we look at narratives and the role of stories in so many of the other areas of language we experience. Aren't many of our conversations and letters full of stories? What makes good ones?

(continued)

A learning log requires that the student become engaged with the daily learning that is expected in every class. I have recently observed that students in most secondary schools do not routinely take notes. This is a skill that should be taught in elementary school and expected throughout the secondary grades. Some students, not expected to take notes, slouch through the "boring" classes, showing disdain for teachers and subject, never realizing that no class is boring when one becomes engaged with the subject. Even a boring teacher can be brought to life with the challenge of a student who asks questions, expresses opinions, and demands clarification from time to time. In many of our secondary schools, students are allowed (encouraged?) to go through the motions, rarely being challenged by school policy to demonstrate engagement in their learning. As a result, some teachers become disheartened and likewise lose engagement.

Any teacher can break this cycle by insisting that students take notes or keep learning logs. Better yet, whole schools might ask all their students (and teachers and administrators) to keep learning logs. Three minutes would be built

Come spring we focus on essays, and by then I have usually connected the students to some kind of telecommunications forum. Here they can exchange opinions, observations, and feedback with a rich community of students both like themselves and wildly different. My students have participated in a powerful nature writing exchange with Tom McKenna's students in the Aleutian Islands, a wildly diverse discussion with other Vermont students about school reform, and an international forum with forty schools about the future of the environment. Again, we talk together from time to time about what makes the good essays good in each of these exchanges.

Teaching for me has come to mean a tightrope walk with accountability on one end and choice on the other. How fully can I follow Donald Graves's urging to "trust the students' obsessions" in my writing workshop? How often should I impose "the" curriculum guidelines to help students experience the range of skills and genres our district's professional consensus has outlined? I wear two hats when I consider these questions. I am a taxpayer and a parent who wants equity and accountability for all children (especially mine). I am also a veteran teacher who knows down to her bones that you can write off a huge chunk of your class unless you plan with an eye toward the individual needs, interests, and opportunities for engagement of your students.

How do you teach to a portfolio? This is as complex as building a culture, since that, in fact, is what a teacher must do to get the stuff that good portfolios are made of. Engage students in projects that suit their needs, their passions, their talents. Link those to the curriculum. (Impossible? That is a separate problem, which *will* demand massive committee meetings and courses.) Bring together your community of writers and thinkers and risk-takers and questioners, and get them moving.

Every now and then, walk by their desks and collect the products of their efforts.

---

into the end of each period, module, or discussion, for participants to write in their logs.

Of course the material in a student's notes or learning log might suggest topics for written exploration, research papers, essays, poems, plays, speeches, explanations, diagrams, and doodles. A content-area teacher might even avoid having to make specific writing assignments (who, after all, wants to read twenty-five student essays on "gravity," or "Albert Einstein," or "the meaning of pi in my private life"?) by encouraging students to review their learning logs from time to time and to create a list of possible topics for the dreaded term paper. Students can share their lists in brainstorming sessions where the teacher's power is limited to vetoing any suggestions that are inappropriate to the intent of the class.

Portfolio Assessment and Report Cards

In *Response and Analysis* (1988), Robert Probst writes: "The problem is not simply that the grade doesn't inform; rather, it misinforms and deceives. It imitates the precision of mathematics, though it is at best only impression and judgment.

In so doing it conceals information that might be useful to students and parents, and trains them to accept an empty symbol as surrogate" (224).

To what extent are the results of a portfolio assessment linked to the grades that are sent home on report cards? This question lies at the heart of many teachers' anxiety about assessment programs, and there is no "one-size-fits-all" answer. The relationship of assessment results and grades depends largely on the teacher's or school's policies, and where large-scale assessment is involved, this distinction becomes especially important.

Take, for example, a student who works very, very hard, but whose skills are not well developed. A large-scale assessment project should demand that the teacher apply the program's standards equally to all portfolios, ignoring personal factors such as family context, effort, or special challenges the student faces. To report reliable information, large-scale assessments require objectivity: standards-based assessment. The classroom teacher may thus, in conducting assessments for large-scale reporting, find some student work at low levels, yet on report cards seek to reward the student for attitude and effort. The results of large-scale assessments should be only as useful as the teacher wants them to be in determining the student's grade. After all, CAT and SAT scores are not generally reflected in report cards!

On the other hand, some small-scale assessment programs are created to provide clear standards on which students' grades will be based. To the extent that the portfolio plays a role in the student's final grade, its contents and ownership may be compromised by the high stakes attached to the results of an assessment. In such cases, I would, once again, strongly encourage the keeping of *two* portfolios: one for the report card and one for work the student doesn't consider appropriate for grading.

From an evolving collection of the student's work in any classroom, a picture of that student as learner emerges that is far more powerful than a report card or the computer printout from a testing company. Any teacher who wants to explain a student's progress to parents needs a portfolio, even if the school is not requiring portfolios for an assessment program!

◆ 6 ◆

Steven's and Abbie's Portfolios

FIGURE 6–1 *Steven's Portfolio*

WRITING PORTFOLIO TABLE OF CONTENTS

Student's Name *Steven Bork*

Grade *4*

Teacher's Name *Mrs. Houston*

School *Wolcott Elem.*

1) Best Piece -- Title: *Me*

2) A letter about the Best Piece ("Dear Reader ...")

3) A poem, story, play, or personal narrative

Title: *Sandals & cemen dont mix*

4) A response to a cultural event, public exhibit, sports event, or to a book, current issue, math problem or scientific phenomenon

Title: *Pros + cons of a Popcorn Busines at School*

5) Writing from any curriculum area that is not Language Arts or English (4th grade: one piece; 8th grade: three pieces).

Title: *Bye, Bye, Birdy!*

Title: _____

Title: _____

6) Other Writing (optional)

Title: *Poetry*

Title: *Writing Reflections = NS*

Title: _____

NS Title: *3rd Grade; Writing Sample - The Bag of Magic Sand!*

Title: _____

For writing that involved more than one draft, all drafts should be stapled together with the most recent draft on top,

All drafts should be dated. **NS = not for scoring**

84

◆

VERMONT WRITING PORTFOLIO ASSESSMENT WORKSHEET

Student: Steven Beach
ID No.:
Reviewer Code No.: N. Houston
Grade: 4 – May 1993

	PURPOSE — the degree to which the writer's response establishes and maintains a clear purpose • demonstrates an awareness of audience and task • exhibits clarity of ideas	ORGANIZATION — the degree to which the writer's response illustrates • unity • coherence	DETAILS — the degree to which the details are appropriate for the writer's purpose and support the main point(s) of the writer's response	VOICE/TONE — the degree to which the writer's response reflects personal investment and expression	USAGE, MECHANICS, GRAMMAR — the degree to which the writer's response exhibits correct • usage (e.g., tense formation, agreement, word choice) • mechanics – spelling, capitalization, punctuation • grammar • sentences as appropriate to the piece and grade level
ENTRY 1 BEST PIECE	No				
	FINAL ASSESSMENT: Best Piece ◉ Extensively ○ Frequently ○ Sometimes ○ Rarely	FINAL ASSESSMENT: Best Piece ◉ Extensively ○ Frequently ○ Sometimes ○ Rarely	FINAL ASSESSMENT: Best Piece ○ Extensively ◉ Frequently ○ Sometimes ○ Rarely	FINAL ASSESSMENT: Best Piece ◉ Extensively ○ Frequently ○ Sometimes ○ Rarely	FINAL ASSESSMENT: Best Piece ○ Extensively ◉ Frequently ○ Sometimes ○ Rarely
ENTRY 2 Type: Letter	E	E	E	E	E
ENTRY 3 Type: Anecdotal Report	F	E	E	F	F
ENTRY 4 Type: Chas popcorn	F	E	E	E	F
ENTRY 5 Type: Len's popcorn	F	F	E	F	F
ENTRY 6 Type: Science R.	F	F	E	F	F
ENTRY 7 Type:					
ENTRY 8 Type:					
	FINAL ASSESSMENT: Portfolio Review ○ Extensively ◉ Frequently ○ Sometimes ○ Rarely	FINAL ASSESSMENT: Portfolio Review ○ Extensively ◉ Frequently ○ Sometimes ○ Rarely	FINAL ASSESSMENT: Portfolio Review ◉ Extensively ○ Frequently ○ Sometimes ○ Rarely	FINAL ASSESSMENT: Portfolio Review ○ Extensively ◉ Frequently ○ Sometimes ○ Rarely	FINAL ASSESSMENT: Portfolio Review ○ Extensively ◉ Frequently ○ Sometimes ○ Rarely

FIGURE 6–1 (continued) Teacher's assessment of the work in Steven's portfolio, using Vermont's initial analytic assessment guide (see Chapter 7).

FIGURE 6–1 (continued)

Me

Yours truly came out of his mother on June tenth, nineteen eighty three in Connecticut. I went camping in Virginia when I was one, I repeat ONE YEAR OLD! Steven Peter Borck moved to Vermont when he was only four!

I think my family is really hungup on the number four, I mean we have four people in the house, four pets and I moved to Vermont when I was four! I have a mother, a father, and a brother, but, thank God, no sisters! My brother is okay, but sometimes he's so incredibly stupid I wonder why he has enough smarts to even talk!

There are only three words to describe shcool boring, boring, boring! Thats what school's like for me. My favorite subject in shcool is art.

When I get out of college, I will be a scientist. I will invent a time machine! I will also invent a way to keep from aging and a way to clean up all the pollution on earth. Well, I hope you enjoyed my story.

by Steven P. Borck

FIGURE 6–1 (continued)

Wollcott Elem. Sch
Wollcott, Vermont
April 28, 1993

Dear Reader

I picked "Me" as my best
piece because it has a lot of humor,
(at least the second grade thought
so!) voice and tone, and it explains my life and possibly the future
of my life. It also introduces
my life before it introduces my
writing. I started "Me" with a
couple of clusters on snow flakes
for each paragraph. Then he
grew into a couple of pages
referred to as a rough draft. We
gave him a sheild. I don't know
why though. Then he evolved into
a more formal form known as a
second draft. Finally, he grew into
a good-mannered young final draft;
but just for the heck of it
we sharp pencil conferenced
him to make him look good. I

FIGURE 6–1 (continued)

writes with humor you see and
my voice and tone are what you'd
expect from a fourth grader who
watches TV too much.

Sincerly,
Steven Borck

FIGURE 6–1 (continued)

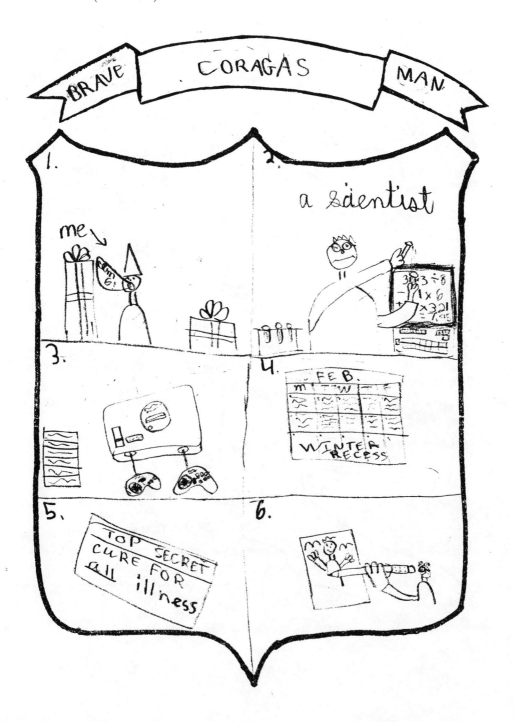

FIGURE 6–1 (continued)

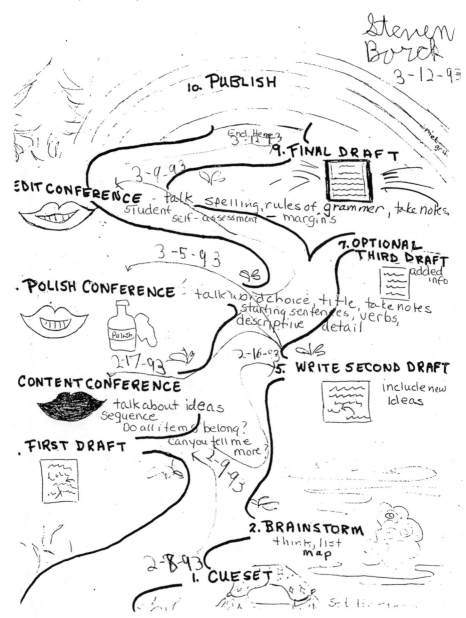

FIGURE 6–1 (continued)

2nd Draft

Steven
Borch
3-4-93

Edit
conf.
2-10-93

Yours truly came out of his
mother on June tenth, nineteen eighty
three. I whent camping in Virginia
when I was one, I repeat ONE YEAR
old! Steven Peter Borch moved to
Vermont when he was four.

in Con-
neticut?

I think my family is really
hung up on the number four.
I mean we have four pets
four people in the house,
and I moved to Vermont
when I was four. I have

family →

a mother, a father, and a
brother and thank God no
sisters. My brother is okay but
some times so incredibly stupid
I wonder why he has enough
smarts to talk!

even

school →
life →

There are only three words
to describe shool – boring
boring boring! Thats what
school's like for me. My faveret
subject in school is art!

FIGURE 6–1 (continued)

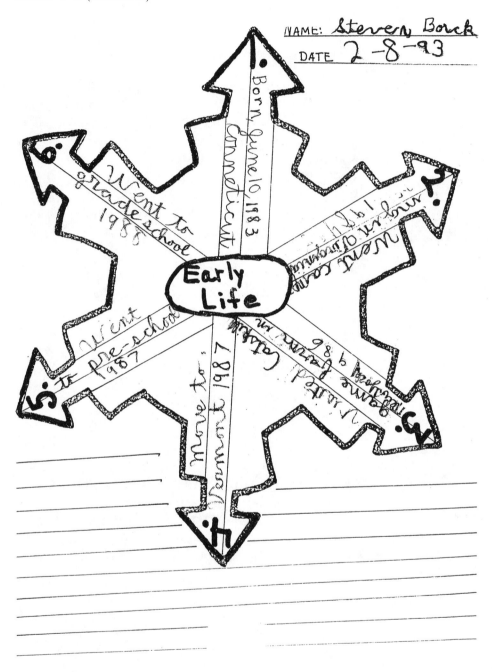

FIGURE 6–1 (continued)

Early life

~~ve out of my mother~~

~~I was~~ ~~born~~ on June tenth nineteen
teen eighty three in C.T. [2] I went

camping in Virginia in 1984.

[3] In 1986 I visited the Catskill

game farm in New York state

[4] I moved moved to Vermont in

1987. [5] I whent to preschool in

1986 [6] In 1988 I whent to grade

school [8] Up until then life was

great, but now its not so great.
~~dum, da da~~

la dum dum, dum dum.

Figure 6–1 (continued)

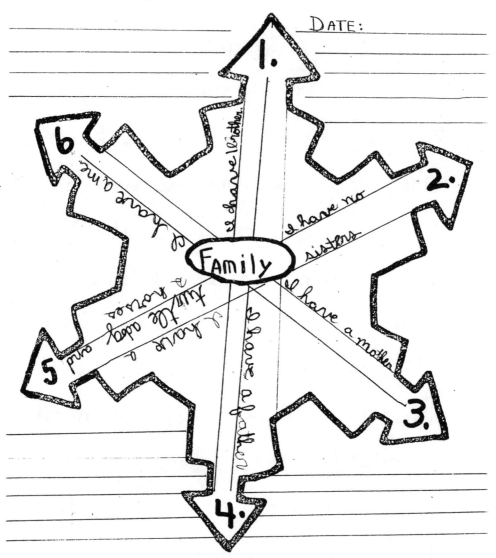

Figure 6–1 (continued)

Family

I have a family of four, four pets, four people (Including me) a brother, a dad, a mom, and a me.

Figure 6–1 (continued)

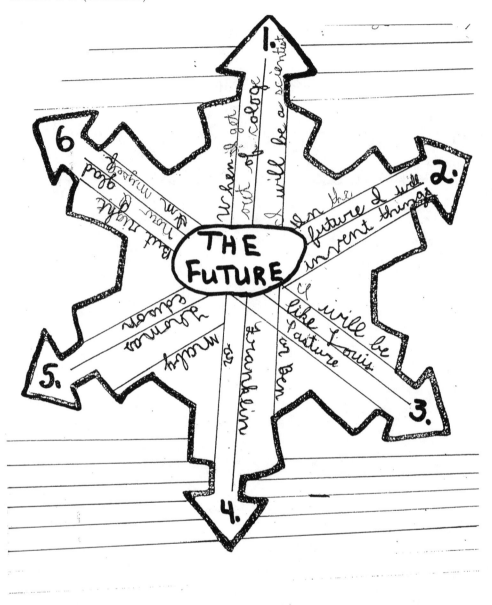

FIGURE 6–1 (continued)

Future

When I get out of colloge I will be a sientist. I will invent a time machine! I'll allso invent a way to keep from aging and a way to klean up all the pollution on earth.

Five titles

1. My life

2. me

3. Who I am

4. This is me

5. Hi im Steven Peter Borck

FIGURE 6–1 (continued)

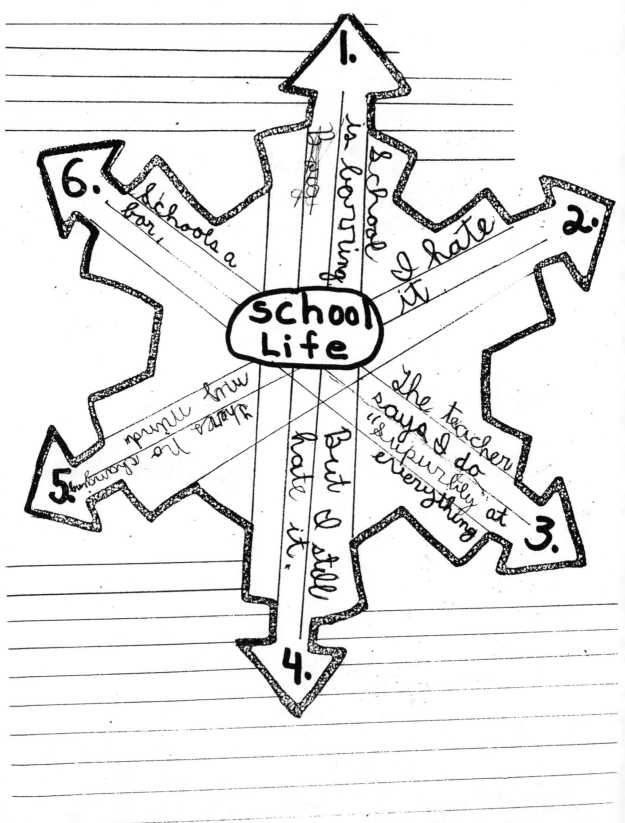

FIGURE 6–1 (continued)

sandals & cement don't mix.
When I was 9 I went to
camp. It was Friday night the
day before we went back home I
was in the shower hanging up
my clothes I was just about
to take off my T-shirt when
I slipped on the cement and
fell out of the shower! With
only a T-shirt and sandals
on! There were two boys standing near the sinks. They started
to laugh at me. I ran back into the
shower, took of my T-shirt and turn-
on the hot water. Whew! I'm glad I
go home tomorrow

by Steven P. Borck
dedicated to greg my
best friend at camp.
9-22-92

FIGURE 6–1 (continued)

Steven Borck 10-26-92

Popcorn at school YAH!
The 4th grade is selling popcorn at school. Wow! I better hurry down there to get that freshly popped, extra buttered, out of this world popcorn!! And they're selling it for only 25¢!!!! WOW!!!!! The whole school is going to be pouring into the 4th grade to stuff themselves silly with popcorn!!!!! The 4th grade will make money and have fun in the process.

Steven Borck 10-28-92

Popcorn? NO WAY!
Does that 4th grade think they could sell popcorn at school? If they do they're dumber than mud! Little kids could choke! Kids would be stealing from each other! Kids would eat too much and throw up! Personally I hate popcorn so I don't mind if they don't sell it! Actually I despise the idea!

FIGURE 6–1 (continued)

Steven B.   Writing   Criteria
Student

Popcorn at school YAH!
+ Popcorn? NO WAY!
title

10–28–92
date

E = extensively   **F** = frequently   **S** = sometimes   **R** = rarely

Skill   Assessment

Purpose: Why are you writing?   E   (F)   S   R

Organization: clear focus? Can we follow your thought pattern? Sequencing?   E   (F)   S   R

Details: Do your details paint a word picture?   (E)   F   S   R

Voice & Tone: Are these words your tongue? Does this writing sound like you?   (E)   F   S   R

GUM: Periods? Punctuation? Capital letters? Noun/Verb agreement? S/NS?   (E)   F   S   R

FIGURE 6–1 (continued)

BYE, BYE, BIRDY!

Figure 6-1 (continued)

Steven
Borch
4-12-93

Geckos have a very wide selection of color. Like the chameleon
the gecko can alter the color of
its skin! Their varity ranges from
brown with black spots to a vivid
yellow and coal black stripes!
Conpare these two geckos:
The fat tailed gecko, a short stuby
fat tailed gecko, and the banded
gecko, a long skinny gecko with
a long pointed tail!
        Geckos live almost every
where! The only places they
dont live in are chilly. The way
they got such a big habitat
is, they become stowaways on
boats! They're welcome on board
because they eat bugs. Thats
why they're popular in gar-
dens too.
        Geckos have so many
cool cool things about them.
They're the acrobats of the
lizard world! There are eight
hundred kinds of them ranging
from an inch to two feet long!
They can hang upside down on
glass because of mini-hair
like bristles on their feet! They
even clean their whole face,
even their eyeballs with their
tongue!

FIGURE 6–1 (continued)

Steven
Borck
4-7-93

Great pets

Extremely fast

Has clear things like contacts on eyes

Chirp, quack, croak, bark

Only animal that pushes off tail to avoid capture

Sheds skin

BIBLIOGRAPHY
Pettit, Jayne, Amazing Lizards
New York, Scholastic Inc., 1990

FIGURE 6-1 (continued)

Final DRAFT

Student Response Booklet
Pets as Friends, Page 14

Now you will revise your first draft. Make sure that you use the comments from your classmates to help you as you write.

Petless

Steven Borck is petless,
Yes petless I say.
He used to have a cat,
But then it ran away.
Then he got a parrot,
Yes a parrot I say,
But when mother whent to
clean its cage it flew away.
Steven Borck is petless,
Yes petless I say,
He used to a hamster,
But then it ran away.
Then he got a turtle,
Yes a turtle I say
But then one day mother
turned to him and said,
It didnt eat Hamburgers
and pizza,
But dead seaweed instead.
Whel there gos all his
pets and he really has
to say,
He's ptless,
Just petless,
Petless I say.

THE NEW STANDARDS PROJECT
1993 LITERACY TASK PILOT

FIGURE 6–1 (continued)

First Marking Period   **Steven B.**
Writing Reflections   Name

What is your favorite part of the writing process:

The brainstorm because I have a good imagination.

As a writer what is the easiest part for you?

The brainstorm because I have a big imagination.

As a writer what is the hardest part for you?

The writing because it makes my hand hurt.

How do you feel about daily journals? I like them because its a way to have kids open up their mind and express their thoughts.

FIGURE 6–1 (continued)

(Writing)/Reading Reflections
Second Quarter

Steven Borck
name
1-25-93
date

What's something new you've learned to do
in writing? I have learned to use descriptive
words.

What would you like to learn so you can
become a better writer? I would like to learn
where and how to use descriptive words.

What's something new you've learned to do in
reading? I have learned to make
reading a habit.

What would you like to learn so you can become
a better reader? I would like to expand
my vocabulary.

FIGURE 6–1 (continued)

Third Marking Period
Writing Reflections

Steven Brock
name
4-27-93
date

1. How have you changed as a writer since fourth grade started? I have changed as a writer since fourth grade started because I now use more voice and tone, humor, and descriptive words.

2. What type of writing do you enjoy most? Why? I enjoy journaling the most because it is a good way to express your thoughts and emotions.

published

3. We've pushed our writing several ways. What was your favorite way? My favorite way of publishing my writing, was when we gave it someone as a gift.

4. A third grader has asked you about writing in Mrs. Houston's room. What will you tell him? I would tell him that you get to use your imagination alot and you have to make your writing interesting.

FIGURE 6–1 (continued)

5. Is there anything you would like to see changed in the way we do writing? No I don't think so. I think our writing process is very efficient.

6. If you had the chance to describe the "fun" part of writing, what would you say? I would say that the "fun" part would be when its all done and I am proud of it.

FIGURE 6–1 (continued)

The BAG of MAGIC SAND!

MAGIC

written and
illustrated by
Steven Borch

FIGURE 6–1 (continued)

One day I was walking and I saw a magic shop. I went in and the shop keeper said "Hello young lad. What do you want to buy?" I looked at the shelves, finally I said "That bag of magic sand." "That will be a penny." He handed me the bag of magic sand some instructions, and a box to carry it all in.

The next morning I read the instructions over and over again.

Figure 6–1 (continued)

but I didn't understand. It said
Hello lucky possessor of the
MAGIC! SAND! Add water and your
own spit, wait one hour, now you
have a MAGIC! ROCK! It will
obey only you. It will do anything
you wish, use it wisely.
I did as the paper said.
The Rock turned out to be a
bright green emerald. It was
butifull I wished I looked

FIGURE 6–1 (continued)

just like it to my suprise I was a emerald exept GIANT Then I shrunk to size of the magic emerald. I looked around I didn't hear anything or see anything Mom was cooking dinner Tom was waching TV and Dad was out in the shop. The magic rock was a human foot away. I knew rocks cant roll by

FIGURE 6–1 (continued)

them selives so somebody would have to pick me up walk or foot and drop me next to the magic rock in order for me to turn back into a human again. I was cold because I shrunk right out of my clothes! Then I felt something. I saw my brother. He was picking me up and the magic rock in the same hand! I wished I was a

FIGURE 6–1 (continued)

human again and I was! Tha
ank goodness the Magic workes
on my clothes!

Brief Comments on the Work in Steven's Portfolio

"Dear Reader" describes the writer's process for writing his best piece. It also shows, especially in the final sentence, the author as a relaxed writer who is willing to inject humor into his work.

"Me," the author's selection as his best piece, indeed proves the assertion in his "Dear Reader" letter that his "voice and tone are what you'd expect from a 4th grader." He's not afraid to be himself in his writing!

Early drafts of "Dear Reader" and "Me" provide a glimpse into the author's strategies for revision.

"Sandals & Cement Don't Mix," written early in the school year, displays a good sense of narrative organization and the author's sense of humor in a brief recounting of what did not, at the time, seem funny. A run-on sentence, a sentence fragment, and the big "jump" in the final sentence are the obvious weaknesses in this piece. One can measure the writer's growth by seeing that similar lapses are less evident in later-dated writing. Although they may be "lapses," the jump jolts the reader into realizing that this was a frightening experience for the narrator, and the sentence fragment adds voice to the piece. Perhaps it's more a matter of helping students to recognize such occurrences in their writing and to use them, when appropriate, as devices.

"Popcorn at School" (Pro and Con). Although he is just a tad more generous, the author's self-assessment of these pieces closely matches his teacher's. I agree that, in all five criteria, the "Popcorn" paragraphs are in the upper range of the rubric.

In "Bye Bye Birdy," his science report, the author uses exclamation points at the end of almost every sentence. The information is otherwise presented without distraction. A reference is cited, but the voice in the writing suggests that the author has assimilated, not paraphrased the material.

The acrostic, "GEHCOS," seems more a webbing activity than a poem. Many elementary-school teachers use fixed forms such as acrostic, haiku, and pantoum as their only approach to teaching poetry, explaining that young students need such structure. But often as not, the imposition of a fixed structure straitjackets the student. Just as a rhyme scheme sometimes leads to nonsense, unwavering adherence to poetic forms can keep writers from discovering what's really on their minds or in their hearts.

"Petless" is a pretty sophisticated poem. The repetition of the first line creates a refrain that is skillfully altered in the final three lines. One error of omission (a recopying mistake?) creates a moment of confusion for the reader, and a few spelling errors might be pointed out to give the writer a "goal" for ensuing work.

"The Bag of Magic Sand" is from Steven's third-grade year. Comparing it to more recent work shows how much he grew, in a single year, as a writer.

F<small>IGURE</small> 6–2 *Abbie's Portfolio*

TABLE OF CONTENTS

Letter of Introduction
Letter About Best Piece
Best Piece–The Mudville Nine That Day
Personal Narrative–
    Stories of the Nude
Response piece–
    Who's the Freak?
Writing from other subjects-
    P.E.–Dream Gym
    Science/English–Arthritis
    Math-Math problems
Journal Entry
We Went on a Hike
7th Grade Piece–Remember When.......

FIGURE 6–2 (continued)

Letter of Introduction

Hey, do I know you from somewhere?

Oh well, maybe not. Allow me to introduce myself. My name is Abbie Foster. I go to Craftsbury Academy, famous for it's excellence in education, outstanding faculty, great students and rubber pizza at lunch.

I live in Stannard, Vt., famous for absolutely nothing, except the highest taxes in the state. It is about the size of my little finger. Don't feel bad if you haven't heard of it, not many people have.

I live in a house (believe it or not) with my older brother, Bert, (who against all popular belief isn't as bad as people think), my younger brother, Gabe, (who all of my friends adore), and my parental unit. There's not much to say about them. I mean moms are moms and dads are dads.

In my spare time, I like to listen to music, talk on the phone, or take part in some social activity—pretty average, huh? I love sports, especially soccer. I also like to watch Monday night football with my dad. Actually, I like to watch anything on television except bridge, chess, croquet and cricket, but they aren't televised too often.

Now you're in for it. This is what I hate. Are you ready? O.K. Here it is: the Cowboys, family reunions, leftovers, the Pledge of Allegiance (not that I'm unpatriotic, but there are lots of confusing terms and big words), and little dogs under 1 foot named Cuddels or Pookie or some obnoxious name like that.

I have a lot more to say and would tell you my life story, but that would bore you, and my pen is running out of ink.

Stay in school and may the bluebird of happiness not fly up your nose.

Abbie
Foster

FIGURE 6–2 (continued)

Letter of Introduction

Hey, do I know you from somewhere?

Oh, well, maybe not. Allow me to introduce myself. My name is Abbie Foster. I go to Craftsbury Academy, famous for its excellence in education, oustanding faculty, great students and rubber pizza at lunch.

I live in Stannard, Vermont, famous for absolutely nothing except the highest taxes in the state. It is about the size of my little finger. Don't feel bad if you have never heard of it, not many people ever have.

I live in a house (believe it or not) with my older brother, Bert, (who ~~is~~ against ~~a racist/sexist~~ isn't as bad as people think), my younger brother, Gabe, (who all of my friends adore), and my parental unit. There's not much to say about them. I mean moms are moms and dads are dads.

all popular belief isn't as ~~known a racist isn't as~~

In my spare time, I like to listen to music, talk on the phone, or take part in some social activity. I love sports, especially soccer. I also like to watch Monday night football with my Dad. Actually, I like to watch anything on television except bridge, chess, and croquet, but they aren't televised too often. ✗

I have a lot more to say and would tell you my life story, but that would bore you, and my pen is running out of ink.

Stay in school and may the bluebird of happiness not fly up your nose.

Abbie Foster

✗ I hate the Cowboys, family reunions, leftovers, the Pledge of Allegience (not that I'm unpatriotic, but there are lots of big words and confusing terms,) and little dogs under 1 ft. named Cuddles, or Pookie or some obnoxious name like that.

Figure 6–2 (continued)

Well hello, and welcome to my portfolio,

Ya know, the world is full of tough choices, and yet another one is staring me in the face. As a state requirement, I have to choose the best piece I have written this year. Trust me on this one, with someome like me who writes everything from Snow White to Michael Jackson, this won't be easy. I have written about 72 million pieces, (or so it seems) and this really is a tough choice.

I would say it is a cross between my letter of introduction and a poem called The Mudville Nine That Day. I would go about choosing this by which one was more fun to write, but I can't because they were both fun. I would also go about doing this by which one I like better, but if I knew that, I wouldn't be having this debate with a piece of paper. So I'll go by which I put more effort into.

Here it is....... drum roll, please.....

The winner is The Mudville Nine That Day!!

No, wait, I changed my mind. Now the best piece is the letter of introduction!!

No, you can't think that I'm serious. The real winner is The Mudville Nine That Day. Written, produced, directed, and co-produced by none other than yours truly!

Now let me give you a little insight to this piece. It is the "true story" to Casey at the Bat by Ernest Lawrence Thayer. It is in poem form, just like the original poem. It was hard to get started, but as soon as I got my motor runnin' and headed out on the highway, it was smooth sailing- or driving in this case.

Well, it's been nice chatting with you. I would stay for some coffee, but I've got to go and write some more final drafts! Happy reading!!

                                                        Abbie Foster

P.S. Are you still reading
this? Well, put it down,
you still have a whole portfolio
to read!!

FIGURE 6–2 (continued)

<u>THE MUDVILLE NINE THAT DAY</u>

```
Please let me inform you about the
    Mudville nine that day.
Let me think, if I remember correctly,
    it was a rainy night in May.
I remember stepping up to bat, and
    falling on my face.
I got into the batters box, and then
    got sprayed with Mace.

As the first pitch whizzed by, I was
    in a daze.
I was totally blinded by all the
    sun rays.
Yes, it was raining, and the clouds
    filled up the sky.
But the sun came out of no where,
    and I don't know why.

The second pitch was way outside,
    so I didn't swing at all.
It really is common sense not to swing
    at a ball.
But this idiotic umpire still called
    it a strike.
I tipped my hat, and threw my bat,
    and told him to take a hike.

We exchanged ideas, and said some things
    I'm sure we didn't mean.
And folks, take my word for this: they
    weren't all very clean.
And just about as sure as the president
    elected,
You're not going to believe it: MIGHTY
    CASEY was ejected.

The crowd did boo and hiss and say
    things I can't repeat.
I stomped off the field, into the dugout,
    and began to remove my cleats.
My coach followed me in with Barrows, my
    friend.
"Casey," They said, with a frown on thier
    face,"I would say this is the end.
    You're substitute is Big Bad Joe Lorenz."

Big Joe stepped up with a count of 0 and
    2.
He had to call time out so he could stop
    and tie his shoe.
He stepped back in and spit his cud.It
    landed on the plate.
Big Joe scowled at the pitcher with a
    gruesome look of hate.

If only he could hit this and drive
    two people in,
That would be enough for them to
    tie the game and win.
In the meantime, as these thoughts
    were rolling through my head,
The pitcher pitched- that was strike
    three- the Mudville nine was
    dead!

As you can see, we lost the game,
    and it was not my fault.
I missed the first, and the second,
    but Big Joe was the one who
    struck out.
Somewhere men are laughing, and some-
    where children shout.
But now there is joy in Mudville,
    because the truth is out.
```

~Abbie Foster~

FIGURE 6–2 (continued)

Stories of the Nude   3/29/93

O.k. Don't go jumping the gun and making assumptions. This is not X-rated and dirty. It is about me when I was two years old. I was always naked. 24 hours a day, 7 days a week. I guess you could call it two-year-old pornography. Even in the winter, I would throw on a coat and a pair of Sorrell boots, just so I wouldn't "freeze my butt off," literally speaking.

There was this one time when I went sledding. I was finely dressed in my ugly brown, yellow and red coat and boots. And I mean only my coat and boots. I headed for the slopes in the front of my house. I hopped in the sled and pushed off. I whizzed down the hill, wipping through the powder of the fresh snow. I was going and nothing was stopping me. I speeded down the hill, across the drive way, and ended up right smack dab underneath the car parked in the driveway. I freaked, I panicked, I screamed. I was horrified until my ever-loving mother pulled me out from under that horrid contraption.

By the time I was four, I was fully dressed 99.9% of the time. I guess you could say I turned out for the best, I mean dressed.

FIGURE 6–2 (continued)

Who's The Freak?   3/10/93

O.k. folks, lets face it. The article in The Burlington Free Press, March 6, 1993, titled Freak Shows a Thing of the Past, Right? was going way overboard. I'm not saying Michael Jackson never used an oxygen tent to slow aging. And I'm not saying that he doesn't bleach his skin. But I'm not saying he does, either. He said he had a skin disorder that affects the pygment in the skin. This is possible. There is such a disease, you know. Besides, who are you to call him a liar, anyway?

Michael Jackson is a living legend, and just because he talks a little high-pitched and he grabs his crotch does not mean he is a "freak," does it? Because you don't have music awards, amusement parks, fame and fortune and live interviews with Oprah Winfrey doesn't mean he's a freak.

Sure, everyone is entitled to his/her own opinion, but this is harsh. Please, desmount your high horse and think how he may feel. Maybe you can't help the way you feel, but do you have to

publish it? I think not.

"Tee-hee-hee, that's personal." What would you say if someone asked you if you were a virgin on national television that 90 million people were watching? Please, give the man a break.

FIGURE 6–2 (continued)

Dream Gym   4/15/93

O.K. Here it is. The ideal physical education class.

To start it off, it would not, I repeat would not be second period. That is way to early in the morning to function. It would be 7th period so it is after lunch, but there is time for my lunch to settle, but late enough in the day so you won't miss your bus because your gym teacher gave you .03 seconds to change.

Then, we could do whatever our little heart desires. We would have to follow one ground rule. This is the most important rule in the history of C.A.

NO SCOOTER HOCKEY, SOCCER, OR ANYTHING THAT HAS TO DO WITH SCOOTERS.

Class would be taught by Dikembe Mutombo. And no matter whatever we were playing — be it ultimate frisbee or korfball, he's on my team. Alongside of Mr. Mutombo would be Jakie Joyner-Kersey. And you know the rules, she's on my team.

We would still have it every other day. There would be no drills or

interludes, we would just play.

Well, that's my ideal gym class. You better like it or Mr. Mutombo will step on you.

FIGURE 6–2 (continued)

ARTHRITIS

BY: ABBIE FOSTER

Mrs. Simmons
Mr. Gutzmann
English/Science
March 8, 1993

Figure 6–2 (continued)

FIGURE 6–2 (continued)

<u>Outline</u>

I. Introduction

II. Definition

III. Signs and symptoms

IV. Causes

V. Effects of Arthritis

VI. Treatment

VII. Current information

VIII. Conclusion

X. Bibliography

XI. Appendix
    a. A normal joint.
    b. A joint with osteoarthritis.
    c. A joint with rheumatoid arthritis.

<u>Introduction</u>

    The purpose of this paper is to familiarize the reader about arthritis. Research will be conducted by reading books, medical journals, periodicals, papers and graphs, and conducting interviews. At the end of this paper, the reader will learn about three main types of arthritis, how a joint works, and how the joint is affected with each different type of arthritis.

FIGURE 6–2 (continued)

Definition

   Arthritis means "inflamed joint". It is named after Arthron, the Greek word for inflammation. Arthritis is not a single disease. There are many different conditions that all can be called arthritis. They all are inflamed, which causes swelling, warmth, redness and pain. Inflammation is the main feature in arthritis.

   About seventy-five million people in the United States have pain in the bones or joints. One out of every three Americans has some sort of pain in the joints, but it does not last long. Over twenty million people have worse pain that does not go away. It causes problems in movement, walking, or using your hands. Treatment is needed to help relieve the pain. Three million people still suffer from pain with treatment. Anyone is susceptible to arthritis, even children.

Warning Signs

Gout: sudden onset of intense pain in the joint, swelling, red- ness and heat. Often first occurs in the big toe.

   · Skin in affected joint may appear red of purple and shiney.

   · Joint may be tender, even to the slightest touch.

FIGURE 6–2 (continued)

4.

<u>Fibromyalgia:</u> aches and stiffness that persist for three months
or longer.

    . `Symptoms may worsen in cold, damp weather.

    . Possibly fatigue, anxiety, sleep disturbances, and
depression.

<u>Ankylosing Spandylitis</u>: pain in the lower back and legs that
develops gradually, in weeks, rather than hours.

    . Early morning stiffness and pain.

    . Exercise relieves symptons and rest worsens them.

    . Symptoms occur for more than three months rather than
occurring in sporadic attacks.

<u>Lupus</u>: fatigue, fever, depression, and joint pains.

    . Hair loss and rashes that worsen with sunlight.

    . Fingers may become blue and white when exposed to cold.

    . Assorted other symptoms affecting major organs.

<u>Lyme Disease</u>

    . Ususally characterized by a distinct rash consisting of
a bump surrounded by a gradually spreading red zone.

    . Flu-like symptoms with fever and chills.

    . In time, arthritis, heart palpatations, or nervous
system disorders.

<u>Who Is Most Likely To Get Arthritis?</u>

    1. Age and sex: Some forms of arthritis seem more likely
and occur more often in one group of people than another; e.g. in
women more than in men. Some forms are seen more in elderly

FIGURE 6–2 (continued)

5.

people, while others are more common in younger people.

2. Lifestyles: People who sit down all day are usually
more susceptible to arthritis than people who get out and
get a lot of exercise. If a person who is active does get arthritis,
it may be easier to treat. It is possible that if you injure a joint,
arthritis may appear in the same joint years later.

3. Family History: Certain forms of arthritis tend to
appear in many family members. Someone who has lots of family
members with arthritis is more liable to get it than someone
with no history of arthritis in the family.

4. Other diseases: People who get certain diseases of the
intestines usually get arthritis at the same time. Doctors are
trying to learn more about why this happens.

How a Joint Works (See Appendix A)
    . The ends of bones are covered with cartilage. They
are like pads on the bones. It is a tough, spongy material.
Their job is to cushion and take the impact of bones crushing
together.

    . The whole joint is enclosed in a capsule (sleeve). It
fits closely around the joint. It is made of strong fibers and
ligaments, strong cords. Muscles give the joint added support.

    . The space inside the capsule is filled with thick fluid
called synovial fluid. It is thick, like the white of an egg.
It, too, helps cushion the bones as well as lubricate the joints
to help them glide without friction. Wherever muscles or tendons
have to slide over each other as the bones in the joints move,

FIGURE 6–2 (continued)

6.

a little sac called a bursa stays between the muscle and the
tendon, and lets them slide.

When a Joint Does Not Work

Every part of the joint is important. Without the cartilage,
the bones would crunch together. Without the capsule and ligaments, the bones would move in ways that could cause great pain
and damage. In the absence of synovial fluid, the joint would
not move smoothly. If there were no bursa, the tendons and
muscles would not move easily.

Osteoarthritis (Degenerative Arthritis)

Osteoarthritis is the most common type of arthritis, but it
does not involve much inflammation at first. You may have pain
and swollen joints. The main problem is that the cartilage gets
worn down and cannot protect or cushion the bone. This is different from all other types of arthritis because it starts in the
cartilage, rather than in the bones. When the cartilage is in its
normal, good condition, it is springy and will go back to its original
shape when it is squeezed. After it is many years old, it may
lose this ability.

Cartilage is made of proteins. These proteins make the
cartilage strong. Years later, small changes may occur making the
proteins weaker. This is when the cartilage starts to break down.
Most people do not have problems because the breakdown is too slight
to notice. Some people have protein differences that make up the
cartilage. These differences cause the breakdown to occur faster.

FIGURE 6–2 (continued)

7.

Osteoarthritis is very rare in ages before forty because
it takes much longer for these changes to occur.

If you look at an X-ray of a joint with osteoarthritis,
(see Appendix E) you will see that the bones are closer together
because they cannot hold as much synovial fluid. As the bones
bump together, tiny cracks occur in the bones under the cartilage.
These are so small that you may need a microscope to see them.
They will not swell because motion in the joints keep forming new
cracks. This constant change causes the ends of the bones to
start forming new bone which grows outward, making the joint
wider and larger as well as stiffer. Exercise helps the joints,
but stiffness usually prevents this.

There are two kinds of osteoarthritis: primary osteoarthritis
and secondary osteoarthritis. The first kind, primary osteoarthritis,
affects many joints throughout the body. These include joints
in the fingers and big toes, the hips, knees, and parts of the
spine. The shoulders, elbows, and wrists are not usually
affected. This is the kind of arthritis that we have been learning
about. Some cases are very mild and enlargement of the joints
may be the only effect. This is most often seen in the elderly.
Bony knobs that form at the end-joints of the fingers are called
Heberdens Nodes. A node is a hard lump and it was named after
Dr. William Heberden who first discovered it over two hundred
years ago. These may be stiff, but they are virtually painless.

In the second type of osteoarthritis, secondary osteoarthritis,
the breakdown of cartilage happens because of some special problem
in the area. An injury, for example, may cause osteoarthritis
later in life. An infection also may cause this, or being over-

FIGURE 6–2 (continued)

8.

weight or a poor blood supply may result in osteoarthritis.
Secondary osteoarthritis may occur in any joint that has had
problems. It does not always affect the joints that are
affected in primary osteoarthritis.

At one time, doctors thought that osteoarthritis was a
simple matter of "wear-and-tear", but they noticed that people
who do hard physical work are less likely to get arthritis than
people who are inactive. But now we know that people with
abnormal cartilage proteins can get primary arthritis and it
takes special causes for secondary arthritis.

Rheumatoid Arthritis

Rheumatoid arthritis patients are often tired and they
suffer from stiffness in the joints and aching in the body.
Six million Americans have rheumatoid arthritis and there are
eighty thousand new cases a year. Three out of four patients are
women and it appears in ages 35-40, but could start at any time.

This arthritis is an inflammation of the synovium, the
membrane that lines the inside of the joint capsule. A healthy
synovium is thin. It folds and bends easily and makes a thick
synovial fluid to cusion the joints. The membrane becomes inflamed,
more and more white blood cells come into the joint, and it gets
swollen and thick. The inflammation leads to damage and that
causes more inflammation. No one knows exactly what causes this,
but doctors believe it might be some sort of a microscopic organism.
Whatever it is, it does not affect many people, and whoever it does
affect, they were probably born with a defect in their immune system.

FIGURE 6–2 (continued)

9.

They cannot fight off the organism, and then the inflammation occurs.

One way to tell if a person has rheumatoid arthritis is they have "rheumatoid factor" in their blood. The immune system makes special proteins called antibodies. Normally, the antibodies fight against harmful bacteria or anything that does not belong there. Rheumatoid factor is an abnormal antibody that works against the immune system. Its presence in the blood is a marker than can confirm the diagnosis of rheumatoid arthritis.

The damaged synovium pours out large amounts of synovial fluid into the joints. Swelling is then caused by two things: thickened synovium and large amounts of synovial fluid. The fluid is made by the damaged synovium, so it is thinner than normal. Therefore it cannot lubricate the joints as well and the bones don't have as much cushion as they are accustomed to. The bones then bump and rub together causing the cartilage to wear down, the space between the joints gets smaller and the ends of the bones wear away . The ligaments are, too, damaged and this causes the bones to slip out of the joint.

Rheumatoid arthritis affects more than the bones. It also affects the eye, the skin, the blood vessels, the heart, the lungs, the muscles, and the nervous system. Many people with this disease feel very tired all the time. Treatment is aimed at fight-ing the inflammation.

FIGURE 6–2 (continued)

10.

Juvenile Rheumatoid Arthritis

Children can sometimes get rheumatoid arthritis. But the
disease called juvenile rheumatoid arthritis is a different disease. It is also called Still's disease, named after Frederic
Still, who was the first person to describe it.

It affects very young boys and girls in equal numbers. When
it starts in older children, girls are often more affected.
Some cases cause a lot of permanent damage to joints, and others
can be treated. The treatment is similar to that for the adult, but
in smaller dosages.

Current Research

There is a lot of research in arthritis, but none of it
will probably lead to miracle cures. People are always looking
for safer and more effective drugs. There is research going on
to develop mechanical joints for the body and other areas, but
these are not cures.

The most important thing is that some kinds of arthritis can
be avoided. For instance, arthritis that is caused by injury
can be prevented by stretching properly and not being overweight.

Treatment will probably be improved through research. The
disease is not curable, but patients can certainly be helped a lot.

Bee Stings

One treatment that very few people know about is honey bee
stings. This was discovered "by accident" by Fred Malone. He
had rheumatoid arthritis in his knees. He got stung on his
right knee and noticed that it felt considerably better than the

FIGURE 6–2 (continued)

                                    11.

left. This is because the venom injected into the person by the bee
has a chemical that helps unstiffen the joints and controls the
amount of pain.

   One precaution you have to take before you have the treatment is to get checked for any allergies to bee stings. This
can cause illness or even lead to death.

   The question was asked to doctors: "Do you use bee venom
in the treatment of arthritis and/or do you know anyone who does?
The results were: 45 doctors were unaware of the treatment, 9
doctors wanted to know more about the treatment, 22 knew it was
being used, and 5 had used it on their patients.

Treatments:

   Aspirin is the most commonly used drug for arthritis and is
a building block for other treatments. A low dose fights pain
and a higher fights inflammation. To relieve a lot of inflammation, a very high dose is needed.

   An alternative for such high doses of aspirin is a drug
called nonsteroidal anti-inflammatory drugs (NSAID). This may
be safer because the dosages are smaller and there may be fewer
side effects, if any. Other drugs are very good at fighting
inflammation, but are very dangerous and can have serious side
effects. These are: corticosteroids, gold salts, penicillamine,
and chloroquine (a drug used to treat malaria, tropical diseases
and found to be good for reducing inflammation in arthritis.)

   Many drugs that help with cancer are also good treatments
for certain types of arthritis, such as rheumatoid arthritis.

FIGURE 6–2 (continued)

12.

Drugs like cyclophosphamide and methotrexate are good at stopping
arthritis from spreading and doing more damage. The problem with
these drugs is that they are extremely dangerous; so dangerous
that treatment with them is not used at all anymore unless the
diesase is damaging the whole body, not just the joints.

Conclusion

     In conclusion, I learned that this incurable disease is not really
life threatening, but extremely painful. Yes, treatment will
probably be improved through research. The disease is not
curable, but patients can be helped a lot by the treatments we
have today.

Bibliography

Crane, Eva. "Honey: Past, Present and Future." American Bee Journal
     3:142 (1977).

Ferdericks, Carlton. Arthritis: Don't Learn to Live With It,
     New York: Grosset & Dunlap, 1981.

Malone, Fred. Bees Don't Get Arthritis, Rutland, VT: Academy Books,
     1979.

Tiger, Steven. Understanding Disease: Arthritis, New York: Julian
     Messner, 1986.

Wallace, Jean. Arthritis Relief, Emmaus, PA: Rodale Press, Inc.,
     1989

FIGURE 6–2 (continued)

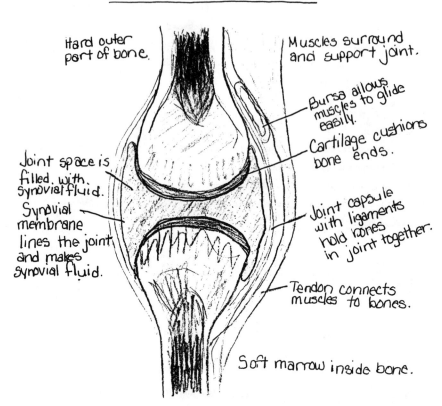

A NORMAL JOINT

Hard outer part of bone.

Muscles surround and support joint.

Bursa allows muscles to glide easily.

Cartilage cushions bone ends.

Joint space is filled with synovial fluid.

Synovial membrane lines the joint and makes synovial fluid.

Joint capsule with ligaments hold bones in joint together.

Tendon connects muscles to bones.

Soft marrow inside bone.

APPENDIX A

Figure 6–2 (continued)

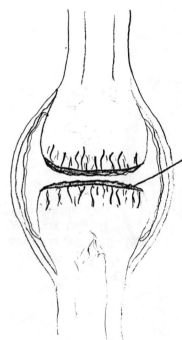

A JOINT WITH OSTEOARTHRITIS

Cartilage pads have broken down. They can not cushion bone ends very well, and microscopic cracks may occur in the bone under the cartilage.

APPENDIX B

FIGURE 6–2 (continued)

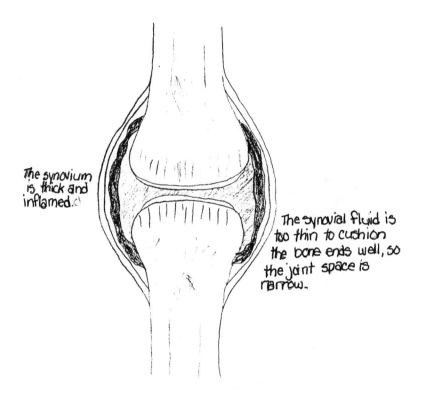

A JOINT WITH RHEUMATOID ARTHRITIS

The synovium is thick and inflamed.

The synovial fluid is too thin to cushion the bone ends well, so the joint space is narrow.

APPENDIX C

FIGURE 6–2 (continued)

NAME: *Abbie Foster*   DATE: 12/2/92

MAKE UP THE PROBLEM

Directions:

Most of the time in school, the teacher or the textbook gives you the problem
and you have to supply the answer. Let's change things around. Here are the
answers. For each of these answers, you make up a <u>wcrd</u> problem.

1. The area is 48 square feet.

Problem: The base of the new staple billboar
Maryjane Jive and Nick just bought
was 6 ft. The height was 8 ft. Ho
many square feet was their ne
staple billboard?

2. The angle contains 16°.

Problem: Maryjane and Nick wanted to build
a triangular bathroom. The first an
was 90°. The second angle was 74°.
How big was the third angle.

3. The answer is 42%.

Problem: Maryjane and Nick had 100 children. 2
of them wanted filet-of-fish for
supper. 18% of them wanted tuna-
wiggle casserole. 11% wanted meat
loaf and cottage cheese. What
percent wanted avacado for
supper?

4. The perimeter is 150 meters.

Problem: Nick and Maryjane wanted to build a
new building for the staple factory. Ea
side was 37½ meters. There are 4
sides. What is the perimeter of
the new building?

5. The weight was 1600 pounds.

Problem: Maryjane was very hungry. She order
30 lbs. of kiwis, 250 lbs. of meatloaf,
63 lbs. of tuna, 310 lbs. of cottage ch
600 lbs. of bananas, 317 lbs. of bruss
sprouts, and 30 lbs. of avacados. How
many pounds did Maryjane order?

FIGURE 6–2 (continued)

PERSONNAL EVALUATION

Which of your problems do you think is the best that you created? (Write
the problem.) Maryjane was very hungry. She ordered 30 lbs. of
Kiwis, 250 lbs. of meatloaf, 63 lbs. of tuna, 310 lb.
600 lbs. of bananas, 317 lbs. of brussle sprouts,
and 30 lbs. of avacados. How many pound
did Maryjane order?

Explain what it is in the problem that makes it your best.

This problem is the best because it has humor and
you have to get every number right to get
the right answer.

Write a solution for your best problem so that any of your classmates will be
able to read and understand it.

$$
\begin{array}{r}
30 \text{ lbs.}\\
250\\
63\\
310\\
600\\
317\\
+\ \ 30\\
\hline
1600 \text{ pounds}
\end{array}
$$

FIGURE 6–2 (continued)

Journal Entry   2/5/92

    I think Snow White and the 7 Dwarfs is a truly unbelievable story. First of all, who would name their kids Grumpy, Happy, Sneezy, Doc, Bashful, Dopey, and Sleepy? I bet their real names were Tom, Dick, Harry, Larry, Curly, Moe, and Bob. Then, they didn't like them, so they changed. For another thing, Snow White?!? Please!! Is that anything like Hail Yellow or Hash Brown? I doubt that. I bet her real name is Filo Lite. Then, some stupid blithering fool from her sophmore class named Eggbert misunderstood. Then, his friend named Dilbert asked who she was, and he said Snow White.

    Another thing, I don't believe in little men wobbling and skipping around singing "Hi-ho. Hi-ho, it's off to work I go." I also don't believe in people biting into apples and dying. Chipping a tooth? Sure! But not dying! Who wrote these fairy tales anyway?

FIGURE 6–2 (continued)

```
         I AM BOUND FOR A DISTANT SHORE

             By Henry David Thoreau


     I am bound, I am bound, for a distant shore.
     By a lonely isle, by a far Azore,
     There it is, there it is, the
          treasure I seek,
     On the barren sands of a desolate creek.




     STANNARD MOUNTAIN
        by Abbie Foster

     There is a little place,
     Not known by many
     Where the people are few,
     But the trees are plenty,
     Where the firds do sing
     And the streams do flow,
     And the bees do sting,
     and where no one goes.
```

FIGURE 6–2 (continued)

7th Grade piece

Remember When....

Remember when you couldn't tie
your shoes?
You would try,
and try,
But it would come
out in knots.
Remember when you couldn't
reach the stuff on
the high shelf.
You would get something
to stand on, but
you would fall off.
Remember when the big
people could swim out
deep? You did
the alligator on shore.
Remember when they
could use the
remote control?
The buttons confused you.
Remember the scratching in
the closet? You could
never go in there at
night.
Remember the big 4th graders?
Don't talk to them or
they'll beat you up.
Remember when you couldn't
sit in the front seat? You

were too small. You were
always too small.

Abbie

Writing Reflection

1. How did you feel when you looked at your grade 7 writing?

2. How has your writing changed?

3. As a writer, what is your strength?

4. As a writer, what is your weakness?

1. I felt like a 7th grader. I think there is a big difference between 7th and 8th, and I felt younger.

2. My writing has changed so much Last year, you would be lucky to see an ounce of voice/creativity, and now I overflow with that.

3. My strength is voice. I seem to have it, even when I don't know it.

4. My weakness is coming up w/a good idea or topic. Sometimes it takes me a few tries to get the topic I want.

Brief Comments on the Work in Abbie's Portfolio

At first I'm not prepared for the casual voice and frequent, humorful asides in "Letter of Introduction" and "Well hello . . . ," but I can feel the author's confidence. I would not credit these pieces as strong evidence of a writer's self-assessment or self-reflection, but they do suggest that I'm about to read the work of a flashy writer.

"The Mudville 9 That Day," based on "Casey at the Bat," captures some of the narrative energy of Thayer's famous poem. The author might be asked why "mace" is used at the end of the first stanza, and might decide to avoid using words solely because they fulfill a rhyme scheme. In this poem, the rhyme is mysteriously abandoned in the final couplet of the fifth stanza. I'd want to ask the author why!

"Stories of the Nude." Using Vermont's analytic assessment guide, I would say the weakest feature of this piece is "Purpose." Why is the author telling this story, and what's the point? It is a cute little tale, but the writer should be challenged to give it some context or consequence. The final paragraph attempts to provide a "summary purpose inferred" *(how I changed between ages two and four)*, but this purpose still seems inconsequential.

"Who's the Freak?" A letter to the editor, this piece maintains a firm sense of purpose and audience, although the statement is muddied in the final sentence of the second paragraph: "Because you don't have music awards, amusement parks, fame and fortune and live interviews with Oprah Winfrey doesn't mean he's a freak." I would ask the author to examine who the "you" is in this sentence, and to rewrite the sentence in a way that makes the reference clear.

"Dream Gym" is listed in the portfolio's Table of Contents as "Writing from Other Subjects," in this case the physical education class. As in most of the work in this portfolio, the author's voice provides evidence of her confidence as a writer. In the second paragraph, this confidence might be blamed for another confusion of personal pronouns. People *do* speak this way, interchanging first and second person; I'd challenge the author to maintain the sense of voice in "Dream Gym" while adhering to the important conventions, such as consistence of person. I might also suggest that she experiment, in a new piece, with "mixed person," seeing whether it's possible to change the person of personal pronouns without confusing the reader. In paragraphs three and four, the author similarly mixes verb moods ("Then, we could do whatever our little heart desires.") Again, I would challenge the author to rewrite these paragraphs into proper English and to experiment in a piece that intentionally mixes moods. Finally, I might ask whether the final paragraph is gratuitous. Reading the piece aloud, the author might discover that the piece has an equally "finished" feel without this paragraph.

"Arthritis" is a remarkable research paper. The author seems to have assimilated information that comes from a variety of sources. The information is thoughtfully organized, presented in fluent prose, and is therefore *useful*. Her voice comes through in a way that does not risk alienating a reader as being "too cute." Anyone wanting a readable, informative report on arthritis will appreciate this report.

"Make Up the Problem." A worksheet response where the author's irrepressible sense of humor rewards the careful reader.

"Journal Entry" feels forced, as if the author couldn't think of anything else to write. This piece might give rise to a minilesson in which topic choice and personal investment are discussed.

"Stannard Mountain," (cited in the Table of Contents as "We Went on a Hike"). An excellent (and somewhat rare!) example of a young person's rhymed poem in which the rhyme seems natural. The slant rhyme of "many" and "plenty" works well, and the humor of the final line is amplified by the rhyming echoes. A typographical error in the fifth line ("firds" for *birds*) will not confuse many readers because the context is so clear. For my taste, the archaic uses of "do" (not for emphasis, I'd argue, but to fulfill metrical demands) jeopardize the poem's chances of seeming a natural expression. I'd ask the author to review the final four lines to see whether she might omit the first two occurrences of "do" (rewriting the lines to maintain the desired meter), and retain the final "do," which (occurring by itself) then *would* seem emphatic, and would add to the humor.

"Remember When," from the author's seventh-grade year, seems formulaic, as in the "I used to . . . , but now I . . ." compare-and-contrast poems and stories so many children are asked to write. The author might write a few paragraphs that reflect on her development as a writer since seventh grade. What new strategies has she learned? Are there elements in "Remember When" that also distinguish her present work? She certainly has *voice*. Is that voice becoming increasingly unique, and what distinguishes it from the voice of other eighth-grade students?

◆ 7 ◆

Developing and
Teaching to
Specific Criteria

M iss Clough, my fourth-grade teacher, could have saved herself a lot of wasted work by focusing, in each paper she "corrected," on only one or two areas. "All I'm going to grade is spelling and content" would have focused her students' efforts and thus given them an interest in the final assessment. Most performance-based assessment programs attempt to isolate a few, specific qualities for which the student should constantly strive.

If an externally designed assessment system is being imposed on your students, discuss the standards of that system as early in the school year as possible. But in the absence of externally designed systems, ask your students what they value in writing: Brainstorm a list of qualities, asking the students to use nouns.

Format for student-nominations of criteria:

1. List on the blackboard nouns that describe the kinds of writing the students like. (Now and then a student will use an adjective. Make a side-list of adjectives, so you are reinforcing an awareness of parts of speech while capturing every idea that is offered.) You can facilitate discussion by asking students to begin each nomination by saying, "A good piece of writing has _____." Depending on the students' age, the responses to this exercise will be more or less abstract, yet will always center on desirable qualities. And there is always room for surprise. A fifth-grade student at Mallett's Bay Elementary School caught me flat-footed one day when he added "empathy" to the list his classmates had been generating.

2. When no one has further nominations, ask whether a single piece of writing could contain more than one, or possibly all, of the qualities that have been listed. Students who answer yes might be challenged to write a piece that proves their assertion.

3. Could a *portfolio*, developed over time, show all these qualities?

4. Suggest to the students that, in the next several weeks, they try to write enough finished work to demonstrate most, if not all, of the qualities

they have listed. They might attach a note to each completed piece of writing, explaining which qualities the writing demonstrates, quoting passages to provide specific examples.

5. Every month or two, students might be asked to create a grid where they list the qualities they know they can easily demonstrate, looking through their portfolios and entering titles in the appropriate places on the grid. They can construct a separate grid where they list the qualities that still challenge them. The spaces in this grid will be filled as the students write new work that meets these challenges.

Qualities I Can Demonstate Easily:			
Good Grammar	Correct Spelling	Suspense	Surprise
Qualities I Will Try to Demonstrate in Future Work:			
Romance	Clarity	Humor	Subtlety

A permanent list on the board of qualities the students admire might provide a set of goals for the first eight to ten weeks of class. "Try to be sure that at least two of these qualities are present in each piece of writing," the teacher might suggest.

According to Donald Graves, if students learn to view their own and each others' work through the common lenses they have developed, it will be be that much easier for them to look later at their own work through lenses that come from external sources. So, along about November, the teacher might introduce a new set of criteria, those used in a large-scale assessment, if one exists, or possibly just a refined set of criteria based on the students' original nominations. Teachers who are not constrained by a large-scale assessment program may want to ask the class, periodically throughout the year, to review and revise its list of criteria. Keeping the students engaged in reviewing their own work, assessing their own progress, is essential; how else will they grow into independent writers, people who continue to write after the school years end?

Graves is very clear on the kind of reflection he wants for students, and he has devised a series of suggestions for them. "Look through your portfolio and find a piece that you are not satisfied with," he might tell a class. "Write 'Not satisfied' at the top of the page. Now look for a piece . . . " (See *Nudges and Valuing,* on page 151.)

Designing Criteria in the Board Room

Any group brainstorming the criteria by which portfolios are to be assessed should be reminded that these criteria will probably be applied to each individual piece as it is composed and revised. Their impact on the curriculum should not be underestimated. And, of course, these criteria should honor the purpose of the program. They might thus seek to measure achievement, or attitude, or longitudinal growth, or the breadth and depth of the teacher's program, all depending on the purpose of the assessment.

NUDGES AND VALUING
A Conversation with Donald Graves

On October 29, 1990, Andrea Alsup, Joan Simmons, and Geof Hewitt, members of Vermont's Writing Assessment Leadership Committee, visited Donald Graves in Durham, N.H., to ask about his work with students and teachers in "valuing" as an early step in evaluation. Graves also spoke of "nudging" students as a means of encouraging them to take on new writing challenges.

Will you say something about how we can give students more experience in practicing evaluation for themselves?

When people make choices from their writing folders, their reasons are often very vague. Students get little practice because the valuing is traditionally done for them, and for teachers the same holds true. Valuing/evaluation is *all reading*. Sorting. Lining up.

Practicing evaluation can be accomplished by forming small groups of students and asking each group to concentrate on a specific element as a peer reads a piece of writing. This reinforces the components of good writing. Rotate the assignments so that each group has an opportunity to listen for each element you seek to reinforce. This is treating students' writing as that of professionals, which helps the students take it seriously.

In a college course I'm teaching, students write twenty ten-minute pieces over a two-week period, which provides them with a kind of instant portfolio. They write two ten-minute pieces a day. Then I offer "valuing-process" suggestions, and this creates a quick profile of the self as a writer and as a thinker.

The suggestions include: Pick out 3 pieces that you just like. Write "Like" at the top of each of those papers.

Pick out 2 pieces that were just plain hard to write. Label them "Hard" at the top.

Pick out 2 pieces where something surprised you during the writing. Label these "Surprise."

Other categories include: "Hang of it," "Writer," "Learn about the subject," "See picture," "First line," "Burn," "Keep going," and "Promise."

Maybe at the end of these tasks they could write a quick three-minute piece about what they'd like to improve in their writing.

Is it a mistake to "import" criteria into the classroom?

We all have our criteria, for better or worse, of what constitutes good writing. We also work hard to get some kind of agreement when we work together to evaluate portfolios. For all our work, however, we forget that the student needs the most practice with applying these criteria that we import. Thus, the student's own written evaluations should accompany the portfolio as it moves ahead.

I keep coming back to experience and practice. The wonderful thing about portfolios is that the portfolio makes clear to us what the job is and — guess what? — *it's a big job*. I can't remember in my whole academic history when this has really been looked at as much as today. And now we're saying "Students can evaluate more."

(continued)

I understand the suspicion and fear among some teachers when something new like this comes along. And I've seen in Vermont's documents how you try to reassure teachers "This is not an individual evaluation." "So it's the school you're evaluating," comes the response, and if the results are not favorable, school personnel may immediately try to figure out who at the school screwed up. Somehow you have to get the message out: Writing instruction is every teacher's and every student's responsibility.

The big question is how to set up a situation of trust, a growth model, and we all work like hell to pull something off that's worthwhile. Is this a growth or survival model you're working with, when the legislature says: "Get it done and on to math!" and where's your support? Okay, it's a long haul, but the trip is worth taking if you can get the time to do the job well.

If students can get good at articulating what it is they've set out to do and why they've selected what they selected, you're well on the way.

If my students kept portfolios that were going to be assessed, as a teacher I'd want the opportunity to write about the work in the portfolios. Make it optional, but allow it. This will provide a good, reflective opportunity for teachers.

Will you explain nudging?

A nudge is a request to experiment. Students ought to be trying new approaches to writing. Nudging helps students to keep their writing fresh and demonstrate a better range of genres and approaches to writing. I nudge as I move around the classroom, talking and reviewing student work in progress.

Here are some examples of nudges: "Take five minutes and underline the verbs in this first paragraph. Okay, then make three of them a little more precise."

"In this piece you have introduced some characters, but I'm curious about what they look like. Take this piece of scrap paper and choose one of the characters. Write for five minutes showing your character. You may decide not to use this in your piece, but try this as an experiment."

"You have two lines of a poem here; take five minutes and run with it on this piece of paper."

Good portfolios demonstrate range and depth. Range from trying new things, which is what nudging is all about. Don't hesitate to interrupt the student. We've underestimated what kids can do, and we need to nudge. Nudge people who are *moving*. Typically, when it's presented to the teacher, it has stopped moving. If the teacher can look over the student's shoulder, as the student is writing, and suggest new directions for the work, so much the better than receiving the work, assigning a grade, and returning it as a *fait accompli*.

If you're nudging you can get all this stuff, but to ask for each bit one piece at a time, you're going to be ill-timed with most of your students. So I say, "I'm just pushing you as a student to show your range and your depth." And, doing this by nudging, rather than saying, "Well, today is the day for all of you to write your poem," makes it possible, I believe, to ask such work even of a first grader.

(continued)

As a teacher, what role would you take in helping students choose work for their portfolios?

I want students to be in on the selections from the beginning and — yes — they are going to make poor choices. I say to the teachers, "You're going to help them learn to value. At the beginning there are going to be lots of mistakes, but it's the students' work and they should be the ones to make the choices."

For nonprofessionals, explanation seems a real opportunity to add experience and valuing to the process. And it's no big deal if they're doing it as they go along, though it might be a real chore to ask them to do this all at one time at the end of the semester. The more you have students writing out their reasons, the more you're going to help them understand how to say these things.

In a class where things are really cracking, and students are writing in response to real issues, it doesn't always fall along neat genre lines. If you look at people who are really writing in life, they learn more from their imbalances and obsessions than from a prescribed, balanced curriculum. Writers develop through imbalance in specific genres, but over a four-year period, it's probably okay, things will balance out. Kids don't understand how different genres apply to the world they're living in and teachers need a lot of help in this area.

Do you think fourth grade is too early to be asking students to write about their best piece?

The best-piece letter is asking a lot of fourth graders if that's the first time they've ever done it. But with experience in valuing and if they've been nudged in all these directions, there's no reason they can't.

As in a third-grade webbing activity, following the rules of brainstorming, the committee should be reminded that this is not a period for comment or discussion. Even a groan or a "yes!" response can have a negative effect on the process. Brainstorming among adults should be enthusiastic, but to the extent possible accomplished with the demeanor of card sharks, poker-faced, efficient. To facilitate this efficiency, the group leader asks for one- or two-word responses and, ideally, requests that they be presented in common form, i.e., "Give me nouns" or "Give me adjectives."

The group leader should record the responses verbatim, even when the responses do not fit the requested form. Adjustments — call them revisions — can be made later. Recording verbatim honors the individual's thought process and encourages other participants to adhere to the prescribed format. If the group leader summarizes or uses synonyms, members of the committee will not be as precise in their responses as they can be. The process picks up speed as soon as the leader establishes ground rules and the rhythm of the session. "A good piece of writing has _____," etc. Responses can build on earlier ideas, or improve on their wording, or intentionally contradict an earlier idea: for example, "broad application" versus "specific focus."

Once the group has run out of ideas, acknowledge that new thoughts can be added at any time. For now, the task is to see which of the nominated criteria are considered essential by a majority of the committee members. This discussion should not immediately follow the brainstorming session: Ideally it happens a week or two later. Everyone copies the list from the board, takes it home, and refines it, listing those criteria that are a "high priority."

At the next meeting, group members read their lists to one another, while the leader keeps track of the ideas on the board or overhead. Through this process of winnowing and refining, the committee can reduce the enormous range of possible standards to a workable few, and can then decide how those standards will be applied and how the levels of student accomplishment will be described. (Although it takes only two or three glib paragraphs to describe this process, it can take many, many meetings to come up with the standards!)

The next question is what the portfolios should contain to demonstrate the standards. Here again, a brainstorming session will elicit a range of responses from which the committee can create a refined list of contents. Is it possible that only a quantitative measure of contents is needed to satisfy the program's purpose? (Purpose: to have each student collect a portfolio of original writing that represents a wide domain of writing styles.) In this case, a checklist is all that is required to accomplish the assessment and the entire section on developing criteria can be ignored.

More often, some qualitative information is sought by the assessment. Usually this information is to be expressed numerically, so that scores can be averaged out and comparisons easily made. Popular systems for such measurement include analytic and holistic scales, or "rubrics." An analytic rubric sets out each standard as a separate entity, to be scored on its own merits, resulting in as many scores for each portfolio as there are criteria. A holistic rubric establishes a single score for the whole of the work, effectively combining the standards that might be judged individually with an analytic system. An analytic rubric might provide a score for mechanics, a separate score for organization, and yet another score for the use of detail. A holistic scale would describe levels of accomplishment combining all three of the nominated standards: "The best work will be nearly without mechanical flaws, will be clearly organized, and will use detail to reinforce the writer's main points."

Because readers are asked to make separate decisions in using an analytic system, analytic assessments take longer to complete and are more complex than holistic assessments. However, analytic rubrics provide useful diagnostic information and can sometimes demonstrate that great writing does not necessarily score highest in every category. Consider how poorly Faulkner might have fared in the "mechanics" column of an analytic rubric and how brilliant his writing might have been judged in "voice," and consider to what extent Faulkner's disregard of conventions might have reduced his score in a holistic system, possibly obscuring his genius.

What I like most about analytic rubrics is that they remind the teacher and the students that there is no single, all-important component to good writing. I know that Vermont's analytic rubric, with its attention to purpose, detail, and voice (in addition to organization and grammar/usage/mechanics), would have driven Miss Clough around the bend. The teachers who designed the program insisted that the criteria not be presented in any sort of "priority order," but they also insisted that grammar/usage/mechanics be last!

Nor do analytic rubrics offer possible rehabilitation solely to the Miss Cloughs of the classroom. A middle-school teacher who is an excellent poet told me that before Vermont's analytic rubric was introduced, she looked at her students' writing only for detail and voice. The analytic rubric was forcing her to pay attention to mechanics, purpose, and organization, too!

For all the benefits an analytic scale brings to the classroom, it can create problems when readers are expected to demonstrate agreement and reliability. Simply because analytic scales require more decisions than holistic scales, the opportunities for disagreement between a first and second reader are multiplied by the number of criteria being applied. If I am ever again asked to help teachers design a large-scale writing assessment, I will probably recommend a holistic approach, and the simpler the better. Or perhaps even better, I'll borrow the best features of both schemes, encouraging analytic scoring in the classroom, but holistic reporting for the large-scale effort.

Regardless of whether a holistic or analytic system is adopted, a design committee is faced with deciding how many levels of accomplishment should be established. Is this is a pass/fail, two-level assessment, an honors/pass/fail system, an honors/high pass/pass/fail system, or *what?* As in everything else, the purpose of the program should help guide this decision, giving the highest priority to the simplest solution that is consistent with that purpose. However, it may be useful to consider the theory that an odd number of achievement levels invites "dumping to the middle," while an even number requires in many cases that the reader make difficult distinctions — for example, on a four-point scale, discriminating between a two and a three. With an odd number of levels, a reader can avoid the tough decision by choosing a midpoint score, i.e., a three on a five-point scale.

Accompanying these pages are three examples of rubrics for the assessment of writing, a holistic rubric (Figure 7–1) followed by two versions (as a way to suggest the types of changes a rubric is likely to require between initial design and subsequent, large-scale use) (Figures 7–2 and 7–3) of Vermont's analytic rubric. More examples could be provided, but the intention here is only to suggest a form, because the local community, whether a classroom of students or the school board, knows best what matters to those people whose work will be assessed. Externally imposed standards are less likely to inspire effort than those derived locally. I'm not about to change my tie if a martian tells me it's ugly; but if my best friend says it looks like a nightmare, I'll probably tear it off as fast as I can.

Some scoring guides attempt to counteract the "standardized" feel of assessment results by including a menu of "commendations" a reader might wish to make after reviewing a student's work. Readers select one or two of these phrases as a way of giving each student a sense of individual response beyond the formal assessment itself. For instance, Maine's statewide writing assessment uses a rubric that lists such phrases as "effective word choice" and "original and/or insightful" as "Commendations." In a separate column, the reader may choose from a corresponding menu of "Needs."

No matter what criteria are ultimately selected, they should be carefully defined; widespread understanding and agreement on their meaning cannot be assumed! Studying the differences between the original and revised versions of

FIGURE 7–1

A 4-POINT HOLISTIC SCALE FOR WRITING

4: A "4" paper is well-organized and fluent, with few grammatical or mechanical errors. Ideas are expressed succinctly and the writer's voice or tone is appropriate to the purpose of the piece, which is clear from start to finish.

3: A "3" paper may be well-organized, but fluency is inhibited by occasional weak transitions or grammatical/mechanical errors. Ideas are evident, and voice/tone suit the writer's purpose.

2: A "2" paper has sufficient lapses in organization and fluency that the writer's purpose is not always clear.

1: A "1" paper is poorly organized or contains so many grammatical or mechanical errors that no purpose can be inferred.

Vermont's analytic rubric, one can see that the descriptors in version one attempted to provide definitions for each criterion. Unfortunately, this required so much detail that the rubric became confusing. For instance, looking at the descriptors for "Purpose," how was the reader to respond to a portfolio in which purpose is "established and maintained" (see "Extensively"), but where "awareness of audience and task" is uneven and "clarity and depth of ideas" is not always evident? Teacher committees recommended a vast simplification of these descriptors, with a written supplement that provides a working definition for each criterion.

Thus, Vermont's revised rubric was published with a brief glossary that gathers the components of the first version's descriptors as a way of providing a common understanding of what each point on the rubric seeks to measure.

Still, it is important to remember that considerable overlap exists among the criteria outlined in the rubric, and this may continue to thwart the dream of high scoring agreement among all participants. For instance, in reviewing the "purpose" of a piece of writing, a reader may discover that its audience is suggested by its *voice or tone*, and that its focus is a matter of how heavily certain *details* are weighted.

(Figure 7–3 continued next page)

"Organization" is often confused with "purpose," since both organization and purpose involve focus. But whereas "purpose" involves intellectual focus,

Vermont Writing Assessment
Analytic Assessment Guide

In Assessing, Consider...	Purpose — the degree to which the writer's response • establishes and maintains a clear purpose • demonstrates an awareness of audience and task • exhibits clarity of ideas	Organization — the degree to which the writer's response illustrates • unity • coherence	Details — the degree to which the details are appropriate for the writer's purpose and support the main point(s) of the writer's response	Voice/Tone — the degree to which the writer's response reflects personal investment and expression	Usage, Mechanics Grammar — the degree to which the writer's response exhibits correct • usage (e.g. tense formation, agreement, word choice) • mechanics —spelling, capitalization, punctuation • grammar • sentences as appropriate to the piece and grade level
Extensively	• Establishes and maintains a clear purpose • Demonstrates a clear understanding of audience and task • Exhibits ideas that are developed in depth	• Organized from beginning to end • Logical progression of ideas • Clear focus • Fluent, cohesive	• Details are effective, vivid, explicit, and/or pertinent	• Distinctive voice evident • Tone enhances personal expression	• Few, if any, errors are evident relative to length and complexity
Frequently	• Establishes a purpose • Demonstrates an awareness of audience and task • Develops ideas, but they may be limited in depth	• Organized but may have minor lapses in unity or coherence	• Details are elaborated and appropriate	• Evidence of voice • Tone appropriate for writer's purpose	• Some errors are present
Sometimes	• Attempts to establish a purpose • Demonstrates some awareness of audience and task • Exhibits rudimentary development of ideas	• Inconsistencies in unity and/or coherence • Poor transitions • Shift in point of view	• Details lack elaboration or are repetitious	• Evidence of beginning sense of voice • Some evidence of appropriate tone	• Multiple errors and/or patterns of errors are evident
Rarely	• Does not establish a clear purpose • Demonstrates minimal awareness of audience and task • Lacks clarity of ideas	• Serious errors in organization • Thought patterns difficult, if not impossible, to follow • Lacks introduction and/or conclusion • Skeletal organization with brevity	• Details are random, inappropriate, or barely apparent	• Little or no voice evident • Tone absent or inappropriate for writer's purpose	• Errors are frequent and severe
Non-Scorable (NS)	• is illegible: i.e., includes so many undecipherable words that no sense can be made of the response, — or — • is incoherent: i.e., words are legible but syntax is so garbled that response makes no sense, — or — • is a blank paper.				

FIGURE 7-2

Figure 7-3

Purpose: Purpose refers to how adequately the author's intent is established and maintained within the writing. The purpose should stand on its own within a piece of writing, and not be dependent upon the reader's knowledge of the actual writing assignment. "Purpose" implies the purpose *within* the writing, rather than the purpose *of* the writing. Important factors that may contribute to the author's success in establishing and maintaining purpose include: consistent awareness of **audience**; consistent **focus** that is appropriate to the audience and the purpose.

Organization: Organization is the degree to which the writer's work illustrates unity and coherence. Writing that displays "unity" does not leave ideas or information hanging; "coherence" exists when sentences are logically and clearly related to one another, and appropriate transitions move the piece forward.

Details: Details contribute to the development of ideas, provide information, evoke images, and elaborate or clarify the content of the writing. When details are "elaborated," they are not simply listed: they advance the purpose of the writing!

Voice or Tone: Voice is the personality of a piece of writing. Tone is the attitude toward the subject, and should vary according to audience, purpose, genre and form. For example, a personal narrative may have a compelling voice and a research paper may have an engaging tone; both can reflect the personal involvement and choice of the author. One way to check for voice is to read a piece aloud: does it have a conversational tone, or a sense of unique involvement? In looking for appropriate tone, ask whether the writing projects a sense of authority or a stance that is consistent to the writing's purpose.

Grammar/Usage/Mechanics: the conventions of writing. In some cases, the writer may intentionally depart from conventional English; where such departure is effective, the writer may be judged to "show command of G/U/M." Where lapses from conventional English are not intentional, the reader should look for patterns. A single word, misspelled once or throughout a piece of writing, counts as a single error; when several words are misspelled, a "pattern of errors" is noted. Similarly, a single type of punctuation error throughout a piece should count as a single error; a variety of punctuation errors constitutes a "pattern." Writing at the "sometimes" level has errors that "distract" the reader — note that these are errors of Grammar/Usage/Mechanics, not of organization or purpose. In a "rarely" piece, the G/U/M errors not only distract, they interfere with the reader's understanding of the writing.

FIGURE 7-3 (continued)

Vermont Writing Assessment
Analytic Assessment Guide

	Purpose	Organization	Details	Voice or Tone	Grammar/Usage/Mechanics
In assessing, consider...	...how adequately intent and focus are established and maintained (success in this criterion should not depend on the reader's knowledge of the writing assignment: the writing should stand on its own)	...coherence: ...whether ideas or information are in logical sequence or move the piece forward ...whether sentences and images are clearly related to each other (Indenting paragraphs is a matter of Grammar/Usage/Mechanics)	...whether details develop ideas or information ...whether details elaborate or clarify the content of the writing with images, careful explanation, effective dialogue, parenthetical expressions, stage directions, etc.	...whether the writing displays a natural style, appropriate to the narrator ...or whether the tone of the writing is appropriate to its content	...the conventions of writing, including: *Grammar (e.g. sentence structure, syntax) *Usage (e.g. agreement and word choice) *Mechanics (e.g. spelling, capitalization, punctuation)
Ask how consistently, relative to length and complexity...	intent is established and maintained within a given piece of writing	the writing demonstrates coherence	details contribute to development of ideas and information, evoke images or otherwise elaborate or clarify the content of the writing	an appropriate voice or tone is established and maintained	As appropriate to grade level, command of conventions is evident, through correct English or intentional, effective departure from conventions
Extensively	Establishes and maintains a clear purpose and focus.	Organized from beginning to end, logical progression of ideas, fluent and coherent.	Details are pertinent, vivid or explicit and provide ideas/ information in depth.	Distinctive personal expression or distinctive tone enhances the writing.	Few or no errors present; *or* departures from convention appear intentional and are effective.
Frequently	Establishes a purpose and focus.	Organization moves writing forward with few lapses in unity or coherence.	Details develop ideas/information; *or* details are elaborated.	Establishes personal expression or effective tone.	Some errors or patterns of errors are present.
	Is author's focus clear within the writing? ┬ Yes ┴ No	*Does the organization move the writing forward?* ┬ Yes ┴ No	*Do details enhance and/or clarify the writing?* ┬ Yes ┴ No	*Can you hear the writer? Or, is the tone effective?* ┬ Yes ┴ No	*Does writing show grade-appropriate command of G/U/M?* ┬ Yes ┴ No
Sometimes	Attempts to establish a purpose; focus of writing is not fully clear.	Lapse(s) in organization affect unity or coherence.	Details lack elaboration, merely listed or unnecessarily repetitious.	Attempts personal expression or appropriate tone.	Numerous errors are apparent and may distract the reader.
Rarely	Purpose and focus not apparent.	Serious errors in organization make writing difficult to follow.	Details are minimal, inappropriate, or random.	Personal expression or appropriate tone not evident.	Errors interfere with understanding.

NON-SCORABLE   * is illegible: i.e., includes so many indecipherable words that no sense can be made of the writing, or
* is incoherent: i.e., words are legible but syntax is so garbled that response makes no sense, or
* is a blank piece of paper
* For Portfolio: Does not have required minimum contents

"organization" attempts to measure how the elements of that focus are ordered, whether the writing "moves forward" in a logical fashion.

Details have a strong impact on whether the writer's purpose is established and maintained, but "detail" and "purpose" are not the same thing. Notice that "depth of ideas," defined as an element of "purpose" in the original rubric, appears in the revised rubric as a matter of "detail."

"Voice or Tone" has been the hardest criterion to define. (In "To Voice or Not to Voice," at the end of this chapter, Andrew Green reflects on the meaning of "voice.") "What is voice? and What do you mean by appropriate tone?" are the questions teachers ask most frequently. "Voice" is the sense one has that the writer's personality is represented in the written language, or that the writer is intentionally manipulating the "sound" of the written narrative to capture the "voice" of dialogue, dialect, or the conventions of a specific genre, such as automobile advertising. "Tone" is the degree of authority a narrator brings to the writing: Is the tone of the writing consistent with its content? Encouraging students to write parodies of a variety of published pieces whose purposes vary widely is the best way I know to encourage an awareness of voice and tone. To help students find a "natural voice," encourage letter writing!

"Grammar/Usage/Mechanics" includes all the mechanical, technical, and grammatical elements of writing. In its revised rubric, Vermont has attempted to accommodate those writers who may intentionally break with writing conventions. Especially in assessing poetry, readers have been confused about how they should respond to writing in which, for instance, the first-person singular pronoun is presented as a lowercase *i*, à la e e cummings. The descriptors for "Grammar/ Usage/Mechanics" refer to "patterns of errors," meaning that the same word misspelled throughout a piece should be treated as a single error. Abundant spelling errors throughout should be considered a pattern, as should continual run-on sentences, etc.

In Vermont's revised rubric, the Writing Assessment Leadership Committee responded to the plea that readers be given some place to "enter" the scoring guide, some quick way of knowing where to look for an initial decision on the writing's merit for each of the five criteria. And thus was created what is now widely known throughout psychometric circles as "the Gordian Wedge," so named because one of Vermont's writing network leaders, Gordon Korstange, suggested that the reader might make a quick decision whether the writing needed work or was pretty close to final-draft form, and thus decide whether to look first at the "Sometimes" and "Rarely" or the "Frequently" and "Extensively" descriptors. Some teachers regard the wedge as the rubric's most significant improvement.

Benchmarking

Once a rubric has been created that suits the program's purpose, a committee should be formed to select "benchmark" or "anchor" papers, specific pieces of student writing that illustrate each level of accomplishment for each of the criteria. Thus, an analytic scale describing four levels of achievement for each of five criteria requires a minimum of twenty benchmark pieces. A six-point holistic scale might require only six pieces, but whether analytic or holistic, the more examples for each point on a scale, the more comprehensive the description of what is meant by any specific scale point. Advisors to Vermont's program have recommended

TO VOICE OR NOT TO VOICE:
AN ATTEMPT AT NARRATIVE EXPOSITION
by Andrew Green

This is the fourth year that many of us have been assessing student writing by the five criteria designed for the Vermont Portfolio Project. And the criterion of Voice/Tone is still the one that seems to be the most difficult to pin down. It's the one category that has engendered the most discussion among us.

This may be because voice is not something that can be taught in a logical, step-by-step process. It is something intrinsic to the writer, the writing, and the writing process itself.

Just what is voice anyway? How do we define it? And what does one have to do to create a sense of voice in a piece of writing?

If only the answers were as easy as these questions. Let's begin with the first question, "What is voice?" As an initial exercise to get students on the right track, I like to ask them all to close their eyes. I tell them that I will walk around the room and tap several people on their shoulders. If you get tapped I tell them, I want you to say out loud, "When can we start writing?" Then I ask the other students to call out the name of the person who just spoke. They all recognize the student immediately and call out the name. After five or six times, I stop and we begin a short dialogue.

How did you know who it was?

By the person's voice.

What about the voice?

We just know that voice.

How?

Because we recognize it.

What do you recognize about it?

And they begin to list what it is that defines that particular voice — it's high, or deep, or timid, or loud, or tough, or soft, or questioning or, well, you get the picture.

After hearing these individual descriptions of voice, I then ask students to talk about how a voice is transferred from vocal chords to paper. And that's where they pause, look at each other, and say (like a Greek chorus) "huh?" We begin by looking at some pieces of their writing. Our discussion revolves around the ideas that will be addressed in the rest of this essay.

The second question is, "How do we define voice?" Anna Quindlen, a columnist for the *New York Times*, says voice is "simply conversation made concrete."

Geof Hewitt says the following about voice: "The mind working alone produces thought; the heart produces feeling; the tongue makes speech and the hand in isolation makes scribble: all four together create voice."

Maya Angelou says that voice is "not what a writer says, but how he says it."

(continued)

Peter Elbow tells us that voice is simply "the sound of someone in your writing. In your natural way of producing words, there is a sound, a texture, a rhythm — a voice — which is the main source of power in your writing. I don't know how it works, but this voice is the force that will make a reader listen to you, the energy that drives the meanings through his thick skull."

These definitions and others, from the students, help inform our discussion, which remains grounded in the student work in front of us.

In that initial classroom exercise we discovered that everyone, that's EVERYONE, has a voice. Therefore, voices take on every shape and size available to the imagination. Voice might be stern and mean. Compelling. Instructional. Lackadaisical. Full of whimsy and fun. Humorous. Ominous. Agitating. Questioning? Commanding!

Finally we get to my favorite question: "What does one have to do to create a sense of voice in a piece of writing?" Let's approach the question from a more concrete angle. Is there voice in this piece of writing that you are reading? Yes? Can you hear a writer here? You can? Are you sure? Then let me ask you, what am I doing in this piece of writing to create a voice? Is my personal involvement (that term sounds like therapist lingo — "are you personally involved in the relationship?") evident in this piece? Or is my integrity, my investment (I'll take one hundred shares of voice at 39 and 3/8 and another fifty shares of tone on margin), my honesty, in here? And what about my personality? Is that coming across on the page? Are you sure? How? Is it because of the words I am choosing to use? For each word I choose, I am rejecting some one hundred thousand in its place. That's a very conscious choice.

What else am I doing to create a voice? Does punctuation affect my voice? For instance, does my use of question marks affect my voice? What about, oh, commas? How about that most often ignored punctuation mark: the colon? How can two dots reveal my voice?

How about my syntax? The way I choose to construct or deconstruct my sentences? Does this add to my voice?

How about the rest of the criteria on the Vermont Analytic Assessment Guide? Does the way I organize this piece, the way my sentences are related to one another, affect my voice? Are the details in here helping to produce a voice? Do they help develop the ideas in this piece? What is my purpose in here anyway? Do I have a focus and is this focus clear? Does this focus, whatever it might be, add to my voice, or the way you perceive my voice? Hmmm.

If you think that all of these things contribute to the creation of voice in this piece of writing, I mean if you think all this nonsense that you have read thus far makes any sense at all, well, check your temperature. Because, remember this: We haven't even started discussing tone. Then again, do we need to? Or is tone just an extension of voice? If voice is the personality on the page, isn't tone the attitude of that personality? And if it is, then what is my tone in this piece? C'mon, I think you have a pretty good idea. G'head. Say it. Out loud! It often helps to read things out loud. That's it. I'm happy for you. Now go do something playful. It's okay. Really, it is.

that several benchmark pieces be provided for each of the rubric's twenty descriptors, involving one hundred or more student papers!

Benchmarks are tangible illustrations of the rubric's abstract language. Benchmark pieces also provide opportunity for review and discussion of the meaning of each point on the rubric, and can serve as foci for some telling disagreements over the application of a program's criteria: "I say the piece that has been ranked a 'two' for Detail is much more richly illuminated than the benchmark piece that is presented as a 'three.'"

"I agree it has more adjectives, but are 'green grass' and 'blue sky' effective and necessary descriptions?"

The benchmark pieces should be used to fuel student discussion of the criteria. It doesn't matter so much whether the students agree with the ratings of the benchmark pieces, their discussion of those pieces and their scores will lead to a fuller understanding of the standards the program hopes to promote.

◆ 8 ◆

The Politics of Large-Scale Assessment

For the sake of continuity, I want to define "large-scale" assessment as any assessment program that involves teachers from more than one school. This is a pretty modest concept of "large-scale," I know, but when more than one school is involved, the challenge of obtaining consistent assessments is the same challenge that faces districtwide, statewide, and national assessment efforts.

Remembering that the root of *assessment* is the Latin *assidere*, "to sit beside," one sees that a true assessment cannot be comprised of a single test, a snapshot. Although an assessment may comprise a series of tests, the ideal assessment is based on several observations, some of which may or may not be tests.

Large-Scale Portfolio Assessment

In almost every large-scale assessment project, some sort of statistical results are intended to reflect what is happening on the local level, with a whole lot of localities involved. "I don't want to know how well my neighbor's child is writing," says the business person or state legislator, "just tell me how well our students are writing and how they compare to other U.S. kids and while you're at it, with the students in Japan."

"Don't tell me how well the students of our state are writing," says the parent, "I want to know how well my child is writing and how that compares to the rest of the country and to the students of Japan."

The larger the scale of the assessment, the more generalized the data become, the more useful the assessment report to a large, central funding source and the less helpful to the individual student. Recently designed large-scale writing assessment programs train classroom teachers to serve as the evaluators of their own students' performance. If teachers can agree to a common set of standards, the thinking goes, they can encourage their students to work toward those common standards, then report objectively to the larger community how well their students are performing.

I believe in this sort of project as long as the funding source, whether it be the P.T.A., the district, or the state, recognizes that professional development for the teachers who will participate must be continuous and responsive to the suggestions of those it serves. Inter-rater agreement, concurrence among scorers, is key to the success of teacher-oriented, large-scale assessment systems. In addition, the scorers' belief in the scoring system is critical to building inter-rater agreement. If participating teachers do not agree that what is being measured deserves to be measured, they are not likely to work very hard to produce reliable assessments. Equally important, the students have to believe in the standards, or they may not work very hard to meet them. The more "local" the standards of an assessment system, the more likely the results will mean something to the people the assessment purports to benefit, the students. The ideal situation is when students develop their own criteria, and when their work is assessed using those criteria. Perhaps these criteria can filter up through other classrooms and eventually become a school's or district's writing criteria. Or perhaps an external system, developed in another classroom or designed by distant professionals, will eventually be adopted. In any case, students who have created their own standards will have an easier time working with an external system than students with no assessment experience.

Here is a list of questions, with a variety of hypothetical answers as examples, that I would use to form broad agreement among all participants in the design of an assessment program. These questions should be answered carefully, and the answers should serve as the bylaws of the program.

Design of an Assessment Program

1. What is the purpose of the assessment? *To improve instruction. Decide whether student gets diploma. Track school's program over the years.*

2. Who is to benefit? *Students will benefit from improved instruction.*

3. How will the assessment serve that purpose? *Teachers will work harder if their students' work is assessed. (This may be inherently unfair, but admit it — some school boards will hire and fire on assessment results.)*

4. How will results be reported? Will they serve the purpose? How will the beneficiary be served by this report? *Percentage of students in a given year who meet the standard. A single number, 1–100, with 70 or above a "passing" score. Percent of students, over the years, who meet the standard.*

5. What are the stakes? *No stakes, just a measure by which we can observe progress over the years. High stakes, no student graduates without meeting the standard.*

6. What will be assessed — a portfolio, or something equivalent? Is it valued by the student as valid and important? *Student writing. Student portfolios. Because this work will be assessed, we assume it will be valued by the student.*

7. Do the school and local community equally value the student's performance as valid and important? *The local school board has been apprised of the plan and supports it. (Realistic schedules are essential here. Don't promise more than you can deliver, and acknowledge that it will take time.)*

8. What are the specific standards of this assessment? Do they match the purpose of the assessment and can they be reported in a fashion that meets this purpose? *Setting the standards is remarkably time-consuming if the teachers and students who will have to live by those standards are involved and if the community is involved. But without this consensual process, who can guarantee that the standards will be honored by those who must work with them?*

9. Is all this manageable? What is a generous, but challenging, time line? *An optimistic scenario for any system involving more than fifty teachers:*

> *Design assessment and set standards: two years*
> *Implement and fine tune, establish teachers' level of "reliability"*
>   *as scorers, publish mock reports: two years*
> *First year of official reporting: year five.*

Answers to these questions, determined as a first step in program design, should form the common principles that guide each participant in refining, implementing, understanding, and measuring the program's success. And they should be constantly reviewed to ensure that the program's focus doesn't stray.

At the most local and best level, as described earlier, the teacher simply walks into the classroom and asks the students to list what they value in a piece of writing. Students' responses, written on the board, become the standards to which they will aspire during the period of assessment, whether it be a single day or the rest of the marking period. The students set the goals. They understand and value those goals.

At the next level, a group of teachers strives to establish standards that will be fair and challenging to the school's student body. Have they included in their deliberations the thoughts of students and parents, the requirements of higher education, the concerns of the school board, the wishes of their district's political representatives? Is a broader committee advisable, one that includes representatives of each of the interested groups?

At the state level, performance-based assessment systems will undoubtedly involve state administrators, curriculum consultants, outside specialists, possibly a state legislator, and, one hopes, a majority of teachers with a principal or two thrown in for good measure. Subcommittees, reporting to a core of teachers with the deepest commitment to the type of performance being assessed, may be essential here.

The larger the number of students whose work will be assessed, the less likely the inclusion of students and the teacher who works with those students in the program's design. And, in district and statewide assessments, the tendency to sway from an assessment's announced purposes requires continual review, given the effects of multiple committees, diverse interests, the comings and goings of specific personalities, and changes in political fortunes. Any one of these factors presents opportunity for distraction and worse: diversion from a noble goal.

Teachers have a responsibility to themselves and their profession to ensure that state- and nationally-mandated systems are reasonable and fair in all senses, and that the students see the performances they purport to measure as valid.

The Demands of Performance-Based Assessment

The formal assessment of portfolios is one type of performance-based assessment. Other examples of performance-based assessment are observing and scoring a student conducting a laboratory experiment and seeing whether a quarter bounces off the newly made bed of a Marine recruit.

Performance-based assessment requires active observations by teacher and student. It is not a single letter grade applied at the end of each marking period. Rather, it is an ongoing conversation during which mutually accepted standards of performance are addressed. Not all standards of performance need be addressed in any single task. What is essential in performance-based assessment is that the tasks that are assessed compose a learning experience; the activity on which the student is assessed is, itself, a real-world performance with relevance beyond the classroom. In a fair performance-based assessment system, the student has repeated opportunities to meet or exceed the standards.

Proponents of multiple-choice tests point out that, although such tests are expensive to create, they can be scored cheaply by machines and results are consistent, "reliable." Multiple-choice test opponents claim that multiple-choice tests are culturally biased and only measure what students know; they fail to show what students can do. Other faults of multiple-choice tests:

1. Teachers "teach to the test" by having students practice on other multiple-choice tests, encouraging the memorization of material that is quickly forgotten. Some teachers estimate that up to six weeks of instruction each year go to preparing students for system-wide multiple-choice tests!

2. There are several ways to cheat on multiple-choice tests.

3. Often returned weeks, if not months, after administration of the test, the data, usually from a distant testing firm, are sometimes misunderstood or otherwise fail to offer any benefit to the student, but are frequently used as a sorting, or gatekeeping, tool.

"Students hate them. Teachers hate them," I heard one superintendent say of multiple-choice tests. "Principals and school boards hate them and parents and superintendents hate them. But ask a principal why her school uses multiple-choice tests and you'll hear, 'I dislike them, but the school board demands this kind of testing.' The school board says 'It's the superintendent!' and the superintendent blames the parents. Multiple-choice testing survives because other forms of testing are time-consuming, and the results are subject to the differences of human judgment among the personalities that are scoring the work."

In fairness we need to look at the liabilities of tests that are based on actual student performance:

1. It takes a long time to make judgments based on real student work. When more than one classroom is involved, more than one reviewer is needed. Often several and sometimes hundreds of reviewers are needed.

2. It is difficult to ensure consistency of human judgment from reviewer to reviewer.

If these two conditions did not cast such formidable shadows on performance-based assessment, multiple-choice tests would have wilted decades ago. But only in the past few years, with experiments across the country beginning to show ways of bridging its shortcomings, has performance-based assessment received national attention.

Models of portfolio-based writing assessment in the United States are generally based on systems devised in Great Britain and Australia, where the classroom teacher assesses student work on the basis of fixed criteria. Teachers bring a sample of student portfolios to "moderation sessions," meetings where the work is exchanged and reviewed by a second teacher. Scores are compared to determine the "inter-rater agreement" among participating teachers. (A high level of agreement provides confidence that scores from portfolio to portfolio, school to school, are consistent, regardless of which teacher happens to score which portfolio.) A sampling of portfolios is taken from this second scoring and rescored by teachers representing a larger cross-section of scorers. Results are again compared to determine whether all regions of an assessment district are "in agreement."

The system is cumbersome. In many cases, student portfolios must leave the control of their authors because photocopied papers are sometimes illegible and because photocopying takes time and money. But its advantages are enormous: The classroom teacher, not a machine, makes judgments about the work that students complete on an ongoing basis. Teachers across a region begin to develop consistent standards, so that a diploma in one district carries the same meaning as one from another district.

Because the system is cumbersome and time-consuming, especially in start-up years when they are learning to use it, teachers need relief from other requirements. Eliminating multiple-choice tests might be an excellent place to start, but many communities want to keep the "secure" measure of past years in place until the new form of assessment proves itself.

My solution to the time problem cuts to the heart of my beliefs about education in the United States. We insist that students spend most of the day behind their desks! As much as one quarter of every school day should be given to upkeep of the school and community. The teacher whose classroom chores are automatically done by students will have at least an extra half hour per day for reviewing student work, or participating in professional-development activities designed to forge a consistent standard.

I believe that any school that wants to improve instruction should find at least an hour's practical work for each of its students, shortening academic instruction accordingly, saving custodial and secretarial costs, allowing teachers more planning time, and giving young minds some experience applying the skills they are learning in the classroom. In a high school, for instance, students should be expected to work in the library, cafeteria, maintenance shop, or anywhere else assistance is needed.

People who deny that performance-based assessment takes time and money are kidding themselves. Some educators advocate hiring teachers on a twelve-month contract, using the summer months for the kind of professional development that a thoughtful large-scale assessment system might require. Developing a reliable portfolio-based assessment system takes administrators' and teachers' time, patience, hard work, and goodwill. But the greatest of these is goodwill: Without it, teachers will not make the necessary effort to derive consistent scores. And, without support from administrators and their understanding of the issues involved, teachers are likely to lose this precious goodwill!

Reliability

Inter-rater agreement is a goal worth working for. Strong inter-rater agreement among teachers in a district or a state indicates that students in one school are held to a standard consistent with the standards of other schools. But assessment designers want more than inter-rater agreement; they want *reliability!* Reliability assures that not only are the scorers consistent in their assessments, but that those assessments are consistent with the established standards. In other words, that what reader number one rates as an excellent portfolio is seen by reader number two as excellent; *and*, that the designers of the program agree with this assessment.

In Oregon, using a five-point, seven-feature analytic rubric to assess prompted writing samples, 420 teachers at eleven district sites achieved inter-rater agreement levels above 95 percent when adjacent or identical scores were construed as constituting "agreement." The state, in turn, certified these scores as reliable by checking the teachers' responses to pre-scored "anchor papers." Reliable large-scale scoring is not a dream, but it takes patience and lots of training!

Who is making the assessments and if two or more people are assessing, how does one ensure they are scoring consistently? It's fairly easy to sell the *idea* of portfolio-based assessment until the question of inter-rater consistency emerges. Certainly the discussions among teachers as they work toward common standards are immensely rewarding to all who participate with a glad heart, but even *they* have to sweat teacups to read through reams of student work, compare it to benchmark pieces, and then assign scores that will be consistent with those of a second reader. Firm guidelines are essential to assure consistency among raters, not only the mind-warp of coming to agreement on what constitutes good writing, but also broad understanding of what, in the portfolio, gets scored and by what criteria a portfolio is deemed "unscorable" or "incomplete." Sometimes, at the expense of dialogue on how to foster a writing community, we ask teachers to practice scoring and learn the guidelines for an assessment program, at which point we jeopardize our cache of goodwill.

The major funding source for assessment efforts usually demands data. Tell us how well the students are progressing and do it consistently from year to year so we can see whether our schools are improving. Foes of multiple-choice testing point to the vulnerabilities of *that* system. Even if such tests invited teaching that engages students in more than "mind bites," they would still be corrupted by how easily they *become* the curriculum and thus are not reliable in measuring beyond the narrow band they test. A machine scores consistently but can only measure what's been loaded into its memory. Can it ensure possession of the qualities we want our children (the very people who will be in charge when we enter our senior years) to have in the twenty-first century? Knowing facts has value, but being able to *apply* them, in combination with other facts, and with feeling — that's what we want. The Boy Scouts and Girl Scouts have strict performance criteria, businesses certainly have theirs: Why can't we establish similar measures for education?

Any system for assessments or testing is subject to major shifts, depending on who's in charge. "We're paying to see data, and you're three years into the program, and still what you're giving us is a little squishy. It's getting better, but it's still pretty fuzzy." The heat is on; you're buying time. There's speculation your program is about to evaporate beneath you. This wouldn't be so bad if you hadn't invested the past five years figuring it out and, most of the time, believing in the whole thing.

This little hypothetical scenario is probably nipping the shins of many educators. A proven system, delivering reliable data, may take years to build if one is counting on the judgments of large numbers of teachers, but without the meaningful involvement of actually assessing the work, teachers are unlikely to have much respect for what the assessment says. The engagement of teachers and students in the rules of the assessment is criticial. If the students or the teachers don't value what's being measured, how can they learn from the results?

So a good assessment system accommodates those essential local classroom or community values, requiring broad teacher involvement in its design and implementation. All such efforts are enlightening, and we should demand open discussion of the failed as well as successful projects. The same statistician who first explained to me the inherent dangers of multiple-choice testing mentioned three major performance-based assessment efforts whose senior administrators were unwilling to release data that showed low reliability in their pilot programs. A less public relations-conscious attitude might have allowed useful information to guide the efforts of ensuing large-scale experiments.

To keep a performance-based system politically viable to data mongers, devise the simplest system you can. Add the complexities later, as teachers, and students, and parents, and the whole community come to embrace the concept. In writing, this might translate into defining as few as two or three qualities that are valued by the community, and possibly having a "yes" and a "no" judgment for each of those qualities.

What, after all, does the funding source want to know? Does it care whether 22 percent of the district's fourth graders keep portfolios of writing that show sustained purpose, and 16 percent write essays that are well-organized, while 20 percent have excellent voice? Or are the hair-splitting measurements of what we mean by "good writing" more properly the concern only of the professionals and their students?

So my recommendation is to promise the minimum data you can get away with promising. If you're working only in a single classroom, not beholden to a formal system, you have the extraordinary opportunity to create the best system of all — one that asks the students for their own assessments. Once we have student acceptance and application of standards, we can turn our attention to other inquiries. The goal of a portfolio program — forget assessment for the moment — should be to show students the value and cumulative mass of their hard work. The self-esteem associated with being taken seriously as a learner, with being asked to include reflective writing on what and *how* one is learning, that alone is the best reason for asking students to keep portfolios.

High vs. Low Stakes

The use of assessment results determines whether an assessment is high or low stakes. Will the results have an impact on the student's academic future? Are we seeking to boil the portfolio down to a number that is entered on a permanent-record card?

OBSERVING AND JUDGING
by Geof Hewitt

Last night I came home from a spirited, two-day "benchmarking" session. I came home to a quiet house, where I celebrated the nearly joyous review by ten teachers of hundreds and hundreds of pieces of fourth-grade writing that had been selected at random from more than six hundred portfolios. The reviewers were searching for work that will show what Vermont teachers consider representative of significant accomplishment in purpose, organization, detail, voice/tone, and mechanics, and will provide examples of specified lower ranges of accomplishment in each of these dimensions. It was two days of reading student work and talking about writing and how we judge it, and the whole time we wondered whether we'd ever be able to finish the job during the time allotted for this retreat.

One teacher at this session told me that, during periods of intense professional work, she doesn't write as much as she otherwise would. What she does to relax in her rare quiet moments is to sketch. Arriving home and finding a clear kitchen table with potted and vased chrysanthemums (try spelling that word without Spelchek!), I took out a basket of colored markers and made a quick drawing. I'm rarely patient enough to get essential detail, though I handle shape and perspective okay. I resolved that I'd draw quickly, the way I tell students to write, and that I'd seek detail with bold strokes, so I swiped the page with yellow ovals then set to giving them shape and dimension with black marker. I'd throw in the

(continued)

Will the teacher's employment status be affected by the results? Will the school lose its license if the results are regularly unfavorable? Will a school's community use the results as justification for refusing the budget? Attaching high stakes to results can compromise the use of portfolios in such a way that students lose their sense of ownership; the portfolio becomes the repository of heavily coached display pieces that the teacher has selected.

The extra burden on the teacher, and the lost opportunity for students to assemble their own evidence of achievement, pretty much defeat the purposes for keeping a portfolio and may well violate the original bylaws of the project. Insist that this issue be addressed as part of the program's governing plan. If it's a high-stakes program, how will you ensure that the portfolio serves a purpose beyond simply delivering scores? How will you ensure that the program's data are not based on the revisions, by anxious teachers, of the work that is to be assessed? And, if *teachers* are to assess the portfolios, will their objectivity vary in direct proportion to the height of the stakes?

When we attach the word *assessment* to the portfolio, we strap on a set of leaden saddlebags. Yet without that assessment — say it in the dark, whisper the word into a candle on the dinner table and the flame will crackle and waver with the three big syllables ASS ESS MENT — without the stick of ASS ESS MENT, stems with a green crayon, then revisit the results with yellow, providing highlights. The yellow ovals, given "shape and dimension" with the black marker, soon looked like automobile headlights covered with ants on a foggy night.

At this point I gave up on the intended product and decided to observe the effect on the piece of changing my strategy. Might I "rescue" the idea of flowers by connecting some of those ants with curvy black lines? Would darkening the green stems and perhaps the vase and the flowerpot lend context, and what was the spirit I might capture with simple, primitive lines? What effect would changing the results of *those* efforts have? I decided to observe the results of my changing strategies, not to judge the final product. Suddenly the drawing was not an attempt to make a picture but a lesson that would inform all future efforts to work without words on paper.

This morning, on a bright sunrise walk through a neighbor's fields, with our dog spiraling away from me in a nose-to-the-ground search for her vision of euphoria, I thought about the potential impact of our ongoing, statewide discussion about the standards of good writing, and I realized that we are born observers who learn through observation, reflection, and practice. So it struck me that our assessment program has to connect observation and reflection with the judgmental component implied by the word *assessment*.

And then I thought about the "best piece," and the letter each student is asked to write about that best piece, and I wondered if those aren't the two most important items in the portfolio, whether or not they are ever reviewed with assessment in mind.

Pass the crayons.

---

some teachers might never ask their students to write, let alone keep portfolios. And without involving teachers in the actual assessment of student portfolios, we'd never have the isolation-breaking conversations among teachers about what constitutes good work!

Teachers are not always well supported in their efforts to find time for performance-based assessment. Generally, the reward for their work rests in the exchange of ideas and values with other teachers and the pleasure of watching students catch on to the new system. Our best teachers may have no problem making time for these rewards and pleasures, but some teachers work within a narrower set of constraints; they do only what their contract requires. As a teacher asked to participate in a large-scale assessment project, I would ask, "What are the benefits for the individual student?" On the basis of the answer to that question, I'd decide whether to commit valuable classroom time to the effort.

Some educators resist participation in large-scale portfolio projects saying, "It's just a fad, just like the other so-called reforms. I'm going to wait until it goes away." Is it fair to point out that whether "fad" or not, such projects are likely to be stepping-stones to further changes in classroom practice? The teacher who resists may, indeed, be resisting *any* change.

An important concept of performance-based assessment is that students know the rules of judgment before they start the task that will be assessed. In the simplest terms, this means that a grade is given on the basis of criteria the student and teacher have agreed on. Miss Clough used to give me a C– and I had to guess whether there was a relationship between that grade and the number of red marks, scattered like measles, she'd incubated all over my pages. It was a guessing game, trying to psyche out what Miss Clough liked. And, worse, I played no role in offering an opinion.

◆ 9 ◆

Portfolios,
Goal Setting, and
Self-Assessment

Performance-based assessment attempts to link assessment with instruction: how much more powerful that link when the student participates! After all, one of the key purposes of keeping portfolios is reflection. While we may think of reflection as an "undisciplined" rereading of the work in a portfolio, a time when the author's mind is free to draw conclusions based on random observations (and this *is* a critical use of portfolios!), self-assessment is where reflection is guided by a series of guideposts — specific criteria established by the author, suggested by classmates, provided by the teacher, or mandated by a formal assessment program.

Self-assessment implies the transition from working with the hope of meaningful response from one's peers and mentors to the state of responding to one's own work. This transition applies to portfolios of all types, indeed to all human endeavor!

Perhaps as much as producing graduates filled with knowledge and skills, we need to ingrain in our students the habits of reflection, of looking back at a given performance and asking, "How could it have been better?" The equivalent of showing the basketball team a video of its most recent scrimmage, students can be asked to read through their portfolios from time to time. Teachers' questions can give focus in the same way as the coach's exhortation to "pay special attention to the position of Murphy's feet on this lay-up." Asking students to reread their portfolios and to single out pieces where, say, the use of detail enhances impact, is a way of guiding reflection and providing a common focus for all participants.

In classroom discussions, the goal is to move beyond the "I like it" stage, past the "I like it because it's interesting" stage, to stage three, "It's interesting because the details are so vivid," and stage four, "The piece interests me because a lot of detail is provided without the overuse of adjectives and adverbs." The shift here is away from a vague, tepid, soft response toward focused observation, from judgment to description. A teacher's conferences with individual students can model the goal of this shift.

"That's Great! That's Horrible!"

What we may be hoping to produce is a student who, as a lifetime practice, looks at a piece of writing and instead of proclaiming, "This is great!" or "This is horrible!" says, "This piece describes the experience adequately, but it might be improved with a supplemental anecdote." This is an attitude, a habit of mind, that can develop if the student is given the verbal tools for such meaningful response. A formal assessment program, or simply classroom agreement for a couple of months on a set of common standards, can provide these tools.

Taking advantage of a system wide vocabulary for assessing students' work, Craftsbury Academy teacher Joan Simmons has created, from her state writing assessment, an opportunity for focused writing exchanges with a neighboring school.

"Students in my classroom begin with self-assessment," writes Simmons. "After they assess their own writing, they exchange pieces with a friend and complete a peer assessment. To do this, students have to become very comfortable with the criteria and in doing so, internalize the qualities of good writing.

"Because my students enjoy assessing their writing, we have formed an exchange program with Darlene Johnson's students at Cabot High School."

An Interschool Writing-Assessment Exchange

Simmons explains that a classroom of students in each school bundles and mails a group of student pieces to its partner classroom, where students read and score each piece. Then, using a fax machine the way pen pals once used envelopes and stamps, each classroom transmits its assessments to the partner students.

"As the fax turns out the scores, we wait with great anticipation," says Simmons. "When the other scorers disagree with the student assessment, frustration reigns; when there is agreement, joy abounds. Always ready to argue the results, students pore over the state's writing rubric and benchmark pieces to prove their position. Some very sophisticated conversations take place. Take, for instance, Rosita's piece, 'Only Memories Are Left.' Rosita is an excellent writer with a wonderful portfolio. But 'Only Memories Are Left' gave her trouble, and I thought it would be good for her to see how someone outside the class would respond. In our own class, she would get minimal help. Because everyone knows she's a good writer, she has difficulty getting an objective conference."

Using the revised Vermont Analytic Assessment Guide, Rosita's classmates gave "Only Memories Are Left" the following scores:

Purpose	Organization	Details	Voice/Tone	G/U/M
Extensively	Frequently	Sometimes	Frequently	Frequently/ Sometimes

"We mailed the piece to Darlene Johnson's class at Cabot School," Simmons explains, "and the response that came back over the fax was not as praising:

Purpose	Organization	Details	Voice/Tone	G/U/M
Sometimes	Sometimes	Frequently/ Sometimes	Sometimes	Frequently/ Sometimes

ONLY MEMORIES ARE LEFT

The killing, the blood, the innocent lives ruined. Why? It's stupid really, Ethnic Cleansing. Who cares if you're Muslim, Croat, Jew or even American. Ethnic cleansing is the dumbest thing ever to happen. Because of this, many people in Sarajevo are dead, many more dying and others watching this beautiful city fall to pieces. The really sad part is that many of these victims are children.

In 1984, the Olympics were held in this wonderful city. It shined with glory and victory. Especially for the U.S. alpine skiiers with Bill Johnson becoming the first U.S. man to win an alpine gold medal. Also winning medals for the men were twins, Phil & Steve Mahre who won the gold and silver medals in men's slalom. For the women, Debbie Armstrong winning gold and Christin Cooper winning silver in giant slalom. Skiing was not everything for the U.S. athletes. Scott Hamilton won the gold medal in men's figure skating. However, this city is now feeling the pain and harshness of bloodshed and U.S. athletes who competed in these Olympics remember all the good memories and share the pain. Unfortunately, this city's Olympic venues will never be rebuilt.

The worst of these attacks that have been happening for 22 months was on February 6. Many people died and the next day was spent as a mourning day for people to share their grief and identify bodies. As the bodies were identified, a list of their names was placed outside the morgue door for people to look at and see which of their relatives died.

No one should have to go through this and I am so sick of these serbian attacks. They wouldn't like it if this happened to them. They should stop thinking they're the greatest and get over the difference.

"Here are the comments that accompanied these scores: 'Purpose: This writer has strong feelings, but lacked a focus. We all had trouble with the second paragraph. It seemed to be disconnected from the rest of the piece. Organization: Lacks transitions, jumps around. Details: We were split. The writing has details, but some of them do not develop the piece. Voice/Tone: First and last paragraphs established a sense of who the writer is, but the voice was not consistent. G/U/M: No comments.'

"And here is the dialogue that ensued once my students reviewed Cabot's response to Rosita's essay:

Purpose

TRICIA   I didn't understand it on the first reading.
MISSY   I felt like it went off the track when it talked about the Olympic situation.
SHERRY   I agree with Cabot when they say the focus is not clear. I can definitely see two topics. I should have scored it with an S.
TEACHER   Would you like to revote?
STUDENTS   Yes. [The revote was an S.]

Organization

SHERRY   The piece is hard to follow, but now I know why. It lacks a focus.
TRICIA   The title is misleading for the piece.
MISSY   We gave it too high a score.
TEACHER   You agree with Cabot's S?
STUDENTS   Yes. [The revote was an S.]

Details

SHERRY   The details are appropriate for the piece.
JASMINE   I was confused about the details of the wonderful city.
MISSY   It's the same problem of focus.
JASMINE   Everything carries over.

Voice/Tone

SHERRY   I hear the writer.
MISSY   She has an appropriate tone. I think Cabot's score is too low!
JASMINE   This is a serious subject. She is using a serious tone.
TEACHER   You think Cabot is confusing voice with tone here?
STUDENTS   Yes.

"I am glad that our statewide system involves analytic assessment," Simmons continues. "This enables the assessment to point out strengths and weaknesses, rather than spit out a number that is relatively meaningless.

"The students' assessments provide a marvelous teaching tool. Looking at the students' judgments, the teacher knows exactly where to place emphasis in instruction."

Short of interschool exchanges, students in a classroom can act as each other's "second reader," confirming or disputing the author's self-assessments in a swap of materials. A second reader, without seeing how the first reader has completed the self-assessment questionnaire, reads and assesses the work. In a conference, the two readers compare and discuss their assessments. This is taking the performance-based assessment process through all its stages; and, in encouraging conversation, it takes the process one step further than most large-scale assessment systems. This final step, conversation about the work, provides a context for the "results," and engages each participant in a focused, three-dimensional view of the writing.

Self-Assessment: Writing About One's Own Writing

One of the most powerful components of the portfolio, a letter or essay the student writes about the work in the portfolio, structures and makes visible the student's self-reflection. In Vermont, this takes the form of a "best-piece letter," in which, after selecting the "best piece" in the portfolio, the student writes about why it was selected as best piece and how it was composed, with any incidental comments the student wishes to make about writing. Such a letter often provides the teacher with valuable insights into the student's learning process and helps the teacher determine the extent to which the student has learned to make decisions that are independent of the teacher's judgments. Some students acknowledge that they have selected the best piece because "it's the one that got the highest grade," but just as often a student will use the best-piece letter as an opportunity to explore personal values and to substantiate an aesthetic framework that may parallel — or be at odds with — the criteria used in the assessment of writing in the portfolio.

Joyce Roof, an eighth-grade English teacher at Woodstock Union Middle School, in Vermont, writes: "When I introduce the best-piece letter to my students, I show that I am excited about, and value, this piece of writing. In fact, I grade each best-piece letter. My students are acutely aware of this. I read a couple of letters to them that I've saved over the years, and I read my own best-piece letter to them. After a brief question-and-answer period, the fun begins.

"I set the scene by telling my students to pretend they are entering a courtroom with their best piece. 'It's up to you to defend your choice,' I tell them. 'You are lawyers; choose your defense carefully. You will be on the witness stand with your piece.'

"As a class, we talk about the letter with a few more specifics. The letter should include how the piece came about (the inspiration), how many drafts (the energy) resulted in the final copy, comments conference partners and teachers made, and any other observations that might contribute to a powerful testimony.

"Usually two class periods are needed to give each student a strong start on the letter; during this time, I circulate around the classroom. I am picky! 'Have you proved to me that this is your best piece?' 'How can you make your letter stronger?' 'Why don't you quote from your best piece to prove to me that you worked on detail, as your letter says that you have?'

"Students are asked to conference with a partner about the letter. This evokes plenty of comments: 'Mrs. Roof, wait until you read Morgan's letter!' 'Read mine, Mrs. Roof, it's great!' The enthusiasm is contagious.

"The conferencing prompts students to excel. Often they write well beyond their ability: I sometimes think their best-piece letter is, indeed, their best piece. I read each letter very slowly; I am picky. (See Figures 9–1 and 9–2.)

"My personal belief is that just as students need time to write, they also need practice writing the best-piece letter. For this reason, I ask my students to write a best-piece letter once every quarter.

"But it is the teacher's natural enthusiasm that sells the letter writing. This is the most important factor!"

A teacher who follows the ten-day plan recommended in Chapter 2 might ask the students to write such a letter to accompany the revised version of their "developed piece," all due on the Monday morning immediately following each ten-day cycle!

A lot of endless debate about what should go into a portfolio might be avoided if we were simply to describe the qualities we hope to find there. For example, work that is well organized, or work that has thoughtful detail and some lifelike dialogue. Asking students to select pieces from their notebooks or working folders on the basis of a set of criteria instead of by genre is one way to allow the contents of the portfolio to show the teacher what has engaged the students. Rather than requiring that a research report be included in the portfolio, for instance, the teacher can determine, by reviewing the portfolios, whether students thought one or two of their research reports deserved inclusion. "Why did so few of you include your research report?" would help break the conspiracy of silence on this crucial subject. Further, asking students to choose work that meets

FIGURES 9–1 AND 9–2   *These letters were written by eighth-grade students. To see what an elementary-level student can do, see Steven's portfolio, reprinted in Chapter 6.*

Connelly Stokes-
2/2/94   Prindle

Dear Mrs. Root,

Without a doubt, I feel that <u>Grampa Makes Five</u> is the best piece I have written this quarter, indeed perhaps ever, despite the cheezy title. The reason for this is also very clear to me – This is the first piece of work I have ever done that is so personal. I actually surprised myself – when I started writing it, the situation with my grandfather was only supposed to cover a couple of paragraphs. But when I tried to put my feelings down on paper, I realized that in order for me to be satisfied with it, it would have to go deeper than a few paragraphs.

The first few pages were very easy for me to write – they literally came pouring out. That was the part where I talked about my grandfather and my family. I think this part was easier because I was able to get some distance. I had no real perspective, though, when I wrote my conclusion. I have often written about my feelings, but never for an audience. The real challenge was writing not just about my feelings, but about myself as a person, and how I think I look to other people.

In the end, I think I succeeded in distancing myself, in fact so much that I learned a bit about myself, as well as about my family, and writing.

            Sincerely,
            Connelly Stokes-Prindle.

FIGURES 9–1 AND 9–2   (continued)

Morgan Macia
English-8
1/20/94

To whom ever it may concern,

If I were to pick one piece that I liked the best, it would be my character sketch.I liked this project the day that Mrs. Roof brought it up.I don't know why, but it just caught my attention.

I wrote about a child named Jed Emerson,a friend that would be considered a counseler to me and a lot of other people.We actually started our life together in the hospital two days after he was born. I had come into this life,November 29,1979.

We were together all of the time and never had any thing come between us.Then it happened, he moved up to the north, and by the time he got back, I left to Reading Vt.

Now we go to school together here at Woodstock Middle school and we are begining to start our friendship all over again.

During this writing I thought that I organized very well,the sentences went good together and I liked the way it sounded,great.

I guess I liked this writing from the day that my teacher brought it up.First she said that we had to make up five characters that are not just the old boring my sister,my mother or my father.This was actually a fun activity,that a teacher brought up!There was a lot of laughter in the classroom,and let me tell you there were some pretty weird descriptions of just made up characters.

Then we got to the hard stuff.We had to write twenty minutes a night,arg!

Well, I guess I had fun with this and I hope we do it again.

Sincerly,

Morgan Macia

given standards will help the teacher to see how thoroughly each student has internalized those standards. For large-scale assessments, this strategy also prevents undue prescription of the curriculum.

Reflection and Goal Setting

"Reflection is the first step toward setting goals," writes Sandra Murphy, who directs the Center for Cooperative Research and Extension Services for Schools at the University of California, Davis, and whose pioneering work in portfolios and writing assessment includes coauthorship, with Mary Ann Smith, of *Writing Portfolios: A Bridge from Teaching to Assessment*. "We can't make wise judgments about where we want to go if we don't know where we are.

"This business about encouraging students to articulate their intentions is important, because too often we forget that students have their own ideas about things and because it's dangerous to assume that they see things the same way we do" (from a letter to the author, Feb. 9, 1994). In *Writing Portfolios: A Bridge from Teaching to Assessment*, Murphy and Smith cite a reflective letter by an eleventh-grade student that "describes her progress as a writer, from changes in her attitude toward writing to improvement in her fluency. She highlights her best piece, chosen because of its personal significance and because the process of writing it enlightened and moved her. It's worth noting that Jennifer's introduction to this piece, like any good introduction, entices the reader" (1993, 47).

Dear Reader,

It took many years for me to enjoy writing. Actually, to tell you the truth, I hated writing for years. I hated it because I had to do it to get a good grade.

When I was younger, for example in eighth grade, my writing was different. We were always given a topic to write about. Now in eleventh grade we're given a topic and learn different perspectives of writing it. I'll give an example. We had to write about Huck Finn in a situation. But you see, we had to write it so the reader is listening to Huck Finn.

The reason I hated writing was also because it seemed I couldn't think of enough information. I don't have a problem anymore. Today I think of too much and get tired of writing it all down. After all these years of writing my imagination has expanded and my grammar and punctuation has improved.

It's easier for me to write in a corner of a quiet room. When I'm thinking about what I'm going to write I don't like to be interrupted because I lose my train of thought. I'd also like to add that the length of writing on my papers has expanded. I remember when I used to have problems writing 3/4 to 1 page. Now I write one page to six pages.

My rough drafts are definitely rough. I read my rough drafts about 2 or 3 times. Each time I see something new.

The all time, best paper that I've written is my Oral History, for many reasons. The paper moved my emotions. I had interviewed my father about the Vietnam War. I never really realized what he went through until after I wrote everything down and reread it later. I cried because I didn't think it was fair that my father had to go through what he did. I took a lot of time to write it. I had a lot of patience which I had acquired within the past few years.

I think I now enjoy writing. It's a way of expressing my feelings. But I'd like to say, I don't like to write every day. (47–48)

In outlining strategies for goal setting, Murphy and Smith cite Linda Rief, the author of *Seeking Diversity*, who teaches at Oyster River Middle School, in New Hampshire. "As teachers, we must listen first to the perceptions our students have of themselves," says Rief. "Ultimately, students show us who they are as readers, writers, thinkers and human beings" (Murphy and Smith, 49).

Rief's strategies for encouraging reflection and goal setting include encouraging students to argue in favor of their portfolio's best piece and to compare it to their portfolio's least effective piece. This leads to goals that are formulated by the following questions:

What goals did you set for yourself?

How well did you accomplish them?

What are your goals for the next twelve weeks?

"Open-ended questions like those Rief poses encourage students to reflect on their long-term as well as immediate goals for writing," write Murphy and Smith (49). "Reflecting on a single piece of writing leads naturally to thinking about immediate goals; for example, specific revisions. But if teachers ask students to reflect on their personal goals in relation to writing collected over a span of time, they are encouraging students to set goals for their own development as writers. Both kinds of reflection are valuable."

We begin to see that where students have been expected to use an assessment vocabulary that specifies important components of their work, they quickly develop the capacity to move beyond the kinds of general goal setting that constitutes little more than empty promises. From "My goal this marking period is to read more books and to write better," a student can set specific goals against which to later evaluate actual progress. In Joyce Roof's eighth-grade English class, a student wrote, in early January, her "Writing and Reading Goals for 1994" (Figure 9–3).

I cannot emphasize strongly enough how important it is to be sure students are practicing their best speaking and listening skills as they read their work to one another. For when students read to one another, they are learning to apply standards to their own and one another's work. They are learning to become critics and to accept criticism. They are becoming partners in assessment and they are learning to look at their own work as they listen to that of others.

Students might begin self-assessment by completing two sentences: The strongest feature of this piece is _____, because _____. The weakest feature of this piece is _____, because _____. For such an assessment, I'd encourage the least formal writing possible, even list making, as long as the student actually cites one or two specific passages for each response. In so doing, students learn to substantiate, in effect to provide benchmarks from their own work to illustrate the standards being addressed.

After three or four such self-assessments, each student should be able to spot trends — areas of strength and areas that need work — and might be asked to provide a summary statement that addresses these key features. On the basis of these summaries, students can be grouped into panels so that those who nominate a specific criterion as their strength can offer help to those who listed

FIGURE 9–3

Nicole Elliott
English 3
1/9/94

<u>Writing and Reading Goals for 1994</u>

This year I plan to improve my reading and writing by doing even more of it! In other years I've always enjoyed reading and writing, and liked doing it, but have always stayed to mainly one style of writing, and have only read books by a few authors, usually writing about a similar subject. This year I want to broaden both writing and reading.

For 1994 I want to find new authors, and new subjects to read about. I want to try mystery and adventure books. I want to read more novels, which I have recently found I enjoy very much. I want to read biographies, autobiographies, and diaries of different people. I want to stop the bad habit I have about choosing books only with nice covers. I may read the front flap of a book, describing it, and be very interested, and then choose a different book because of a better cover. I'm sure I have missed many wonderful books by doing this, and read many bad books with just nice covers.

I've made the same mistakes

As for writing, I want to experiment with different styles of writing. I want to be more descriptive in my writing. I would like to write more poems, and try different ways of writing poems. I want to write more stories and letters also.

Hopefully I will be able to stick to these goals. Since there are so many books out there, I've realized I better get reading a wider range of books soon! I want to read as much as possible. I also have to get writing. Even if it's just more journal writing, it will be a start.

I learn so much from reading and writing. The more I read, I find, the more I know. Reading helps me to write. It gives me a variety of styles of writing, different ideas to write about, and the many ways an author can keep you interested in a story. I had thought of being an author a few years ago, and the more I read, the more I will know about writing, and finding a style of writing.

It seems 1994 should be full of books, and full of my writings, from the goals I want to accomplish. Hopefully by the end of this year, I will have tryed many styles of writing, written many things, and have an endless list of books I've read by a large variety of authors!

that criterion as a weakness, while the rest of the class observes. If the list of criteria is kept short, it's likely that every criterion will be covered in these discussions. "How I handle voice" or "How I handle organization," for instance, can be the subject of a brief discussion led by each student who has named voice or organization as a strength. Students who listed these features as weaknesses can question the experts. Asking each student to read a self-assessment, with its citations, also accomplishes this sort of exchange.

One other feature of students' self-assessments is that they sometimes open the door for clarifications that might not otherwise be made. The opportunity to write a "Dear Reader" letter gave one student a chance to clear the air about a piece that had stirred his classmates beyond his expectations (Figures 9–4 and 9–5).

"New Standards"

Performance-based assessment gives students a full picture of what the assessment will attempt to measure. The rules of the test are, in effect, revealed before students prepare for the test. Performance-based assessment continually seeks fairness for all participants. It is especially vigilant on behalf of the subject of the assessment because it seeks to recognize positive attributes and to have the entire performance be a learning experience.

One of the most ambitious national performance-based assessment programs is the New Standards Project that, since 1991, has been working with partner states and school districts that enroll more than half the country's public-school students. The New Standards Project seeks to involve, on a voluntary basis, schools across the country that will submit student performance tasks, projects, and portfolios (sometimes called "The Three Ps") for review by specially trained teachers who will decide whether the work qualifies for a Certificate of Initial Mastery. Behind this daring plan is the desire to hold students across the country to a common, high standard, without special allowance for demographic factors that might traditionally excuse lacklustre performance.

In the name of fairness and equity, the New Standards Project is developing performance-based assessments that outline daily activities for the teacher to use in preparing the students for the performance tasks. Week-long assessment projects enter the classroom and, in the interests of fairness, teachers across the country are asked to administer these projects in a uniform fashion. If we are serious about creating a classroom culture that honors the performances required for these assessments and if we are serious about restructuring our schools, a number of traditional expectations must be dropped from the teacher's lesson plan.

And if we're really talking "New Standards," let's articulate those standards as succinctly as we can, and give our students and their teachers the opportunity to select the work that best exemplifies those standards. The standards can *suggest* human activities, but local communities and the students themselves should be encouraged to choose the activities they feel best exhibit their skills and knowledge.

Engaging students in selecting work that meets those standards is another way of giving them ownership of their work, of accommodating local initiative. Encouraging them to write about their selections — how and why various examples of their work were chosen — gives students an opportunity to reflect on their own processes and standards, effectively providing ownership of the program's assessment criteria.

FIGURE 9–4

Why Grampa?

Why did Grampa smoke?
Why did God take him away?
Why is it always me?

He was doing so well
Then it hit him one night
Another heart attack.

He lived only six months
Pale, gray, short of breath
Helpless, he sat in a chair.

Then his time came
He was gone
I found myself at the funeral.

My cousin was sitting with me
She was crying
I held her hand.

I tried to reassure her
Everything would be all right
But I cried, too.

FIGURE 9–5

Dear Reader,

My best piece is "why Granpa"
because it has voice and detail and shows
what happens when you love someone.

The interesting point is this poem
was not true. I fooled everyone in my class
and even the teacher "M.   .Then
I read it to the Principal when he came
to visited the class. They all **Tried** so hard
to express sympathy. I had to tell them
the truth. So I chose this piece because
I thought it must have been pretty
good writing if everyone thought it
was true.

I hope you like reading it
because I had fun writing it.

Sincerely,
Chad

◆ 10 ◆

How Soon Reliability?
(A Little Jab at
the Statisticians)

"The worst thing that can be said about any assertion in our culture is that there is no scientific evidence to support it; conversely, when there *is* scientific evidence, we must accept it at face value . . . . Finally, because science is putatively value-free, adherence to the scientific paradigm relieves the evaluator of any moral responsibility for his or her actions" (Guba and Lincoln 1989, 38).

In the name of "science," statisticians demand a percentage of accuracy that may be unattainable in some performance-based assessment projects. What level of precision is necessary for scores to be deemed "reliable"? Has there ever been a real difference between a ninety-five and a ninety-six on a language arts test? Who's kidding whom?

At the same time, there has to be *some* meaning behind all the data.

Aside from the major challenge of ensuring inter-rater reliability, an assessment system depends on several other crucial factors. Any system involving more than one reader must have clear, simple instructions and widespread understandings. It does no good to have impeccable reliability if, for instance, reporting forms are confusing and result in spoiled data. I know of one large-scale program in which an important segment of the data was rendered unreliable by a confusing report form: When only column one should have been used, some readers bubbled column one and some bubbled column two. Thus, when all subsequent responses should have been reported in columns two, three, etc., an undetermined number of column two responses were entered starting in column three, creating a domino effect of useless information.

I also know of one large-scale assessment program in which scores were entered in reverse order on the contractor's computers and submitted for statewide release. Luckily, an administrator observed "unlikely patterns" in the data before the report was published, and the computers were consulted a second time. When I told this story to one contractor, she said "I'd better call my office to be sure we didn't just do the same thing!" I found this response far more reassuring than "Oh, that would never happen with *our* system!"

Aside from such matters of administrative error, the struggle for reliable data will probably remain the biggest challenge to large-scale performance-based assessment systems. Participants in these efforts need to be candid and forthcoming with their discoveries, sharing techniques for overcoming reliability problems, collaborating to build systems that work. Hiding unflattering reliability figures is academically irresponsible. As Guba and Lincoln write in *Fourth Generation Evaluation*, "It has been said that research means doing one's damnedest with one's mind; it also means doing one's damnedest to prove oneself in error" (70).

At the same time we struggle to produce reliable data, we should be asking ourselves how we present the data. A measure of humility and the thoughtful presentation of benchmark pieces to illustrate the data can build public understanding and tolerance for what traditional statisticians sometimes call "soft information." Guba and Lincoln present this challenge in positive terms: "To substitute relativity for certainty, empowerment for control, local understanding for generalized explanation, and humility for arrogance, seems to be a series of clear gains for the fourth generation evaluator" (48).

Standards of Reliability

Yet, like it or not, we still live in an educational environment shadowed by the levels of reliability claimed by objective tests. Take, for instance, a four-point analytic scale for writing that reports whether the student is a "one," a "two," a "three," or a "four" — four options for each of, say, six criteria. The reviewer makes twenty-four choices (four times six) to reach six decisions, reporting out six scores. A second reviewer of the same work also faces twenty-four choices to make six decisions. How many times do the two reviewers need to agree before they demonstrate an acceptable level of inter-rater agreement? Is it statistically defensible to have them come up with a single score, an average of their six scores, and to determine their "agreement" on the basis of that number?

One question is whether "adjacent" scores are acceptable. Statisticians point out that, on a four-point scale, where readers have four choices to reach a single decision, sixteen possible combinations are possible in the responses of two readers: Two people making random guesses will be adjacent or in agreement an average of ten out of sixteen times, or 62.5 percent of the time! Thus, a four-point system that accepts adjacency is allowing a 62.5-percent fudge factor, hardly likely to instill confidence in the people who have to act on the data! On the other hand, one might suggest that 62.5 percent be accepted as the figure of expected agreement, and measure progress from that point upward. Any agreement below 62.5 percent would show that the readers are so unfamiliar with the program's standards that they'd be better off guessing; agreement above this threshold might measure, over a couple of cycles, growing progress in accepting a common standard.

One factor of a community's standard of reliability is the use of resulting data; how high are the stakes? If the assessment is being used as a test that the student must pass, then we want to make darn sure that the scores are reliable. But if the data are being used to paint a picture of a group of students, while each individual's score is accepted only as an approximation of personal achievement, the system can tolerate a little wobble, and data might be reported with acknowledgment of this wobble built in.

"We found that teachers were in 97-percent 'agreement' when we accepted adjacent scores, as follows: 6 percent of our students' portfolios rate only a '1'; seven percent were scored as a '1.5'; 13 percent were scored as a '2.'

"Teachers were in 78-percent agreement when the definition of 'agreement' required that their scores be identical. Here are the findings from that 78 percent of assessments where exact agreement was recorded . . . ."

In this way, the report carries two sets of information. The first set describes the readers' progress in coming to agreement on the standards; the second set describes the students' progress, as judged by the readers.

In "Nontechnical Assessment," Peter Johnston writes, "The social nature of literate activity in the classroom influences children's assessments of their own literate activity. For example, when I asked Tara, 'What sort of reader are you?' she told me she was 'pretty good.' When I asked her, 'What makes you say that?' she said, 'I'm in the Red group.' Sheila, in a different classroom, drew her description from a different framework: 'I like funny stories and books about animals, but often I just kind of get stuck on the same author for months at a time.' Students who evaluate their reading and writing in the simplistic normative terms ('I'm good at writing') will view reading (or writing) as a talent that one either has or does not have, a view that is neither motivating nor instructive.

"The propensity for those outside the schools to ignore all this and pose assessment as a technical matter is problematic enough, but as teachers we have lived with this thinking for so long it has become part of us. It is reflected in our own formulations of assessment problems and in the language we use. For example, we formulate the problem of 'accountability' instead of the problem of 'responsibility.' These words reflect entirely different metaphors. You are *held* accountable whereas you *are* responsible. To arrange for responsibility, you focus on building communities, involvement, trusting relationships, and self-assessment. To arrange for accountability, you focus on building external assessment, a power differential, and some means for those in power to mete out consequences based on outcomes.

"As a second example, we refer to our own observations as 'subjective,' 'informal,' and 'anecdotal,' whereas we refer to tests as 'objective' and 'formal.' Our own language devalues the close knowledge we have and values distance. It would be more helpful if we referred to our own assessments as 'direct documentation' and test-based assessments as 'indirect' and 'invasive.'

"These uses of language are far from trivial. They show that we do not value our own assessment knowledge. Our unfortunate cultural concern for control, distance, objectification, and quantification is a legacy from Kant, Bacon, and Descartes (Field, 1991) and it does not favor teachers, whose knowledge is often intuitive, usually nonnumerical, more inclined to the narrative, and gained through personal involvement. Not valuing our own knowledge leaves us continually insecure and easily made defensive, which makes learning difficult" (*The Reading Teacher*, 1992).

Performance-based assessment requires that humans make the judgments and often, indeed, *several* humans. How can we be sure that these humans are making judgments that are consistent with one another? Not only that, but in some districts the teachers are assessing their *own* students' portfolios! And it's all so subjective! People who raise this argument may or may not have faced up to the fact that report cards themselves are usually based on subjective judgments. The effort behind performance-based assessment programs is to diminish, if not eliminate, this subjectivity by measuring student work against published standards.

Reducing subjectivity requires crystal-clear rubrics with finite, terse descriptors and undisputable benchmark pieces to exemplify each score point. All scoring participants need to have studied these materials and to have practiced using them on pre-scored calibration pieces until their scores match the "official" scores at or above the desired percentage of reliability. Thoughtful consideration has to be given, in advance, to what will happen with readers who never reach the reliability target, and plans are needed to ensure that readers deemed "reliable" are checked often for the scourge of large-scale assessment projects, "rater's drift."

Keeping It Simple

Keeping the system as simple as possible will help. Obviously, the fewer decisions a reader has to make, the greater the chances that a second reader's decisions will be in agreement and the easier it is to train to that level of agreement. At its simplest, then, the system would require only a yes or no answer: "Does the work meet or exceed the standard?" A piece of student work that just misses the standard would serve as the benchmark for "no." A piece that meets the standard, but only barely, would be a benchmark "yes." Scorers would simply compare the pieces they review with those benchmarks and call them a "yes" or a "no" on the basis of that comparison. Because most written work will be significantly better or notably weaker than the benchmarks, teachers and even untrained participants will probably be able to score the work with a high level of reliability if only because so much of that work, presuming a random sample of, say, thirty or more writers, will fall well below or above the level exemplified by the benchmark pieces.

But matters are complicated by the problem of providing a verbal description of what makes the difference between "yes" and "no" work. Again, one can easily describe the extremes on the scale, but how does one define, preferably in rubric language, work that only barely makes it or that barely fails to meet the standard?

The temptation is strong to use such a seemingly reliable system as a gate-keeping or sorting device. This may be fair to students whose work is at the extreme points of the scale, but what about those students whose work falls in the center? Here is a case where a system that looks highly reliable to the public may be used to the detriment of those unlucky students whose skills fall too near the line. But one tenet of performance-based assessment is that the student has repeated opportunities to meet or exceed the standard. In this way, no one is unduly penalized for a lacklustre performance; students are constantly challenged to meet or exceed the standard. Perhaps most important, the human being who is scoring the work, knowing the student will have repeated opportunities to "pass," is not tempted to "go easy." Just as objective tests cannot guarantee that students will retain the knowledge they have demonstrated, performance-based assessment does not assure repeated performances at a certain level. Rather, performance-based assessment certifies that the student has performed at the prescribed level and thus, most likely, can perform at that level again.

An advantage of systems that are more complex than the yes or no structure is that they provide more information. How about a three-point scale? Again, there will be borderline cases, but here we've created two borders. Most holistic systems involve four or six carefully defined levels of achievement and accept scores as reliable if they are "on target" (four-point scale) or on target or "adjacent" in a larger (five- to eight-point) scale. If found reliable, the first and second readers' scores are averaged or simply totaled for the purposes of reporting. Because even a six-point holistic scale requires relatively few choices and only one decision (the single score the reader gives the work), holistic systems are often chosen for large-scale assessment projects.

The more points on the scale, the harder it is to obtain inter-rater agreement, but accepting adjacent scores dramatically reduces instances of disagreement. In their simplicity, some holistic systems may look reliable without requiring much understanding on the part of the people who assign the scores. Worse, holistic scales do not provide specific information about strengths and areas needing improvement. Typically, a holistic score is only one step better than the traditional letter grade at the top of the paper. It tells "how you did," but better than the letter grade, it represents a point on a rubric that is supplemented by benchmark pieces.

Analytic scoring, with a four- or six-point scale, provides lots of useful information for the student and teacher, but establishing reliability with analytic systems is much harder than in holistic systems.

At this point, designers face some critical decisions. Can they keep it simple for reporting purposes and still accomplish some good in the classroom? Are the results going to be used in such a low-stakes way that high levels of reliability are not crucial, at least during the system's formative years? This is an excellent time to revisit the bylaws of the project to be sure that, during the design process, the system has not taken on a purpose of its own.

Given a low-stakes program, where no one is being penalized (or praised!) on the basis of the results, there is an excellent chance that these results can be used to improve instruction and student performance, which is, after all, the usual avowed purpose of an assessment program. Where the stakes are high, people tend to get a little edgy, and the dialogue may be more defensive than constructive. For this reason, I argue for the least threatening possible systems, and because the stakes are low, systems that seek to provide information that is sufficiently complex to be of use to the individual student. Emphasizing that the system attempts to provide rich information, I would acknowledge that its complexity requires a certain humility in how we present and use the resulting data. It's the difference between a report that says "Here is how well our students write" and "Here is how well, *in our assessment*, our students write." To this information, I would add figures that explain the level of inter-rater agreement and reliability.

The more complex the system, the more time, over years, it will take to develop inter-rater agreement and reliability. Some large-scale systems use an intensively trained, small group of readers to verify a sample of the classroom teachers' assessments, and some projects report only the assessments made by a small group of intensively trained teachers. Once again, it's a question of the purpose of the program and what types of data are needed to satisfy that purpose.

Reporting Results

The more complex the system, the more difficult the task of reporting results. At its simplest, such reporting is for a student's benefit only; at its most complex, the report represents the performance of a large group of participants. The larger the group of participants, the less useful the results to the individual. "But we don't care how well individual students write," whine the editorials, "we want to know how well they write compared to students in other states!" National efforts like the National Assessment of Educational Progress and the New Standards Project are grappling with such demands.

Designers of local writing assessment programs often borrow heavily from large-scale models in anticipation of the day a national program will be mandated. "Let's get the jump on a national trend. Best we design our program with an eye toward the day the feds will take over . . . ."

Keeping an eye on national trends makes sense, for sure, but it may be helpful to recognize that "national trends" are likely to become yesterday's fad on any day the voters go to the polls or a new commissioner takes the vows. Further, at least for the moment, designers of national assessment systems acknowledge the unlikelihood of a "national test" or of a single, specific assessment system being selected for national implementation. Instead, as with the New Standards Project (see Chapter 9), the vision is for large-scale, statewide or district wide assessment systems that are linked to provide national verification of local results. Since no national test is currently in design, there is no way to anticipate what such an assessment might entail, unless it be a Neanderthal shift back to multiple choice. Once again, the strongest indicators of quality remain what best helps students, teachers, and parents. What does the local community value and what skills and knowledge are important in the outside world?

If numbers are used for a holistic scoring, they can simply be averaged to provide a mean score for all participants. Thus, over the years, assuming the standards are held to the benchmarks established at the program's inception, a community can compare student progress to baseline figures and theoretically determine whether its programs are improving.

Analytic results can be averaged, giving the same information that holistic scoring provides. But this defeats the entire reason for making the extra effort to score a student's work analytically. For this reason, Vermont's statewide writing assessment program reports its levels of accomplishment not as numbers, but as words. The student's work "Rarely," "Sometimes," "Frequently," or "Extensively" demonstrates mastery of each of the program's five criteria. A student's portfolio may "Rarely" show effective use of detail, for instance, but "Frequently" demonstrate and maintain purpose. The teacher committee that designed this system not only insisted on a verbal scale that would resist averaging and the subsequent ranking of students and schools, but suggested the use of adverbs to describe the levels of achievement. Using adverbs keeps the focus on the act of writing, providing a little personal distance between the assessment and the person whose work is being assessed.

For systems in which designers do not seek a single number, but wish to provide a rich array of information, group scores can be represented as the percentage of students whose work is assessed as falling at each point on the program's scale.

◆ 11 ◆

The Future
of Portfolio-Based
Writing Assessment

A s I write this, I've just returned from New Jersey, where I presented an
introductory workshop to groups of thirty teachers for districtwide in-service
"coverage" (the superintendent called it "awareness-level training") on portfolioassess-
ment. My sessions were mandatory on a gorgeous day, the first warm, sunny day
of the spring after a miserable winter. Why are mandatory in-service programs
inevitably scheduled for such days?

As one might imagine, the teachers showed varying amounts of interest,
mostly arms-folded-across-the-chest attentiveness, but three or four teachers in
each group turned out to be enthusiastic about being part of a portfolio-based
assessment project. And three or four teachers in each group provided brief
displays of childish, distracting behavior, giggling and whispering, which was little
different from what I imagine their students occasionally dish out to them.

I finally pushed one of these teachers to articulate her skepticism. "We tried
all this ten years ago. For five years I had a portfolio-based classroom," she said,
her voice quavering. "It was a good program, and it worked beautifully in my
classes. But then the administrators lost interest, and at the end of the year the
portfolios stayed in my room. No one even looked at them!

"Now they're asking us to go through the whole thing again."

I certainly share this teacher's frustration with the fickleness of administrative
mandates, but she was unable to explain why — if portfolios were working so
well in her classes — she abandoned their use just because her administrators no
longer cared whether her students kept portfolios. Just because a program loses
official currency, its value does not necessarily diminish!

Portfolios, in existence since the cave people, are not going to be stamped
out by the failure of a fad of the 1990s, which is how portfolio assessment may
be remembered if our experiments don't pan out. Because reviewing portfolios
takes time, our educators are trying to find ways to provide abstract information
gleaned from time-consuming reviews, so that not everyone has to read every
portfolio. But abstractions may obscure work with real promise. Just look at the
portfolio! Because portfolios are not efficient deliverers of standardized data, their
future as a tool for large-scale assessments is far from assured. But now that

thousands of teachers and students across the country have experienced the benefits of portfolios, their continued use for a teacher's and a student's assessments, however informal those assessments may be, is virtually certain.

Performance vs. Multiple Choice

Recently, Howard Gardner visited Vermont to speak at a conference on arts education, and during the question-and-answer period following his address, I asked him about the "reliability problem," which had been dogging Vermont's efforts to report useful data on the assessments of students' writing portfolios. "Are there new models for reliability?" I asked. "We know that traditional testing has created a presumption of accuracy; will performance-based assessment give rise to a new way of determining the reliability of judgments?"

"It took more than a hundred years and billions of dollars to bring multiple-choice testing to its present state of development," he responded. "So there may be some wisdom in giving performance-based assessment more than five or ten years to prove itself."

In my role as writing consultant for a program that was being publicly inspected as the nation's first statewide attempt to develop reliable data from the professional judgments of all participating teachers, I took heart from Gardner's comment. I rushed back to the office to pass the word on to my supervisors, who remained unmoved by such reasonableness, given that a body of citizen lawmakers approves our funding year to year and the appropriations are vulnerable, indeed.

The publicity attending Vermont's pioneer effort has proven a mixed blessing. One might better design a program without such attention. Media reports (indeed, one's own publications!) tend to freeze perceptions of the program, which is evolving in response to the experience of students and teachers. Our writing committee once mailed a rubric, in draft form and clearly marked as such, to hundreds of teachers, requesting their ideas for improving the draft. Four years later, long after a vastly improved rubric had been devised (thanks to all that teacher response), the draft was published in a text that labeled it "Vermont's Rubric." On several occasions in the past year I've been offered condolences from out-of-state colleagues who have heard that our program has been abandoned. Well, let's have a sense of humor about negative press and about misinformation, and get on with the revolution. I believe we *are* in a race to establish the credibility of performance-based assessment, and those multiple-choice test publishers whose well-being depends on their established, "objective" view of testing are lurking in the corners of national conventions with their bad news about our fondest dreams.

The positive part about the publicity surrounding Vermont's program is that parallel efforts across the country can benefit from our mistakes and take portfolio-based assessment to a higher level. Perhaps by then, Vermont will have undergone the complete cycle described by the frustrated teacher in the New Jersey school district where portfolios were mandated, dropped, and are possibly returning. The conviction of administrators that assessing portfolios will keep portfolios in the curriculum will go a long way toward keeping such experimentation sizzling while the New Standards Project's commitment to portfolio assessment will provide a high-profile, nationwide attempt to obtain consistent assessments of student portfolios. The experiment is only now warming up, and a few years of bad press (and good press, too!) about Vermont's program will be but a footnote in the books as larger numbers of districts and states design programs that work and programs that do not.

Some of the adversarial atmosphere dividing the advocates of standardized testing and performance-based assessment is possibly being kindled by the theory/ hope that student testing should simply be one or the other. Standardized testing companies may want to disprove the early efforts of performance-based assessment projects, but I doubt many performance-based assessment advocates want to abolish all standardized tests. Rather, it is the prominence such tests play in sorting students and the time they require for the teaching of trivia that have made them so odious. A balanced, districtwide assessment system might include, among its components, a single battery of "objective" tests for students who are halfway through their primary, middle, and secondary years.

Partnerships between the standardized testers and those educators who work in performance-based assessment projects will assure a blended assessment strategy in which, through performance-based assessment, response is available almost immediately to the student. Performance-based assessments will offer an ongoing set of judgments that provide continued opportunity to do one's best, rather than the "objective" test snapshot whose immediacy is often so long past that we merely enter it into a file without further consideration.

Given that formal portfolio assessments take time — lots of time if inter-rater reliability is to be cultivated — we need programs that anticipate this time commitment. Is it worth it? Can we trust our teachers (hiring outside experts is costly and would violate the performance-based assessment precept of linking assessment to instruction) to give us reliable assessments of their own students' work?

Putting aside the issue of whether one can trust such assessments, consider the impact of all teachers focusing on a common set of standards. Once again, we see the possibility of enormous classroom benefit that cannot, at this writing, be documented in a reliable fashion. Vermont's fourth- and eighth-grade teachers, frustrated as they often are by the bureaucratic and psychometric demands of the portfolio program, are nearly unanimous in acknowledging the positive changes it has brought to their classrooms. For one thing, students are writing a whole lot more!

Included in conversations spurred by large-scale, portfolio-based assessment efforts is an enormous variety of educators, from teachers who want nothing that will pull them from the syllabus established by a favorite textbook, to those who believe a writing portfolio is the only text a student needs. These conversations, which might never occur without the perceived mandate of a large-scale program, are probably more valuable than the data the program proposes to offer to the taxpayer. They are an unintended consequence. But for these conversations to bear fruit, we need to allow plenty of time for all participants to express themselves, to rethink and refine their positions, and finally (one hopes) to come to a state of accommodating the program that gave rise to the conversations in the first place.

"Aha!" cries the skeptic, the one who has stock in a standardized testing company, "you're going to beg for time so you can slide into retirement before your fancy scheme is seen for the sham that it is!"

Yes, beg for time. If the portfolio is itself an unmistakable way of presenting the real evidence, then someone — great mercy — has to provide the time to allow the system to take root. School boards and administrators often neglect to put one or two outmoded or unnecessary requirements on the chopping block (or at least on the shelf) to make room for their teachers' thoughtful commitment to new programs.

You ain't gonna get teacher reliability without teacher buy-in. Imagine being told, "These are the standards, use them!" if those are not your standards. This is why developing local standards is so critical. And, as expressed elsewhere in this book, the more local the better. If you are the one being assessed, you deserve a say in the standards!

I'm convinced that the future of portfolio-based assessment rests first with our teachers and second with members of the press. Teachers are going to have to embrace and champion a reasonable alternative to what they find intolerable. If what's intolerable is the multiple-choice test, teachers need to push for an alternative and show that it works!

Our fellow writers, the journalists, have an enormous responsibility in presenting and fairly using the abstracted information that portfolio assessment data represent. Can we make "results" clear to all participants, even with the misprints that public documents are likely to contain? Clear communication is the key in a profession that has become infused with jargon — language that sometimes causes even the educators to misunderstand one another, language that confuses and alienates parents and the community.

As for the politicians and the higher-up administrators who call out for "accountability," it will come, but only when the people being held accountable believe in the validity of the measures being used. Merely testing students does not guarantee that their education will improve or, in the words of a variety of commentators on America's addiction to testing: "Weighing the pig does not make it heavier."

Can we communicate to parents and students, to retired taxpayers whose children and grandchildren have long since left the expensive local school, that we have a way to teach writing and of assessing that writing, and that it's really a community affair? Yeah, I'm a writing zealot who thinks that half of every town or school board meeting should be given over to writing — that participants should be guided by a culture that encourages them, within its sense of democracy, to organize and hone their thoughts before presenting them in public.

Because I believe Grant Wiggins's exhortation "What's valued is assessed, what's assessed is valued," I am naturally in favor of writing assessments. My journey into finding ways to accomplish such assessments has taught me that the wide involvement of all teachers, administrators, and students in a program's design is key to its acceptance. Take the problems to the constituents, don't try to hide those problems from them! We'll accept an imperfect solution if we are part of forging the compromise.

Committees around the country, some as "local" as a teacher and a roomful of students, are wrestling with the questions of what goes into a writing portfolio and how it should be asssessed. Other groups, some as "national" as the New Standards Project, are debating the contents and assessment strategies for a "literacy portfolio" that will allow students to show themselves as readers, speakers, listeners, and writers. And some groups, attending to the broad academic goals evolving from several states' "common core" documents, are discussing a "learning portfolio" that would allow the student's accomplishment in all academic work to be reviewed. "I worry that as soon as we come up with a program, some other committee is going to devise the Better Mousetrap," is a fear I've heard from many program designers. And it may be so. But, just as students benefit from devising and applying criteria to their own work, our designing a variety of systems will provide a common base of understanding upon which future efforts can build.

The Standardized Portfolio

As districts, states, and the nation wrestle with the design of portfolio-based assessment systems and their reliability, an understandable temptation is to standardize the contents of the portfolios. The degree of such standardization may be relative, but as the experiment in large-scale portfolio assessment unfolds, it may be found that high levels of inter-rater agreement are possible only with strict controls over the type of work being assessed. It will be a cruel irony, indeed, if portfolios, whose strength lies in showing each student's unique capabilities, become — in the interests of scoring reliability — little more than long-winded standardized tests. A solution to this potential dilemma, addressed in Chapter 5, is that students keep *two* portfolios, a "Master Portfolio" and an "Assessment Portfolio." Selections from the Master Portfolio are made to meet the demands of the Assessment Portfolio.

Until issues of reliability and efficiency are resolved, performance-based assessment will carry an Achilles heel that swells in direct proportion to the size of the assessment. Yet, on a large scale, performance-based assessment offers the possibility of simply validating the classroom teacher's judgments by saying, in effect, "This teacher's assessments of student work are consistent with the assessments other teachers are fairly making of *their* students." For many people who are struggling to develop reliable systems, the goal is equity from school to school, district to district, state to state.

Many teachers faced with the prospect of mandated assessments fear that results will be used to evaluate the *teacher's* performance. "Don't give *me* credit for the positive results," one teacher in Vermont told her principal when her students' writing scores were among the highest in the state. "Next year, things may go the other way, and both years I'll have been working with students whose backgrounds include seven previous years in school with a variety of other teachers!"

It's teachers who have to do the work; it'll be teachers who have to agree on common standards and how to judge student work consistently. It'll be teachers who have to shift their curriculum to accommodate a common assessment system. It'll be teachers who've been using as many as six weeks a year to coach students for objective tests who'll be told the objective tests will stay in place as we phase in this new, experimental system.

What's missing here is the level of institutional imagination, vision, and commitment that's at the heart of whether performance-based assessment will make it to the year 2000. As we talk of restructuring our schools, have we gone further than just adding neat, new ways of doing things? Do we have new things to do? Have we abandoned stale activities to allow time for a thoughtful fulfillment of our new, restructured ways?

While it may be the teachers who ultimately put thumbs up or down on assessment by portfolio, it is administrators who can create the atmosphere in which portfolios are used as the reflective, student-controlled learning tool they should be. And if those administrators ask for those portfolios to be assessed, assessed consistently, by the members of that community, they have to be willing to shift the school's expectations. They have to allow time, lots of time, and to regard the teachers as fellow researchers whose study asks, "How can I allow my students to do their best work every day?"

As I once heard Donald Graves say, "The real curriculum is what happened; and we don't pay enough attention to *that*." Teachers need systems that afford them time to reflect on their students, just as students need time to reflect on their portfolios.

♦

<hr>

Appendix

A Glossary of Terms Used in This Book

Agreement/reliability When two or more readers score the same piece of writing identically, they are "in agreement." When this agreement is in accord with scores that have been assigned to prescored "check" papers, the results are deemed "reliable." Obtaining inter-rater reliability requires substantial group training, with carefully worded rubrics and frequent reference to the benchmark pieces.

Analytic scoring A system in which an independent score is reported for each criterion of the assessment. Thus, for instance, a student's writing may be assessed as grammatically excellent at the same time it is assessed as poorly organized. Analytic scoring is especially effective as a diagnostic tool and works best if the scores are not reported as numbers (which can be averaged into a single score, resulting in the loss of integrity of each individual criterion) but as words. Using adverbs instead of adjectives keeps the results focused on the act of writing and helps prevent the labeling of students.

Assess/assessment Regrettably, *assessment* is frequently used as a euphemism for *test*. It is important to remember that the Latin root of *assess* (*assidere*) means "to sit beside." Although some assessments may result from a series of tests, most people do not produce their best work under testlike conditions. For this reason, portfolio assessment has become an important way to measure the development of young writers. Note that *portfolio assessment* is two words: Large-scale assessment systems based on students' portfolios are still in the experimental stage. If the experiment fails, the portfolio will remain as a centuries-old, proven tool for helping students witness and reflect upon their progress.

Benchmarks Pieces of writing that serve as exemplars for each level of achievement on an assessment scale. Often used only by the people conducting the assessment, benchmark pieces should be shared with students and interested parents. In selecting benchmarks, it is important to find work that demonstrates the mid-range of each point on the scale, especially for the highest and lowest points. Selecting the work of a prodigy as a benchmark for the highest point, for instance, might set an unattainable goal for most students.

Descriptors Short phrases that describe each level of achievement on an assessment scale.

Holistic scoring In holistic scoring, the reader is asked to assign a single score based on an overall impression. A holistic rubric typically defines four or six points on a single scale. The advantage of holistic scoring is its simplicity; its disadvantage is that it offers little diagnostic information.

Performance-based assessment Performance-based assessment is a form of active observations by teacher and student. It is not a single letter grade applied at the end of each marking period. Rather, it is an ongoing conversation (between teacher and student; among students; between teachers and themselves; and between students and themselves) in which mutually accepted standards of performance are addressed. Not all standards of performance need be addressed in any single task. What is essential in performance-based assessment is that the tasks that are assessed themselves comprise a learning experience. Thus, the assessed activity is itself a real-world performance, with relevance to the student and to the community. In a fair performance-based assessment system, the student has repeated opportunities to meet or exceed the standards.

Portfolio A collection of work. The first known portfolios have been found on the walls of the homes of the cave people. Graphic artists often use portfolios as a way of showing their best work to potential clients. For the purposes of this book, we are considering the *writing portfolio* only, as distinguished from a *writing folder*, which contains work in progress and pieces of writing that may not represent the author's best efforts. A portfolio is a selection of work in which the writer takes pride; a portfolio is the result of considerable reflection or self-assessment.

Prompt A "writing starter." A prompt may be a graphic image, the first sentence of a story, a specific topic, or a challenge: "Write an essay about the importance of voting without using the word *you*." Many large-scale writing assessments use a prompted writing sample; that is, a writing test. Although a uniform prompt may generate writing that can be scored more reliably than a portfolio, it may not deliver valid results. A portfolio reflects the student's work over a period of time and shows what the student values. A prompted writing sample shows how well a student writes under testlike conditions, and is further limited by whether the prompt happens to engage the student. Bad prompts elicit mediocre writing. Comparing the results of annually administered writing prompts, even when they have been scored reliably, requires careful consideration of the variability of prompts. One of the best features of portfolios is that they reflect the value or futility of each prompt a student has been given. For this reason, the student's portfolio provides an excellent learning opportunity for the teacher.

Rubric An assessment scale. A rubric defines the criteria of an assessment system and establishes the levels of achievement.

A Glossary of Writing Techniques
reprinted from Barry Lane's *Writing as a Road to Self-Discovery*

Body Mapping Find a friend, a life-size sheet of paper and a magic marker. Lie down on the paper and have your friend trace your outline, the same way they do it for murdered people in movies. This is your body map. You can use it to stand back from the body you live in. Try writing memories from different parts of your body. Hang your body map on a wall near your writing desk. When you remember a bodily memory write it on the map. Try giving a voice to the parts of your body.

Brainstorming Make a quick list of memories, ideas, details, questions or anything. Don't be critical. Let all your thoughts get to the paper. The power of brainstorming is that you give yourself permission to write everything down on the paper.

Cavewriting As a cross between doodling and brainstorming, cavewriting is a technique to get you playing with thoughts on paper with more than words. Begin by making a sketch of something you are writing about. Next add words to the paper. Let your words and drawing reflect your emotions like an expressive cartoon. Try to get all your feelings and ideas down on the paper.

Chant This is a poem with a repeating line as a chorus. The line can repeat as often as you want it to. Try writing a chorus that explores early memories, voices from the past, phrases, slogans, hopes, dreams. For example:

> Go away
> I'm coming closer
> Go away
> don't take a step
> Go away
> you don't know me
> Go away
> why should I stay
> OK
> Go away.

Core Moments This is a moment in your life when something important happened, something you will always remember. Try exploding a core moment and see what you remember.

Core Story A core story is an essential story that replays itself over and over again in your life with different characters and different settings. We find our core stories by learning to stand back and see the patterns in the stories we tell over the years. Finding our core stories can help us to get a handle on the central questions of our lives and begin to answer them.

Exploding Moments We explode a moment by returning to a short but important moment in our lives and expanding it over several pages, adding as much detail as we can to make the moment last. Think of yourself as writing in slow motion. Remember that writers have a great advantage over any camera because they can include smells, sounds, tastes, thoughts and feelings (emotional *and* tactile) along with what they see.

Express Letters An express letter is simply a letter that expresses what is in your heart. Try writing one to someone you have always wanted to tell your feelings to.

Firewriting This technique can be used to make wild comparisons that may or may not lead to a greater understanding of a given situation. You begin by thinking of a subject you wish to explore. Then you start writing, all the time thinking of ways to connect what you write to something else to make a spark — a connection. Don't plan your sparks, let them occur in the flurry of free association. For example:

I am looking at the blue sky, it's the color of faded jeans, the Caspian Sea. Why is the sky blue? Who painted it blue? Blue is the color of the sky and sadness. Why is the sadness blue? The earth turns to the left, spinning blue jean oceans . . . .

Freewriting Write faster than you can think. That's the one rule of freewriting. Pick a block of time, say seven minutes. Sit down with your pen and paper and write without stopping for that length of time. Don't screen out thoughts or erase anything. If you get stuck just write down your thoughts and wait for the next idea.

Hand Mapping Hand mapping is a technique for discovering ideas. Trace your hand onto a piece of blank paper. Write a feeling or aspect of your personality inside each finger. Draw lines from each finger and connect them with places, people and events. If you have children, trace their hands onto your hand map. Write down childhood needs for all of your children's fingers. Think of your own childhood and compare which needs got met for you with what you are providing them. Let your thoughts trigger memories. Write them down on the chart.

Leads A lead is a journalistic term for the first line or two in a piece of writing. A strong lead pulls both the writer and the reader in. Practice writing leads that make you want to write more. Try growing leads from questions by simply answering the question. For example, Why didn't I do anything? Lead: I don't know why I just sat there when everyone else was screaming.

Leap Essays/Poems A leap essay is when the writer makes analogies between disparate things to make a point. Begin by making a list of ideas and branch off with metaphors and analogies when possible. Compare things. Leap from one topic to another. Then look for the connections.

Lyndy Loo Stories If you are sick of writing in the first person, try writing in the third person about a character like yourself. This is a Lyndy Loo story. Give your character the problems you don't want to write about and see what happens.

Pain Poem Poems can cut to the heart of a painful experience quicker than any other form I know. A pain poem is simply a poem about a painful experience. Here's one written by a fourth grader. Think about how many more words the writer would have to use if this weren't a poem.

My burnt arm

Caps in a plastic bag
hot day
bang
bye three layers of skin
Clinic
doctor
bandage for a month
arm better but have scar.

Potato A potato is my term for the thing that makes a writer want to keep writing even when the lights go out. It is the thing the writer is trying to figure out.

Scenes A scene is when two or more characters are talking to each other in a piece of writing. Scenes are usually composed of dialogue, thoughtshots and snapshots. For example:

Snapshot: He stood by the counter.
Dialogue: "Hi, Joe."
Thoughtshot: He hadn't seen Joe in years. Joe hadn't changed.

Shifting Contexts A context is the frame around any given experience. We shift contexts by creating a new frame. For example, a societal context might tell men they shouldn't cry, but an individual man can create a new context that says all men should cry. This new frame sheds light on the macho society that says men shouldn't cry. Shifting contexts helps us to reexamine the original context with new ideas. Try reframing yourself in a new context. Write about how it changes your perceptions of the original world.

Shifting Points of View Imagining ourselves as others helps us to see the big picture. We shift points of view by simply pretending we are the other person's point of view and looking at the world through that person's eyes. Try experimenting with unique points of view. Notice how a new point of view can change an old story.

Snapshots A snapshot is a word picture of anything. As writers we possess magic cameras that can show us far more than light, color and shape. We can put smells in our pictures — thoughts too. Snapshot essays and poems are strings of word pictures held together by their association with each other.

   Begin writing a snapshot as if you are focusing a pair of binoculars on your subject. If you get stuck, ask yourself a question to turn the knob on the binoculars for a clearer picture. Try writing several snapshots of the same subject. Notice how sometimes the smallest detail can open up a new way of seeing the subject.

Splitting Personalities Think of the different aspects of your personality and give them specific names — for example, the Jester, the Procrastinator and so on. Write a dialogue between them involving a decision you have to make. Try splitting the personalities of people you know.

Story Circle Invite friends to your house and pass around a group-appointed talking stick. The stick gives you the right to talk. Everyone else listens. Note that this ritual is different from conversation because interruptions are not permitted. Notice and delight in how one story sparks another.

   Try focusing story circles on themes. Practice the joy of really listening to each other.

Story Cycle Stories that get told and retold often change in meaning. This is what I call a story cycle. Discovering a story's movement through time is one way to understand the evolving meaning of that story. Try remembering how you told a particular story to different audiences at different times of your life.

Thoughtshots A thoughtshot is a thinking report of a writer or a character. We write a thoughtshot by simply writing down the thoughts of an author or character. Thought-shots can add reflection to a piece of writing. Practice writing down your thoughts in twenty-minute freewrites.

Web Chart or Webbing Webbing is a way to take a helicopter ride above a subject. Begin by putting your subject in the middle of a blank page. Free associate words, ideas and memories as "strands" from the subject. Relax and don't censor yourself. When one strand runs out go back to the nucleus and free associate another strand. Stand back and look for connections and areas of intrigue in your web. Freewrite about those areas and look for more areas of interest in your writing.

Obvious Principles for Large-Scale Portfolio-Based Writing Assessment I Wish Someone Had Given Me Four Years Ago

1) Time is precious, and writing assessment takes time.

2) Developing a program takes more time than usually estimated, much more time.

3) Articulate the program's purpose and test every component against that purpose.

4) When teachers are fearful, the learning is slow and the portfolios are less interesting.

5) Keep it public, but don't believe all the headlines.

6) If teachers have to live by it, they should be its inventors.

7) Students should have access to the same information the teachers have and teachers should share their biases with the students.

8) Beware of experts.

9) Share what you're learning freely.

10) Don't just inform administrators, *train* them.

11) Learn whether flexibility is wishy-washiness and whether consistency is rigidity.

12) All portfolios are not alike.

13) One can support, but not dictate, good teaching practices.

14) Large-scale assessment requires objective use of a common set of standards; if teachers are asked to report their assessments of the students, they should not equate assessment results with grades, which usually consider student effort, and other concerns the assessment is not designed to measure.

Works Cited

Berry, Wendell. 1974. *The Memory of Old Jack*. Harcourt Brace Jovanovich: New York.

Bullock, Sir Alan, F.B.A. 1975. *A Language for Life, Report of the Committee of Inquiry appointed by the Secretary of State for Education and Science*. Her Majesty's Stationery Office: London. 162–169.

Fox, Elizabeth. May-June, 1993. "Talking on the Pigback." *Teachers & Writers* magazine. Teachers & Writers Collaborative: New York. 7-11.

Graves, Donald. February, 1991. "Nudges and Valuing," an interview with Geof Hewitt, Andrea Alsup, and Joan Simmons, reprinted from *Intervals*. The Vermont Department of Education: Montpelier, VT. 2–9.

Green, Andrew and Barry Lane, eds. 1994. "Rules for Revising Our Concept of Revision," reprinted from *The Portfolio Source Book*. Vermont Portfolio Institute: Shoreham, VT. 92.

Green, Andrew. March/April, 1994. "To Voice or Not to Voice," reprinted from *Intervals*. Vermont Department of Education: Montpelier, VT. 5–6.

Guba, Egan G. and Yvonna S. Lincoln. 1989. *Fourth Generation Evaluation*. Sage Publications: Newbury Park, CA. 38–70.

Hewitt, Geof, ed. 1972. "Movies," "Untitled," and "A Schoolteacher's Story," reprinted from *Living in Whales: Vermont Public School Stories and Poems*. Vermont Council on the Arts. 37–41.

Hewitt, Geof. June, 1991. "Observing and Judging," reprinted from *Intervals*. Vermont Department of Education: Montpelier, VT. 11.

Hewitt, Geof. 1990. "Improvised Drama," reprinted from *Ideas Plus, Book Eight*. The National Council of Teachers of English: Urbana, IL.

Johnston, Peter H. September, 1992. "Nontechnical Assessment," excerpt reprinted from *The Reading Teacher*. International Reading Association: Newark, DE. 60–61.

Lane, Barry. 1993. "Glossary of Writing Techniques," reprinted from *Writing as a Road to Self-Discovery*. Writer's Digest Books: Cincinnati, OH. 184–189.

Lane, Barry. 1993. *After THE END*. 1993. Heinemann: Portsmouth, NH.

Malcolm, Janet. 1994. *The Silent Woman: Sylvia Plath and Ted Hughes*. Alfred A. Knopf: New York.

Murphy, Sandra and Mary Ann Smith. 1993. *Writing Portfolios: A Bridge from Teaching to Assessment.* Pippin Publishing Ltd: Markham, Ontario. 47–49.

Paulson, F. Leon and Pearl R. Paulson. 1994. "The Four Stages of Portfolio Growth," reprinted from *A Guide for Judging Portfolios.* Multnomah Education Service District: Portland, OR.

Probst, Robert. 1988. *Response and Analysis.* Heinemann: Portsmouth, NH. 224.

Raffalli, Mary. August 1, 1993. "Classwork Vs. Tests as a Measure." *Education Life.* The New York Times: New York. 5.

Rothman, Robert. December 16, 1992. *Education Week:* Washington, DC. 1.

Squire, James R. 1984. "Using Computers in Teaching English," reprinted from *Computers in the English Program: Promises and Pitfalls,* ed. by Charles R. Chew. New York State English Council: Liverpool, NY. 1.

Thayer, Ernest Lawrence, 1949. "Casey at the Bat," cited in *Best Loved Story Poems,* selected by Walter E. Thwing. Halcyon House: Garden City, NY. 742–743.

Bibliography

Books on Writing and Teaching Writing

Applebee, Arthur (1993). *Writing in the Secondary School: English and Content Areas.* National Council of Teachers of English.

Atwell, Nancie, ed. (1990). *Coming to Know: Writing to Learn in the Intermediate Grades.* Heinemann.

Atwell, Nancie (1987). *In the Middle: Writing, Reading, and Learning with Adolescents.* Boynton Cook Publishers.

Ballenger, Bruce and Barry Lane (1989). *Discovering the Writer Within: Forty Days to More Imaginative Writing.* Writer's Digest Books.

Bissex, Glenda and Richard Bullock, eds. (1987). *Seeing for Ourselves: Case-Study Research by Teachers of Writing.* Heinemann.

Brannon, Lil and Melinda Knight (1982). *Writers Writing.* Boynton Cook Publishers.

Bullock, Sir Alan, F.B.A. *A Language for Life: Report of the Commission of Inquiry appointed by the Secretary of State for Education and Science under the Chairmanship of Sir Alan Bullock, F.B.A..* Her Majesty's Stationery Office, London.

Calkins, Lucy McCormick (1985). *The Art of Teaching Writing.* Heinemann.

Carson, Patti and Janet Dellosa. *Cartloads of Creative Story Starters.* 8488 Glenridge Ave., Clinton, Ohio.

Collins, John. *The Effective Writing Teacher.* The NETWORK Inc.

Collom, Jack. *Moving Windows: Evaluating the Poetry Children Write.* Teachers & Writers Collaborative.

Daniels, Harvey and Steven Zemelman (1985). *A Writing Project: Training Teachers of Composition from Kindergarten to College.* Heinemann.

Dickerson, Mary Jane and Karen Burke LeFevre. *Until I See What I Say: Teaching Writing in All Disciplines.* IDC Publications.

Duke, Charles R., ed. *Writing Exercises from Exercise Exchange, Vol. II.* National Council of Teachers of English.

Elbow, Peter (1981). *Writing With Power: Techniques for Mastering the Writing Process.* Oxford University Press.

Elbow, Peter (1973). *Writing Without Teachers.* Oxford University Press.

Emig, Janet. *The Composing Process of Twelfth Graders.* National Council of Teachers of English.

Emig, Janet (1983). *The Web of Meaning: Essays on Writing, Teaching, Learning, and Thinking.* Boynton Cook Publishers.

Eschholz, Paul and Alfred Rosa (1993). *Subject and Strategy: A Rhetorical Reader.* St. Martin's Press.

Fadiman, Clifton and James Howard. *Empty Pages: A Search for Writing Competence in School and Society.* Fearon Pitman Publishers.

Ferrara, Cosmo F. *The Art of Writing.* RandomHouse.

Fulwiler, Toby, ed. (1987). *The Journal Book.* Boynton Cook Publishers.

Fulwiler, Toby and Art Young, eds. *Language Connections: Writing and Reading Across the Curriculum.* National Council of Teachers of English.

Fulwiler, Toby (1987). *Teaching with Writing: An Interdisciplinary Workshop Approach.* Boynton Cook Publishers.

Fulwiler, Toby and Art Young. *Writing Across the Disciplines: Research into Practice.* Boynton Cook Publishers.

Garrison, Roger (1990). *How a Writer Works* (Revised Edition). HarpCollege.

Gere, Anne Ruggles, ed. *Roots in the Sawdust: Writing to Learn across the Disciplines.* National Council of Teachers of English.

Goldberg, Natalie (1986). *Writing Down the Bones: Freeing the Writer Within.* Shambhala Publications.

Graves, Donald, Jane Hansen and Thomas Newkirk, eds. *Breaking Ground: Teachers Relate Reading and Writing in the Elementary School.* Heinemann.

Graves, Donald (1984). *A Researcher Learns to Write: Selected Articles and Monographs.* Heinemann.

Graves, Donald (1989). *Writing: Teachers and Children at Work.* Heinemann.

Hall, Donald, and D. L. Embleno (1993). *A Writer's Reader.* HarpCollege.

Hall, Donald, and Sven Birkets (1993). *Writing Well.* HarpCollege.

Handbook for Planning an Effective Writing Program. California State Department of Education.

A Handbook of Poetic Forms. Teachers and Writers Collaborative.

Hansen, Jane (1987). *When Writers Read.* Heinemann.

Higgins, William. *The Haiku Handbook: How to Write, Share and Teach Haiku.* McGraw-Hill Book Co.

Hubert, Karen (1976). *Teaching Writing and Popular Fiction: Horror, Adventure, Mystery and Romance in the American Classroom.* Teachers and Writers Collaborative.

Hunkins, Francis. *Questioning Strategies and Techniques.* Allyn and Bacon, Inc.

Koch, Kenneth and Kate Farrell (1982). *Sleeping on the Wing: An Anthology of Modern Poetry with Essays on Reading and Writing*. Random House.

Lane, Barry (1992). *After THE END: Teaching and Learning Creative Revision*. Heinemann.

Lane, Barry (1993). *Writing as a Road to Self-Discovery*, Writers Digest Books.

Langer, Judith and Arthur Applebee. *How Writing Shapes Thinking: A Study of Teaching and Learning*. National Council of Teachers of English.

Levertov, Denise. *The Poet in the World*. New Directions.

Long, Littleton, ed. *Writing Exercises from Exercise Exchange*. National Council of Teachers of English.

Macrorie, Ken. *Telling Writing* (4th Edition). Boynton Cook Publishers.

Macrorie, Ken. *Writing to Be Read*. Boynton Cook Publishers.

Martin, Nancy, ed. (1975). *Writing Across the Curriculum*. Boynton Cook Publishers.

Moffett, James (1981). *Active Voice: A Writing Program Across the Curriculum*. Boynton Cook Publishers.

Moffett, James (1988). *Coming on Center: Essays in English Education*. Boynton Cook Publishers.

Mohr, Marian (1984). *Revision: The Rhythm of Meaning*. Boynton Cook Publishers.

Murray, Donald (1993). *Read to Write*. Harcourt, Brace.

Murray, Donald (1990). *Write to Learn* (2nd Edition). Holt, Rinehart and Winston.

Murray, Donald (1984). *A Writer Teaches Writing: A Practical Method of Teaching Composition*. Houghton Mifflin Co.

Myers, Miles. *A Procedure for Writing Assessment and Holistic Scoring*. ERIC, National Council of Teachers of English.

New York State English Council. *Computers in the English Program: Promises and Pitfalls*.

Newkirk, Thomas, ed. (1990). *To Compose: Teaching Writing in the High School*. Heinemann.

Perl, Sondra and Nancy Wilson (1986). *Through Teachers' Eyes: Portraits of Writing Teachers at Work*. Heinemann.

Petty, Walter and Mary Bowen. *Slithery Snakes and Other Aids to Children's Writing*. Prentice-Hall.

Ponsot, Marie and Rosemary Deen (1982). *Beat Not the Poor Desk: What to Teach, How to Teach It and Why*. Boynton Cook Publishers.

Ponsot, Marie and Rosemary Deen (1985). *The Common Sense: What to Write, How to Write It and Why*. Boynton Cook Publishers.

Rainer, Tristine (1979). *The New Diary: How to Use a Journal for Self-Guidance and Expanded Creativity*. J.P. Tarcher.

Rico, Gabriele Lusser (1983). *Writing the Natural Way*, Houghton Mifflin Co.

Rief, Linda (1992). *Seeking Diversity: Language Arts with Adolescents*. Heinemann.

Romano, Tom (1987). *Clearing the Way: Working with Teenage Writers*. Heinemann.

Sears, Peter. *Gonna Bake Me a Rainbow Poem: A Guide to Writing Poetry*. Scholastic.

Self, Judith, ed. *Plain Talk about Learning and Writing across the Curriculum*. Virginia Department of Education.

Strunk and White (1979). *Elements of Style* (3rd Edition). MacMillan.

Trimble, John (1975). *Writing with Style*. Prentice-Hall.

Tsujimoto, Joseph I. *Teaching Poetry Writing to Adolescents*. National Council of Teachers of English.

Welty, Eudora (1979). *The Eye of the Story*. Vintage.

Willis, Meredith Sue (1984). *Personal Fiction Writing*. Teachers and Writers Collaborative.

Zinsser, William (1990). *On Writing Well*. Harper and Row.

Zinsser, William (1989). *Write to Learn*. Harper and Row.

Zinsser, William. *Writing with a Word Processor*. Harper and Row.

Books with Record-Keeping Suggestions

Atwell, Nancie (1987). *In the Middle: Writing, Reading, and Learning with Adolescents*. Boynton Cook Publishers.

Baskill, Jane and Paulette Whitman. *Evaluation: Whole Language, Whole Child*. Scholastic.

Goodman, Kenneth, Yetta Goodman and Wendy Hood (1988). *The Whole Language Evaluation Book*. Heinemann.

Graves, Donald H. (1989). *Writing: Teachers and Children at Work*. Heinemann.

Hansen, Jane (1987). *When Writers Read*. Heinemann.

Newkirk, Thomas and Nancie Atwell, ed. (1987). *Understanding Writing: Ways of Observing, Learning and Teaching*. Heinemann.

Parry, Jo-Ann and David Hornsby (1988). *Write On: A Conference Approach to Writing*. Heinemann.

The Primary Language Record Handbook for Teachers. Heinemann.

Routman, Regie (1988). *Transitions from Literature to Literacy*. Heinemann.

Turbill, Jan. *Now We Want to Write*. Heinemann.

Zemelman, Steven and Harvey Daniels (1988). *Community of Writers: Teaching Writing in the Junior and Senior High School*. Heinemann.

Books Addressing Writing Portfolios and/or Writing Assessment

Archbald, Doug A. and Fred M. Newmann. *Beyond Standardized Testing: Assessing Authentic Academic Achievement in the Secondary School*. National Association of Secondary School Principals, Reston, VA.

Belanoff, Pat and Marcia Dickson, eds. (1991). *Portfolios: Process and Product*. Boynton Cook Publishers.

Brown, Carol Smullen and Susan Mandell Glazer (1993). *Portfolios and Beyond: Collaborative Assessment in Reading and Writing*. Christopher-Gordon.

Cooper, Charles R. and Lee Odell. *Evaluating Writing: Describing, Measuring, Judging*. National Council of Teachers of English.

Gentile, Claudia. *Exploring New Methods for Collecting Students' School-based Writing: NAEP's 1990 Portfolio Study*. U.S. Department of Education.

Graves, Donald H. and Bonnie S. Sunstein, eds. (1992). *Portfolio Portraits*. Heinemann.

Green, Andrew and Barry Lane, eds. *The Portfolio Source Book: How to Set Up, Manage and Integrate Portfolios in the Reading/Writing Classroom*. Vermont Portfolio Institute, Shoreham, VT.

Guba, Egan G. and Yvonna S. Lincoln (1989). *Fourth Generation Evaluation*. Sage Publications, Newbury Park, CA.

Harp, Bill (1991). *Assessment and Evaluation in Whole Language Programs*. Christopher-Gordon, Norwood, MA.

Murphy, Sandra and Leo Ruth (1988). *Designing Writing Tasks for the Assessment of Writing*. Ablex Publishing Corporation, Norwood, NJ.

Murphy, Sandra and Mary Ann Smith (in press). *Writing Portfolios: A Bridge from Teaching to Assessment*. Pippin, Markham, Ontario.

Tierney, Robert J., Marck A. Carter, Laura E. Desai (1991). *Portfolio Assessment in the Reading-Writing Classroom*. Christopher-Gordon, Norwood, MA.

Wiggins, Grant. *Assessing Student Performance*. Jossey-Bass Publishers, San Francisco.

Yancey, Kathleen Blake, ed. (1992). *Portfolios in the Writing Classroom*. National Council of Teachers of English, Urbana, IL.

Periodicals

English Journal, National Council of Teachers of English, 1111 W. Kenyon Road, Urbana, IL, 61801.

FairTest Examiner, National Center for Fair & Open Testing, 342 Broadway, Cambridge, MA, 02139–1802.

Portfolio Assessment Newsletter, Northwest Evaluation Association, 5 Ceterpointe Drive, Suite 100, Lake Oswego, OR, 97035.

Portfolio News, Portfolio Assessment Clearinghouse, c/o San Dieguito Union High School District, 710 Encinitas Boulevard, Encinitas, CA, 92025.

The Quarterly, National Center for the Study of Writing and Literacy, 5513 Tolman Hall, School of Education, University of California, Berkeley, CA, 94720.

The Reading Teacher, International Reading Association, 800 Barksdale Rd., P.O. Box 8139, Newark, DE, 19714.

Teachers & Writers, Teachers & Writers Collaborative, 5 Union Square West, New York, NY, 10003.

Index